CONNECTED COMMUNIT

Creating a new knowledge landsc

G000163062

COMMUNITIES, ARCHIVES AND NEW COLLABORATIVE PRACTICES

Edited by
Simon Popple, Andrew Prescott
and Daniel H. Mutibwa

First published in Great Britain in 2020 by

Policy Press
University of Bristol
1-9 Old Park Hill
Bristol
BS2 8BB
UK
t: +44 (0)117 954 5940
pp-info@bristol.ac.uk
www.policypress.co.uk

North America office:
Policy Press
c/o The University of Chicago Press
1427 East 60th Street
Chicago, IL 60637, USA
t: +1 773 702 7700
f: +1 773-702-9756
sales@press.uchicago.edu
www.press.uchicago.edu

© Policy Press 2020

British Library Cataloguing in Publication Data
A catalogue record for this book is available from the British Library

Library of Congress Cataloging-in-Publication Data
A catalog record for this book has been requested

978-1-4473-4189-5 hardback
978-1-4473-4194-9 paperback
978-1-4473-4195-6 ePub
978-1-4473-4193-2 ePDF

The right of Simon Popple, Andrew Prescott and Daniel H. Mutibwa to be identified as
editors of this work has been asserted by them in accordance with the Copyright, Designs and
Patents Act 1988.

All rights reserved: no part of this publication may be reproduced, stored in a retrieval system,
or transmitted in any form or by any means, electronic, mechanical, photocopying, recording,
or otherwise without the prior permission of Policy Press.

The statements and opinions contained within this publication are solely those of the editors
and contributors and not of the University of Bristol or Policy Press. The University of
Bristol and Policy Press disclaim responsibility for any injury to persons or property resulting
from any material published in this publication.

Policy Press works to counter discrimination on grounds of gender, race,
disability, age and sexuality.

Cover design by Clifford Hayes
Front cover image: iStock

This book is dedicated to all our funders, partners and community members who helped us to realise this project. Thank you!

Contents

List of figures, tables and boxes

Figures

Table

Boxes

Notes on contributors

Lianne Brigham is a founder and administrator of York Past and Present, which is a Facebook group but also so much more. Now with over 28,000 members, York Past and Present enables people to share photographs, memory and knowledge about York's past and, through this, contribute to shaping York's present and future.

Richard Brigham is also a founder and administrator of York Past and Present.

Andrea Capstick is a Senior Lecturer in Dementia Studies at the University of Bradford and teaches on the MSc Advanced Dementia Studies programme there. Her research interests centre on arts-based approaches to social research and public involvement in dementia, narrative, human rights and historical trauma.

Jez Collins is the founder and director of the Birmingham Music Archive CIC, a cultural and creative arts organisation that captures, documents and celebrates the musical culture of Birmingham and develops associated projects such as exhibitions, tours, talks, youth and community focused projects and broadcast media (films and radio). Collins is also a co-Director of Un-Convention CIC, a global grassroots music network that helps build sustainable music infrastructures. He is a Trustee of the National Jazz Archive, a member of the Advisory Board for the Community Archives & Heritage Group and sits on the Heritage Committee panel for Birmingham Civic Society. His work on music archiving practices has been published in a number of journals and books.

Paul R.J. Duffy is an archaeological consultant and independent researcher based on the beautiful Isle of Bute on the west coast of Scotland. Between 2009 and 2012 he was the deputy project manager responsible for archaeology for the Heritage Lottery funded Discover Bute Landscape Partnership Scheme, a project that sparked a decade long interest in exploring how new relationships between communities and heritage can be enabled. His current research interests include exploration of the rural landscape of Bute and the role of residents in heritage preservation, which he pursues alongside a rich portfolio of consultancy work.

Kelly Foster is a London Blue Badge Guide. Kelly is a member of *Transmission* – a group of five individuals who share thoughts and ideas on the current heritage landscape. *Transmission* is developing a framework for interrogating what it means to be a Black archive, advocate and/or archivist in the 21st century with a view to sharing skills and to building capacity within the sector.

Helen Graham teaches heritage studies at the University of Leeds, and uses action and participatory approaches to research the politics and practices of heritage and democracy.

Vicky Green was a researcher on the Inclusive Archive of Learning Disability History project. Vicky previously worked for Mencap, is currently Co-Chair of her local Learning Disability Partnership Board and volunteers three mornings a week in a charity shop to raise money for cancer research.

Ian Gwilt is Professor of Design in the School of Art, Architecture and Design at the University of South Australia. He is interested in design for communication and knowledge mobilisation, data visualisation and the potential to design hybrid digital/physical experiences, from museums to human–robotic interactions, and design in the health care environment. He is also interested in how we can incorporate visual communication design practices into interdisciplinary research teams and in better defining design research practices.

Kim Hammond is currently a Research Consultant on the AHRC project Sounding Coastal Change in Geography at The Open University. This work includes running deliberative workshops with environment institutions and other public groups on the north Norfolk coast, organising a travelling exhibition and other public engagement events; and she is also leading the SCC multimedia e-books. She was project manager and research associate on two recently completed AHRC-funded projects: Stories of Change and Earth in Vision. Both projects benefited from Kim's first career as an environmental scientist and her more recent engagement in the cultural dimensions of environmental change. She has published both as a scientist and a cultural geographer. She led the Earth in Vision multimedia e-book team.

Pip Hardy is a director of Pilgrim Projects Ltd., co-founder of the Patient Voices Programme (www.patientvoices.org.uk) and honorary lecturer at Manchester Medical School. Pip has a BA (Hons) in English literature, an MA in Lifelong Learning and a PhD, which investigated the impact of digital storytelling in healthcare. She is co-editor of *Cultivating Compassion: How Digital Storytelling is Transforming Healthcare* and *Digital Storytelling in Higher Education: International Perspectives*. She has authored chapters in these and several other books and has published a number of papers about digital storytelling in healthcare and healthcare education.

Kassie Headon is a Virtual and Extended Reality artist who worked on the Inclusive Archive project through a role at the Rix Centre.

Victoria Hoyle was, at the time of the project, City Archivist for York Explore Libraries and Archives and a PhD researcher at the University of York. Victoria has since completed her PhD and is currently a Research Associate at UCL on an Arts and Humanities Research Council project on the information rights ecology in the public and voluntary sectors, focusing especially on social care records.

Nigel Ingham is a community oral historian, with a strong interest in the social history of learning disability. On the Living Archive Project Nigel was one of the Research Associates. In 2019, he is a Visiting Research Fellow with the Open University, developing a research grant application that will draw upon personal testimonies and life histories to investigate educational selection.

Hannah Ishmael is a doctoral candidate at University College London. Hannah is a member of *Transmission* — a group of five individuals who share thoughts and ideas on the current heritage landscape. *Transmission* is developing a framework for interrogating what it means to be a Black archive, advocate and/or archivist in the 21st century with a view to sharing skills and to building capacity within the sector.

Tom Jackson is a Lecturer in Digital Media in the School of Media and Communication and the Academic Lead for Cultural Engagement with the Centre for Immersive Technologies, both at the University of Leeds. His research addresses issues and debates related to sensory experience, technology and communication. Combining theoretical interests including neurological studies of cross-modal perception, ethnographic methods and the critical analysis of digital media platforms with a practice-led approach to research, he designs and evaluates digital methods for studying social, cultural and environmental phenomena through the lens of sensory experience.

Vanessa Jackson is a former BBC series producer and now course director of the BA (Hons) Media Production at Birmingham City University, teaching practical television production skills to undergraduates. She completed her practice-based PhD in television historiography at Royal Holloway, University of London in 2018. Her research interests include the history of television, as well as the uses of social media in community history projects. She has also published on the use of social media in enhancing student employability and student engagement.

Tricia Jenkins is co-Director of DigiTales Ltd and an associate lecturer on MA Arts Administration and Cultural Policy at Goldsmiths, University of London. She is a PhD candidate at Middlesex University and works regularly with participatory video company InsightShare. She is co-editor of *Digital Storytelling Form and Content* and author of 'Ageing Narratives' in *Digital Storytelling in Higher Education* (Palgrave Macmillan, 2018 and 2017). She is a researcher specialising in digital storytelling and participatory video as visual/participatory research methods. Current research interests include working with indigenous communities, older people and migrant women, and the impact of their personal stories in effecting change.

Etienne Joseph is a doctoral candidate at the University of Sussex. Etienne is also an archivist and independent practitioner. He is a member of *Transmission* — a group of five individuals who share thoughts and ideas on the current heritage landscape. *Transmission* is developing a framework for interrogating what it means to be a Black archive, advocate and/or archivist in the 21st century with a view to sharing skills and to building capacity within the sector.

Sue Ledger was a researcher on the Inclusive Archive project, where she led on the inclusion of people with high support needs or people with profound and multiple learning disabilities in archives. Sue is a Visiting Research Fellow with the Open University and freelance researcher. She has recently completed an inclusive evaluation project funded by Wellcome and is working on developing a website to support the inclusion of people with profound and multiple learning disabilities in public archive collections.

Melanie Levick-Parkin is the MFA Design Programme leader at the Sheffield Institute of Arts, Sheffield Hallam University. She also supervises doctoral candidates across Art & Design. Her research interests focus on making and visual communication practices, particularly in relation to intangible heritage and heritage and archaeology. Most of her work is about visual and material language and is informed by her feminist stance. She is particularly interested in how gender manifests in/affects how meaning is made within the public sphere, both materially and visually. Her work is situated within design anthropology and participatory design practices. Her latest publications include 'The values of being in design' (2017) and *Freedom to Make* (2018).

Katherine Ludwin is a freelance researcher and editor with an interest in documentary film-making and gender and LGBT studies. From 2013 to 20-15 she was a researcher on the NIHR-funded study Can Participatory Video enhance social participation and well-being for people with dementia in long-term care.

Patrick McEntaggart is a Senior Lecturer in Visual Communication at Sheffield Institute of Arts in Sheffield Hallam University. He has an evolving body of work that includes both practice (interactive installations/media) and publications. Past enquiry explored relationships between technologically mediated memory and the ways in which narrative might consequently be (re)constructed. The projects have focused on sites of memory (real world and virtual) with a particular interest in modes of transmission and moments of transition. Much of the work resituates collected memories within a new frame or interface, finding perspectives on the relationship between users and content. Recent enquiry includes psychological exploration with enquiry around creativity and individual differences.

Andy Minnion is Professor of Media Advocacy at University of East London, where he runs RIX Research & Media, a research and development centre dedicated to exploring the use of digital media for the benefit of people with intellectual and learning disabilities. Andy led the RIX Centre team's contribution to the Inclusive Archive project, hosting inclusive co-production workshops and 'sandpit' sessions, coordinating the development of a highly accessible prototype of an Inclusive Archive and trialling this with learning disabled people and collections that helped to represent the social history of this community. Andy is now supporting an inclusive group called the purpleSTARS at the RIX Centre to provide training and develop strategies to make museums, libraries and archives more inclusive and engaging for users with different abilities. RIX is pursuing support with partners for a national model of the Archive for the Social History of people with learning disabilities.

Niamh Moore has a background in interdisciplinary feminist research and is currently a Senior Lecturer in Sociology at the University of Edinburgh. Her research is informed by ecofeminist theory and practice, explored in a range of different settings and modes. As well as focusing on environmental justice, Niamh is also committed to supporting the creation of archives as a crucial site for sustaining knowledge, especially knowledge which might not otherwise be documented. Books include *The Changing Nature of Eco/feminism*, *The Archive Project* and *Participatory Research in More-than-Human Worlds*.

Ralph Morton is a freelance researcher who has worked at universities across the Midlands (UK), most recently at Loughborough University, where he researched barriers to (and enablers of) communication and engagement in the youth justice system. His research interests include corpus linguistics, forensic linguistics, institutional discourse, linguistic identity, language change and language in the youth justice system.

Daniel H. Mutibwa is an Assistant Professor in Creative Industries and Digital Culture in the Department of Cultural, Media and Visual Studies, University of Nottingham, UK. Daniel researches and teaches in the areas of media and communication, creative industries, digital culture, arts and citizenship and (new media) transformations in communities and culture. Daniel is author of *Cultural Protest in Journalism, Documentary Films and the Arts: Between Protest and Professionalisation* (2019) and has published work in key journals such as *Convergence: The International Journal of Research into New Media Technologies*, *European Journal of Cultural Studies*, the *International Journal of Media and Cultural Politics* and the *International Journal of Communication*, among others.

Hilary Nesi is Professor of English Language at Coventry University. Her research interests include language corpora, academic writing, academic speech events, dictionary design and use, English for specific purposes and English for academic purposes.

Simon Popple is Director of Impact and a Senior Lecturer in Photography and Digital Culture at the School of Media and Communication, University of Leeds. His primary research interests include community archives, digital storytelling, photography and archival theory. He is particularly interested in how archives can be used to make community history and in the relationships between institutional archives and communities.

Andrew Prescott is Professor of Digital Humanities in the School of Critical Studies, University of Glasgow. From 2012 to 2019, he was Theme Leader Fellow for the AHRC Digital Transformations strategic theme.

George Revill is Senior Lecturer in Geography, the Open University. George's background is in historical-cultural geography, particularly landscape as a way of understanding past and contemporary experiences of place and environment. These ideas have developed in his work through interests in geographies of travel, transport and mobility on the one hand, and a long-standing interest in sound, music and auditory spaces on the other. His current research centres on bringing issues of sound, mobility and landscape together. George has worked on several large multi institutional AHRC research projects, including Earth in Vision and most recently leading on Sounding Coastal Change; and he is Co-Investigator on the EPSRC project Next Generation Paper.

Nathan E. Richards is a doctoral candidate at the University of Sussex. Nathan is a member of *Transmission* — a group of five individuals who share thoughts and ideas on the current heritage landscape. *Transmission* is developing a framework for interrogating what it means to be a Black archive, advocate and/or archivist in the 21st century with a view to sharing skills and to building capacity within the sector.

Row Richards acted as Vicky Green's personal assistant during the Living Archive project.

Anna Sexton is a Lecturer in Archives and Records Management in the Department of Information Studies at University College London. Her research interests are primarily focused on participatory and trauma-informed approaches to archives and record-keeping, particularly in the context of mental health and social care. Her broader research interests include the intersections between ethics, rights, and social justice across archives, record-keeping, data management and cultural heritage settings.

Joe Smith was Professor of Environment and Society and Head of Geography at the Open University before becoming Director of the Royal Geographical Society on 1 May 2018. His academic work was focused on environmental communication, history, policy and politics. Joe has led several large multi-institutional AHRC research projects including Earth in Vision and Stories of Change.

Ego Ahaiwe Sowinski is an independent archivist and artist. Ego is a member of *Transmission* — a group of five individuals who share thoughts and ideas on the current heritage landscape. *Transmission* is developing a framework for interrogating what it means to be a Black archive, advocate and/or archivist in the 21st century with a view to sharing skills and to building capacity within the sector.

Liz Tilly was Principal Investigator on the Inclusive Archive of Learning Disability project and is a senior lecturer in health and social care at the Open University. Her research and teaching interests include learning disability, advocacy, the interface between disability and sexual and reproductive health, and death, dying and bereavement. Liz has a particular interest in historical perspectives, ethics and participatory methods in health and social care research.

Jonathan Wood is currently a Senior Lecturer in Graphic Design at Sheffield Hallam University. Throughout his meandering career path, Jonathan has actively enjoyed the roles of a graphic design student, full-time musician, managing director, multimedia design student, digital artist, freelance designer, teacher and lecturer. After initially studying graphic design he moved towards motion graphics and multimedia design. During this period, he started teaching the subject part time but after winning awards and industry accreditation he went on to work for RealtimeUK, responding to the creative multimedia challenges of a variety of high-profile corporate clients, including Jaguar, Sony and Rolls Royce.

Acknowledgements

The editors would like to acknowledge the commitment and enthusiasm of all our authors. We would also like to extend our gratitude to the anonymous reviewers of the manuscript as well as to Sarah Bird and Amelia Watts-Jones at Policy Press and Elizabeth Stone at Bourchier for their brilliant support throughout.

Series editors' foreword

Around the globe, communities of all shapes and sizes are increasingly seeking an active role in producing knowledge about how to understand, represent and shape their world for the better. At the same time, academic research is increasingly realising the critical importance of community knowledge in producing robust insights into contemporary change in all fields. New collaborations, networks, relationships and dialogues are being formed between academic and community partners, characterised by a radical intermingling of disciplinary traditions and by creative methodological experimentation.

There is a groundswell of research practice that aims to build new knowledge, address longstanding silences and exclusions, and pluralise the forms of knowledge used to inform common sense understandings of the world.

The aim of this book series is to act as a magnet and focus for the research that emerges from this work. Originating from the UK Arts and Humanities Research Council's Connected Communities programme (www.connected-communities.org), the series showcases critical discussion of the latest methods and theoretical resources for combining academic and public knowledge via high-quality, creative, engaged research. It connects the emergent practice happening around the world with the longstanding and highly diverse traditions of engaged and collaborative practice from which that practice draws.

This series seeks to engage a wide audience of academic and community researchers, policy makers and others with an interest in how to combine academic and public expertise. The wide range of publications in the series demonstrate that this field of work is helping to reshape the knowledge landscape as a site of democratic dialogue and collaborative practice, as well as contestation and imagination. The series editors welcome approaches from academic and community researchers working in this field who have a distinctive contribution to make to these debates and practices today.

Keri Facer, Professor of Educational and Social Futures,
University of Bristol

George McKay, Professor of Media Studies,
University of East Anglia

Community archives and the creation of living knowledge

Simon Popple, Daniel H. Mutibwa and Andrew Prescott

> How do we move from an archival universe dominated by one cultural paradigm to an archival multiverse; from a world constructed in terms of 'the one' and 'the other' to a world of multiple ways of knowing and practicing, of multiple narratives co-existing in one space?
>
> (AERI and PACG, 2011: 73)

> an archive needs to be a yarning, a conversation, with all the tacit protocols involved in a conversation between people, the respect in engagement that allows a conversation to continue over time, to be returned to, to grow and deepen, within a shared creative space. Yarning implicitly acknowledges the various contributors, embraces their contributions. It is by nature co-creative.
>
> Allison Boucher Krebs,
> cited in Faulkhead and Thorpe (2017: 5)

The Archival Multiverse

Since the 1980s, a traditional monolithic view of the nature of archives and record-keeping, largely derived from European and American bureaucratic traditions, has given way to a more fluid and pluralistic conception of archives that better reflects the diversity of the societies that create them. The rise of this archival multiverse has transformed the way in which collective memories are curated, recapturing forgotten and suppressed voices, reshaping our view of what archives are and how they function, and challenging old assumptions about the role of professionals in mediating and sharing common heritages (Gilliland, 2017).

The growth of the archival multiverse reflects many intellectual, cultural, technological, social and political currents. This book focuses on one of the most important of these developments, the growth of community archives and the active participation of ordinary citizens in their formation. The boom in community archives over the past 30 years has been important in allowing people to take control of their own histories and share their experiences, knowledge and expertise.

As community archives have become more widespread and influential, the professional archive community has started to radically rethink many of its own assumptions about how archives are created, preserved and made available. The roles of archivists, academic researchers and citizens have begun to coalesce and overlap, and the boundaries between these spaces have become more porous. Projects run by communities, archives and museums in partnership seek to break down the barriers between citizens and archival collections, adding previously excluded voices and memories and developing shared interpretations and understanding.

This volume seeks to capture the range and vibrancy of community archives through a series of case studies that illustrate their variety of subject matter, voice, form and method. These case studies partly (but not exclusively) derive from work undertaken in recent years by two major funding programmes, including a joint workshop held at the University of Edinburgh in November 2016. Connected Communities was a Research Councils UK programme led by the Arts and Humanities Research Council (AHRC), which from 2010 has funded over 300 projects, bringing together over 700 academics and more than 500 collaborating organisations from the wider community to explore how community and university expertise can be combined to better understand how communities are changing, and the roles that communities might play in responding to the problems and possibilities of the contemporary world. Digital Transformations was an AHRC strategic theme from 2010 to 2018 that funded 100 projects exploring how digital methods offer new opportunities for arts and humanities researchers, and also the critical, social and ethical issues presented by the increasing reliance of society on digital technologies.

Connected Communities was distinctive in its commitment to encouraging exploratory and open-ended projects that involve collaboration between university and community partners at all stages of the process. The topics covered by Connected Communities research projects range from festivals to community food, from everyday creativity to care homes, from hyperlocal journalism to community energy. Connected Communities and Digital Transformations organised a joint call in 2013 on 'Community Research Co-Production in the Arts and Humanities', which sought to unleash the creative power of communities to work with academic researchers in order to use the opportunities offered by digital innovations to strengthen communities, forge new networks, improve quality of life and reduce inequality. The success of this prompted the Digital Transformations theme to emphasise similar collaborative components in its subsequent Awards Amplification call.

A major lesson from these research funding activities is that working with communities as equal research partners, fully engaged in shaping research questions and methods, is a powerful means of using research to drive social, cultural and economic transformation. Technologically driven research often struggles to achieve transformative social impact because of its 'top-down' nature. Deeper transformation enhancing the quality of life and creating a more equal and just society is more likely to come from the type of collaborative activity that is a feature of Connected Communities, Digital Transformations and the other AHRC strategic themes active from 2010.

There are major institutional and cultural barriers that impede this 'participatory turn' in research, including limited funding for providing time to build collaborative dialogues, lack of diversity in universities themselves and a need for more investment in civil society's public learning infrastructure. The lessons learnt through Connected Communities on community–university relationships and the participatory turn in the production of knowledge were summarised in *Creating Living Knowledge* (Facer and Enright, 2016), which offered a template for the creation of 'the sorts of ongoing, productive conversations that enable both academics and communities to reframe their assumptions, build living knowledge and create embodied and lasting legacies' (Facer and Enright, 2016: 153).

Heritage is potentially an important meeting ground for communities, academic researchers and policymakers. Many museums have sought to build active links with their community. While there are many success stories, such as the community partnerships of Hackney Museum, equally, as a 2011 report sponsored by the Paul Hamlyn Foundation pointed out, there are many cases where curators see community activities as an optional extra or are reluctant to allow communities full participation. Curators stress funding difficulties and the challenges of dividing up a small cake, prompting community groups to ask 'whose cake is it anyway?' (Lynch, 2011, 2014).

The experience of creating, developing and ensuring the long-term sustainability of community archives also reflects some of these tensions, but nevertheless the number and varied nature of community archives mean that they provide valuable case studies in the issues associated with fostering the 'participatory turn' in research. Through

3

presenting a selection of recent and ongoing projects, our authors explore the current state of research and practice in relation to a range of community archives. They provide an overview of current thinking around the relevance of the archive as both a communal and institutional space and as a site of experimentation and collaboration. They assist in the development of a critical frame to help understand the theory and practice of the archival multiverse, and suggest how we can use digital resources, data and collaborative working to continue to foster an increasing diversity of voice and memory in the archive.

The community turn

The notion of 'community' is a slippery one. Facer and Enright (2016: 13) observe in respect of the Connected Communities programme that it is tempting to say that the term is so vague as to be unhelpful. They note that 'it is a word that is often infused with a nostalgia which masks processes of oppression and exclusion and produces unhelpful generalisations that mask real differences' (Facer and Enright, 2016: 13). Preferring a very broad definition of community as 'the very wide range of virtual, physical, geographic, interest and accidental groups that are formed around interests, issues, places, histories, cultures and professions' (2016: 13), Facer and Enright note how the use of the term 'community' is invariably politically loaded.

Crooke (2007, 2011, 2015) argues that discussion of community in relation to museums and heritage falls into three main areas. The first is community studies, which examines the way in which a sense of identity and belonging is generated. By acting as custodians of memory, museums and archives play a fundamental role in shaping community self-perceptions. A second area in which the term community is applied in museums and archives is in the development of public policy. Governments frequently see community action as an important means of enhancing local and national services. However, the term 'community' can frequently be used by government as an 'aerosol can' to give a more sympathetic and progressive cachet to reduced or limited services, as with community care or community policing (Cochrane, 1986: 51).

The final area of intersection between heritage and community identified by Crooke is the community as a vehicle for social action:

> Here one will encounter the community of resistance, and community as a form of protest and as underpinning the formation of a democracy. Community groups have

used heritage and museum activity as a vehicle for protest and as integral to their social and political campaigns. Involvement of community in this context is about the creation of new 'circuits of power' and sustainable networks that promote access and inclusion and are accountable to diverse communities. (Crooke, 2007: 28)

It is this social activism and community self-organisation that is the distinguishing feature of the community archive. The most commonly used definition of community by writers on community archives is that offered by Flinn et al, which again stresses the looseness of the communal links: 'all manner of collective self-identifications including by locality, ethnicity, faith, sexuality, occupation, shared interest' (Flinn et al, 2009: 75). These shared interests are less important than the fact a group self-identifies as a community. To quote Flinn et al again, 'A community, in short, is any group of people who come together and present themselves as such, and a "community archive" is the product of their attempts to document the history of their commonality' (Flinn et al, 2009: 75).

It is this independence, the way in which a group of people sharing common characteristics and interests seek to create their own archive on their own terms, which is the chief feature of the community archive. The 19th and 20th centuries saw the establishment in many countries of an elaborate network of national, local and specialist archive repositories. International standards governing the storage, retention, processing and cataloguing of these archives were put in place. Professional training and qualifications were created, and professional and scholarly literatures were produced. While community archives may make use of these networks and may pay attention to professional standards in matters such as cataloguing, they do not feel bound to follow these procedures and regard their independence as crucial. The importance of the community as the primary agent in the creation and control of the archive is stressed by Flinn et al (2009: 73):

the defining characteristic of community archives is the active participation of a community in documenting and making accessible the history of their particular group and/ or locality on their own terms. These terms range from complete autonomy from the 'mainstream' to the delegation of the custody and preservation of their materials to public-sector archivists and a wide range of options in between.

Community archives are independent grassroots efforts to document and record shared experiences that fall outside the frameworks of the conventional mainstream archive. They are archives 'for the people, by the people, that often eliminate the traditional middlemen of the professional archivist and university or government repository' (Caswell, 2014: 32).

The reason for the creation of these independent archives was an awareness that the formal corporate archive ignores or obliterates many people, a process described by Michelle Caswell as symbolic annihilation, a term widely used in feminist and queer criticism (Caswell, 2014: 27). Thus, the Black Cultural Archives were created in Brixton in 1981, the year in which heavy-handed policing in South London led to major riots in that part of the city. By documenting and disseminating the culture and history of the peoples of Africa and Caribbean ancestry living in Britain, the Black Cultural Archives sought to combat the omission of Black people from British histories, which contributed to 'a sense of frustration and alienation from British society' (Flinn, 2007: 157). Particularly influential in encouraging this movement to create a more diverse sense of the British inheritance was a 1999 lecture by Stuart Hall, which criticised policy on cultural heritage as 'intended for those who "belong" – a society which is imagined as, in broad terms, culturally homogeneous and unified' (Hall 1999: 6). Hall noted 'a decline in the acceptance of the traditional authorities in authenticating the interpretative and analytic frameworks which classify, place, compare and evaluate culture, and the concomitant rise in the demand to re-appropriate control over "the writing of one's story"' (Hall, 1999: 7–8).

This demand to 'write one's own story' extended to many different groups. Internationally, the way in which government archives excluded or ignored the histories and memories of indigenous peoples in colonised territories such as Australia and North America has been particularly important in challenging canonical perceptions of the archive. Traditional archives privileged the written record and excluded oral memory, performance and story. Yet for many indigenous groups it is this oral memory that is the most significant. The landscape itself forms part of their archive:

> A responsibility and belief that seems to be shared by all Indigenous nations of Australia is the connection between the land and the people. This is both a physical and an emotional connection that relates to specific areas of land with stories and oral knowledge dating back thousands

of years telling us of the responsibility of belonging to the land. These stories explain land boundaries and methods of caring for people and land, for flora and fauna, and for places of significance, such as cemeteries. The responsibility also includes caring for the oral stories necessary for land care and ownership. (Faulkhead and Berg, 2010: xvi)

For the native American Allison Boucher Krebs, it was essential that indigenous peoples themselves took the lead in the endeavour to rethink the archive to encompass this knowledge:

It is these Indigenous institutions, their founders, administrators, staff, and communities that will be writing the next chapters of policies and procedures sourced from deep within the multi-verse of Indian Country. It is these institutions and their founding communities that live their protocols. It is these institutions that will struggle with integrity to align their policies and procedures with their ways of knowing. It is here, at the grassroots of Indian Country that the face of the information fields of libraries, archives, and museums will be altered, shape shifting in meaningful ways in service of peoplehood, in service of a relational accountability built from ground up in a new sprouting of trust. (Krebs, 2012: 189)

This clarion cry on behalf of indigenous peoples expresses the moving spirit of community archives. The belief in the importance of grassroots action in the archive animates the chapters in this volume, generating new ways of thinking about the archive, its nature and potency as a source of shared and fluid historical narrative. Such activities unmake traditions of ownership and disrupt formal architectures and curatorial orthodoxies (Borowiecki et al, 2016). Community archives are reshaping the ontological nature of the archive and becoming the focus of growing research, data generation and digitally enabled interactivity.

The 'community turn' in archives is paralleled in many other areas of heritage and memory work, particularly museums where there has been a long-standing interest in opening them up to a more collaborative dialogue with the communities they serve (Crooke 2015; Lynch 2014). However, there are some distinctive features of the archives work described in this volume that are worth emphasising.

First is the range of communities represented. While much of the initial impetus for community archives came from under-represented groups such as black communities or lesbian, gay, bisexual, transgender or queer (LGBTQI+) groups, community archives nowadays increasingly represent almost any type of bond which draws people together. The archives represented in this volume include those formed by groups sharing an interest in particular music, who worked in the same place or shared common forms of illness. Community archives have become a way of celebrating different forms of connectedness and illustrate the variety our communities take.

Many of these community archives are not intimately linked to recognisable forms of social activism, but they nevertheless express the wish of varying groups of people to document the phenomena that link them together. In this way, community archives themselves become a form of social activism because of the way in which they forge and consolidate such a wide range of social links. Community archives are a means of forming and exemplifying community feeling in a world where the older forms of community such as workplace and locality have become less important and social connections are more dispersed, fragmented and fluid.

A community archive has become a new sort of space for communities to be formed and developed. One issue in the interaction between museums and communities has been the continued curatorial control of the museum space and the sense that the community's access to the museum is still subject to the whim of the curatorial gatekeeper. A striking feature of the community archives discussed in this volume is the extent to which they are spaces formed on community initiatives. While such archives pose many issues of sustainability and dependence on commercial solutions, nevertheless they are created by communities and help sustain the community. In these ways, community archives offer many pointers as to the development of new types of shared knowledge and pedagogical spaces of the type proposed as a result of the Connected Communities programme.

Turning the archive

The conventional 20th-century archive derived from models developed in such European countries as France and Germany (Gilliland, 2017) and was famously codified in the *Manual for the Arrangement and Description of Archives* published by the Dutch archivists Muller, Feith and Fruin in 1898 (Ketelaar, 1996). This model of the archive focused on the written official record and emphasised the importance of reflecting the existing bureaucratic structure of the *fond*. Official custody was seen as significant in confirming the authenticity and evidential value of the record, with the English archival theorist Hilary Jenkinson going as far as denying full archival value to documents which had strayed from government custody and were held in libraries and museums (Jenkinson, 1965).

In such a context, it is easy to understand how archives came to be seen as complicit with power. The Latin *archivum* derives from the Greek *arkheion*, which was 'a house, a domicile, an address, the residence of the superior magistrates, the *archons*, those who commanded' (Derrida, 1998: 9). Documents were filed in the house of the magistrates because of their official position. As Derrida comments, 'It is thus, in this *domiciliation*, in this house arrest, that archives take place' (Derrida 1998: 9). As David Bate (2009) has noted in his work relating to the photographic archive, the ownership and curation of public and social memory lie at the heart of political control.

Work such as that of Thomas Richards (1993) and James Ryan (1997) on the imperial archive exposed the ways in which archives were used to control and regulate those narratives and ideological controls that were the building blocks of empire. A stark illustration of the use of the archive to support and reinforce state power was the way in which the state archives of South Africa were sanitised by the apartheid regime to justify its actions (Harris, 2007). Even the archives of democratic countries such as Canada and Australia reinforce existing inequalities and injustices by the omissions and silences inherent in the close relationship of the archive to state bureaucracies (McKemmish et al, 2011; Morse, 2012; Hunt, 2016; Luker, 2017). Increasingly those groups that are excluded or muted in the archive – ethnic groups, indigenous populations, women, disabled, LGBTQI+ – protest at their absence from the major repositories of social memory. The work of Truth and Reconciliation Commissions in South Africa and Canada and the debate around indigenous archives in Australia have been major drivers in recent discussion about the nature, structure and ownership of archives (Harris, 2007; Ghaddar, 2016). The decolonisation of the archive has direct links to other decolonisation campaigns such as the Rhodes Must Fall movement (Kros, 2015).

The current relationship between civil society and the archive is being reshaped by many factors in addition to perceptions of social exclusion. At an institutional day-to-day level, many local record offices find themselves under great pressure as they struggle with reduced resources, demands for new digital services and the difficulties of preserving and curating new types of information (Summers, 2011).

However, at the same time, there are exciting new developments. Activities such as family history are generating a stronger sense of shared ownership of the archive, encouraging a greater sense of community engagement and an understanding of how archives embody shared memory. Digital access to catalogues and to images of records is becoming more widespread. Increasingly, users can take their own images of records and share them.

In this context, the archive is ceasing to be an institutional treasure chest and is emerging as a collaborative space bridging traditionally segregated institutions and communities of users. This is reflected in the increasing range of media falling in the purview of the archive. The primacy of the written record was challenged first by the rise of new types of media, including sound, photographs, film and now digital media. The importance of audio-visual archives in social memory became increasingly apparent during the 20th century, but traditional archival methods were by no means suited to the appraisal, description and preservation of this material. As archives increasingly dealt with a wide range of media, archival theories predicated on written records came to seem increasingly outmoded.

At the heart of the community archive, and evident in this volume, is a much more wide-ranging view of the content of the archive:

> an archive can variously be a building, cardboard-box, photograph album, internet website, or discourse of interconnected ideas such as community heritage and shared memory; and it holds or contains documents, which can take the form of written texts, photographs, sound recordings, postcards, medical records, printed materials, material objects…and not just official records, nor necessarily things on paper either. (Moore et al, 2016: 1)

In this context, an archive is defined by how far a community sees it as embodying its own social memory:

> Let anything be 'as archive' and let everyone be an archivist. The important question is not 'what is an archive,' but how does this particular individual or group perceive and understand an archive? […] The creator, the user, and the archivist find meaning and make meaning in an archive and those meanings help in structuring and restructuring the relationship between the self and "the larger order of things. (Ketelaar, 2017: 239)

This view, which allows anything archival value and proclaims everyone to be an archivist, is far removed from the emphasis of older theorists on official custody and the primacy of corporate records as evidence. This liberation of the archive from house arrest described by Derrida is one of the great achievements of community archives.

Many writers included in this book are pushing forward this process of reinventing the archive by working with communities to provide a home for excluded voices, building strategic partnerships that challenge hegemonic traditions and establishing a new community turn in relation to archival theory and collaborative practices. This is, of course, not an entirely new approach. The network of record offices established in Britain in the 1930s was based on local government units such as counties and boroughs, and many record offices have worked assiduously to record local community life beyond the formal local government record (Flinn, 2007: 154–8). In the USA, county historical societies have also played an important part in curating local memory. The work of local archivists created that awareness of the importance of the archive in community life that sowed the seeds of modern community archives. Much groundwork was also laid through the development of history from below methodologies, people's history projects and pioneering co-creation work fostered through the History Workshop movement (Samuel, 1994; Scott-Brown, 2017).

Central to our current concerns, and drawn from such democratic precursors, is the transformative power of the stories that can be (re)made from the archive and of the new archives that can be joint endeavours and held in common. They embody a sense of challenge and empowerment that seeks to remake the archive and offer innovative collaborative models of ownership and curation within evolving theoretical models of the archive. These new archives are reshaping the epistemological nature of the archive and becoming the focus of growing research, data generation and digitally enabled interactivity.

As established organisations revalue their archives, there is a drive towards more collaborative partnership, experimentation and risk-taking, as can be found in the Manchester Libraries Archive Plus (www.archivesplus.org), where traditional boundaries between archives, libraries and museums have been collapsed into a single integrated and public space. Digital technologies encourage the creation of more porous archives where the boundaries between creator, participant and user break down and there are opportunities to reflect and comment on the archive (Popple, 2015; Duffy and

Popple, 2017). The challenge that community archives and archival partnerships now face is to find an effective voice in a range of attempts to play a central role in the decolonisation of the academy and, in the most marginalised and excluded contexts, to establish disruptive and counter archives. It is striking how there are parallel discussions around these themes within libraries, museums and archives, but these debates remain in separate cultural silos, and another major challenge is to connect these different discussions to create a more integrated approach to community engagement with the past.

Archives are fundamental to the re-creation and co-ownership of knowledge. They are becoming less 'closed' or elite spaces. Archives increasingly belong to those who are represented in them, and archivists are increasingly seeking to explore the potential of these community activities (Theimer, 2015). The archive is increasingly emerging as a driver of political change at a time when the ability to 'speak back' to hierarchical, racial and gendered orthodoxies has never been more important.

The digital turn

A major force in the growth of community archives has been the availability of digital tools. While the community archive movement pre-dates the personal computer, as the Black Cultural Archives in Britain demonstrate, the development of the World Wide Web and the way in which it made it possible to publish digital resources with minimal technical know-how was vital in promoting the growth of community archives (Flinn, 2010: 42–5; Chenier, 2016). A wide range of community groups was now able to share and curate objects, including images, video, sound and text, and to provide their own narratives. A good example is Chile SCDA (www.chilescda.org), the website of Chilean refugees who fled General Pinochet's regime and settled in South Yorkshire. The way in which this website combines news and information for the Chilean exile community with documentation of their stories, such as video interviews with those who fled from Chile in 1973, is characteristic of many community archives.

The use of digital tools has been a major factor in enabling the archive to extend beyond the written record. Websites have proved a flexible and easy way by which community groups have been able to share and preserve a variety of different formats such as video interviews, family photographs and representations of material artefacts such as quilts and tapestries. Digital archives also have the possibility of incorporating new levels of interpretative and contextual sources, by enabling community comments and commentary on objects. This can open out the sort of conversation around the archive, the sort of 'yarning' about the archive that Allison Boucher Krebs suggested was important in exploring the wealth of stories and memories embodied in the archive.

The development of such participative spaces presents many issues and challenges. They may offer a contested and contestable version of events, shaped by historical accident and a variety of institutional and community factors. The curation and documentation of open-ended and multi-vocal commentary as an inherent part of the archive is a demanding proposition, generating complex and shifting bodies of metadata (Flinn, 2010: 46–9). The proliferation of web and social media-based archives poses major issues of discoverability – of finding out what archives have been created and what they contain. Detailed cataloguing of archives poses major resource issues, and there is a risk that documents can be effectively lost because of poor or inappropriate cataloguing. Nevertheless, such digital archives provide opportunities to offer insights into the mediation and reception of particular events, so that the different perspectives of various social groups and institutions in relation to major events such as strikes or terrorist attacks can be explored.

While digital affordances have been important in driving the growth of community archives, the use of digital tools by community archives is a conflicted and complex question, and the way ahead is not necessarily clear. As the web has become increasingly carved up by large commercial interests, many community archives have started to use commercial platforms for their archives. The enormous growth in special interest groups on Facebook is an illustration of this. Many of these groups use Facebook to share memories and archival objects of various sorts, and the conversation on the groups is a potentially major resource for the study of particular communities (Sheffield, 2018). However, the sustainability of these Facebook archives is a major issue. Groups can be suspended for a variety of reasons and the long-term sustainability of these archives is entirely dependent on the longevity of Facebook (Sheffield, 2018: 106–13). The issues surrounding the sustainability of community archives using other social media, such as Instagram, or commercial blog platforms, is equally complex. Simple failure to renew a domain registration can potentially make an archive inaccessible.

These issues of sustainability pale by comparison with the wider issues about the health of the internet and abuse of social media. The way in which Facebook, for example, uses algorithms to manipulate and polarise reaction to discussions is by now well known, and the dangers posed by the hijacking of social media to promote extremist and racist views are familiar to all users. The increasing risk of abuse might cause community archives increasingly to restrict their membership and become less open. More complex and difficult to evaluate is the way in which algorithmic manipulation might affect the membership profile of archives and the way in which members of community archives interact with each other. There is a strong case that community projects should avoid the use of platforms such as Facebook altogether and develop more open solutions, but for some communities the development cost and lack of appropriate expertise may be off-putting.

It is unclear what use Facebook and other social media platforms are making of the information contained in community archives housed by them. This can potentially be an enormous problem if politically sensitive information about (for example) activist groups is stored in the archive. In the case of community archives associated with, for example, the Arab Spring, information on social media sites has disappeared quite quickly as a result of government action, although attempts have been made to conserve this information by institutions such as Brown University in the United States (Sheffield, 2018: 112). The use of digital platforms for archiving heritage items of minority groups can present complex ethical problems and the frameworks for dealing with these have not yet been fully articulated. For example, a cassette tape from a Native American archive might contain songs that are not supposed to be heard by outsiders, requiring special restrictions to be put on the circulation of the tape (Christen, 2015).

These and other issues mean that community archives inevitably become engaged with debates about the overall health of the internet. Discussions about privacy, reuse of data, use of commercial platforms and centralisation of data all impinge heavily on the development of community archives. An annual 'Health of the Internet Report' to act as focal point for monitoring these issues has recently been established by the Mozilla Foundation (https://internethealthreport. org), and Mozilla has been active in providing leadership to groups and individuals concerned with the health of the internet through its festivals, fellowship schemes and other activities. It might be that in the future the social activism that has been a feature of the development of community archives will cause them to become more identified with digital activism.

Conclusion

As Emerling (2011) notes, it is what we bring to the archive that is often as important as what we take from it. And it is in the creative elision of community and archival institution that the true value of the archive can be realised. The current-making, interrogation and reshaping of the archive is an attractive prospect, but not without its own challenges. Issues such as digital optimism, the renegotiation of power relationships and voice, curatorial ethics, working practices, data and intellectual property are among the current key concerns.

Our aim in this volume is to consider the changing nature of the archive through the lens of a carefully selected portfolio of projects that, because of their emphasis on co-creation, provide insights into the shifting patterns of engagement with the archive and its potential as an innovative collaborative space. All the chapters seek to distil the latest thinking about the relationships between communities and institutions and reflect on where we now stand. They describe a range of approaches to the practice of co-research and co-creation within this developing context and consider the issues presented by the problems of liberating cultural resources from formally closed and resistant institutions. As emergent dialogues about the role and function of the archive are played out through a rapidly changing series of technological, political, methodological and cultural paradigms, the authors reflect the opportunities and challenges of working across and through different sectors. This represents a novel way of combining both critical thinking and the lessons of practical community-based experience.

The projects discussed in this book demonstrate the need for a commitment to partnerships between communities (defined in their broadest sense) and institutional partners to develop models of co-curation, creative exploitation and access models that open up cultural resources and reinstate lost and excluded voices. They highlight the need for openness, honesty and the ability to listen as well as speak, and demonstrate how the archive comes alive when it contains plural voices and we learn how to make the archive a yarning.

References

AERI and PACG (2011) 'Educating for the archival multiverse', *The American Archivist*, 74(1): 69–101.

Bate, David (2009) *Photography: The Key Concepts*, Oxford: Berg.

Borowiecki, Karol J., Forbes, Neil and Fresa, Antonella (eds) (2016) *Cultural Heritage in a Changing World*, Switzerland: Springer Open.

Caswell, Michelle (2014) 'Seeing yourself in history: community archives and the fight against symbolic annihilation', *The Public Historian* 36(4): 26–37.

Chenier, Elise (2016) 'Reclaiming the lesbian archives', *The Oral History Review*, 43(1): 170–82.

Christen, Kimberly (2015) 'Tribal archives, traditional knowledge, and local contexts: Why the "s" matters', *Journal of Western Archives*, 6(1), Article 3.

Cochrane, Alan (1986) 'Community Politics and Democracy', in Held, D. and Pollitt, C. (eds) *New Forms of Democracy*, London: Sage, pp 51–75.

Crooke, Elizabeth (2007) *Museums and Community: Ideas, Issues and Challenges*, London: Routledge.

Crooke, Elizabeth (2011) 'Museums and Community', in Macdonald, Sharon (ed.) *A Companion to Museum Studies*, London: Wiley, pp 170–85.

Crooke, Elizabeth (2015) 'The "Active Museum": How Concern with Community Transformed the Museum', in Message, Kylie and Whitcomb, Andrea (eds) *The International Handbooks of Museum Studies: Museum Practice*, London: Wiley, pp 481–502.

Derrida, Jacques (1998) *Archive Fever: a Freudian Impression*, Chicago: University of Chicago Press.

Duffy, Paul R.J. and Popple, Simon (2017) 'Pararchive and Island Stories: Collaborative co-design and community digital heritage on the Isle of Bute', *Internet Archaeology*, 46, Available from: https://intarch.ac.uk/journal/issue46/4/toc.html [Accessed 21 October 2019].

Emerling, Jae (2011) *Photography: History and Theory*, Abingdon: Routledge.

Facer, Keri and Enright, Bryony (2016) *Creating Living Knowledge: The Connected Communities Programme, Community-University Relationships and the Participatory Turn in the Production of knowledge*, Bristol: University of Bristol and AHRC Connected Communities.

Faulkhead, Shannon and Berg, Jim (2010) *Power and the Passion: Our Ancestors Return Home*, Melbourne: Koorie Heritage Trust.

Faulkhead, Shannon and Thorpe, Kirsten (2017) 'Dedication: Archives and Indigenous Communities', in Gilliland, Anne J. McKemmish, Sue and Lau, Andrew J. (eds.) *Research in the Archival Multiverse*, Clayton: Monash University Publishing, pp 2–15.

Flinn, Andrew (2007) 'Community histories, community archives: Some opportunities and challenges', *Journal of the Society of Archivists*, 28(2): 151–76.

Flinn, Andrew (2010) 'Independent community archives and community-generated content', *Convergence*, 16(1): 39–51.

Flinn, Andrew, Stevens, Mary and Shepherd, Elizabeth (2009) 'Whose memories, whose archives? Independent community archives, autonomy and the mailstream', *Archival Science*, 9(1–2): 71–86.

Ghaddar, J.J. (2016) 'The spectre in the archive: Truth, reconciliation, and indigenous archival memory', *Archivaria*, 82: 3–26.

Gilliland, Anne J. (2017) 'Archival and Recordkeeping Traditions in the Multiverse and their Importance for Researching Situations and Situating Research', in Gilliland, Anne J., McKemmish, Sue and Lau, Andrew J. (eds) *Research in the Archival Multiverse*, Clayton: Monash University Publishing, pp 31–73.

Hall, Stuart (1999) 'Whose heritage? Un-settling "the heritage", re-imagining the post-nation', *Third Text*, 13(49): 3–13.

Harris, Verne (2007) *Archives and Justice: A South African Perspective*, Chicago: Society of American Archivists.

Hunt, Dallas (2016) 'Nikîkîwân 1: Contesting settler colonial archives through indigenous oral history', *Canadian Literature/Littérature Canadienne*, 230: 25–42.

Jenkinson, Hilary (1965), *A Manual of Archive Administration*, 2nd ed., London: Lund Humphries.

Ketelaar, Eric (1996) 'Archival theory and the Dutch manual', *Archivaria*, 41: 31–40.

Ketelaar, Eric (2017) 'Archival Turns and Returns', in Gilliland, Anne J., McKemmish, Sue and Lau, Andrew J. (eds) *Research in the Archival Multiverse*, Clayton: Monash University Publishing, pp 228–68.

Krebs, Allison Boucher (2012) 'Native America's twenty-first century right to know', *Archival Science*, 12(2): 173–90.

Kros, Cynthia (2015) 'Rhodes must fall: Archives and counter-archives', *Critical Arts: South-North Cultural and Media Studies*, 29: 150–65.

Luker, Trish (2017) 'Decolonising archives: Indigenous challenges to record keeping in reconciling settler colonial states', *Australian Feminist Studies*, 32: 108–25.

Lynch, Bernadette (2011) *Whose Cake Is It Anyway? A Collaborative Investigation into Engagement and Participation in 12 Museums and Galleries in the UK*, London: Paul Hamlyn Foundation.

Lynch, Bernadette (2014) 'Whose Cake Is It Anyway? Museums, Civil Society and the Changing Reality of Public Engagement', in Gourievidis, Laurence (ed.) *Museums and Migration: History, Memory and Politics*, London: Routledge, pp 68–80.

McKemmish, Sue, Faulkhead, Shannon and Russell, Lynette (2011) 'Distrust in the archive: Reconciling records', *Archival Science*, 11(3–4): 211–39.

Moore, Niamh, Salter, Andrea, Stanley, Liz and Tamboukou, Maria (2016) *The Archive Project: Archival Research in the Social Sciences*, Oxford: Routledge.

Morse, Bradford W (2012) 'Indigenous human rights and knowledge in archives, museums, and libraries: Some international perspectives with specific reference to New Zealand and Canada', *Archival Science*, 12(2): 113–40.

Popple, Simon (2015) 'The new Reithians: Pararchive and citizen animateurs in the BBC digital archive', *Convergence*, 21(1): 132–44

Richards, Thomas (1993) *The Imperial Archive: Knowledge and the Fantasy of Empire*, London: Verso.

Ryan, James (1997) *Picturing Empire. Photography and the Visualisation of the British Empire*, London: Reaktion Books.

Samuel, Raphael (1994) *Theatres of Memory I: Past and Present in Contemporary Culture*, London: Verso.

Scott-Brown, Sophie (2017) *The Histories of Raphael Samuel: A Portrait of a People's Historian*, Acton: Australian National University Press.

Sheffield, Rebecka (2018) 'Facebook live as a recordmaking technology', *Archivaria* 85: 96–121.

Summers, Anne (2011) '"A continuing supply of history": Thoughts from the archive', *History Workshop Journal*, 72: 249–55.

Theimer, Kate (2015) *Appraisal and Acquisition: Innovative Practices for Archives and Special Collections*, Plymouth: Rowman and Littlefield.

2

Disorderly conduct:
the community in the archive

Simon Popple

Clearly archives are not neutral: they embody the power
inherent in accumulation, collection, and hoarding.

(Sekula, 2003: 446)

Introduction

The 'Finding Myself in the Archives' (2017) project undertaken by
the Ward Museum in Canada is illustrative of creative approaches to
opening up the 'Archive' to new forms of scrutiny and new interpretive
voices. It does so in a way that allows for collective reorientations of
history, culture and witness through innovative curatorial practice.
Students who had taken part in the project were asked to research
and find the 'stories' connoted by 54 objects from the collection
of the University of Toronto. They were to relate the objects and
associated stories not just to their own lives but also to the lives of the
marginalised communities those objects touched.

While the participants were students studying on a museum
programme, they were a 'community' in their own right, a professional
community in the making, one that would shortly form part of a
new generation of archival professionals, guardians of knowledge and
potential gatekeepers. This and many other recent projects, such as
those undertaken as part of the Research Councils UK Connected
Communities programme and Digital Transformations theme, point
to a sea-change in institutional and community relationships that
increasingly foregrounds collaborative approaches (Facer and Enright,
2016). Such approaches increasingly invite the community into the
institutional archival space and legitimise the non-institutional archive,
recognising the reciprocal value and authority of the community and
the vibrant potential of collaborative dialogues that challenge traditions,
innovate new practices and share the inherent power of the archive
in all its emergent forms (Crooke, 2007; Flinn, 2010; Hacker, 2013).

The archive as community

The archival space is one populated by communities of all sorts: those represented, those who curate and care for its contents, those who excavate and interpret, and those curious about what, if anything, it has to say about their own lives and histories. These roles, often separated and oppositional in the past, are increasingly disrupted and interrogated by a combination of new approaches, materialities, digital technologies and the pressures of the prevailing economic climate. The potential to collect, connect and challenge knowledge, remix materials, share responsibilities and flip boundaries is palpable and ongoing (Smith, 2007). In many respects traditionally defined protocols, articulations of power and conceptions of ownership and responsibility have been blurred. Historically, and across a whole raft of historical precedent and archival theory, they were in competition around contested histories, practices and the archival space itself (Moore et al, 2017). As Pollock has demonstrated in relation to women's art, new articulations of the archive, perhaps through a digital reimaging, afford new histories and shifts in the control of meaning and interpretation (Pollock, 2007). Whilst still contested and often hierarchical, institutionally and at community level, there are exciting changes taking place, new challenges and opportunities to be embraced and archives to be 'activated' (Buchanan and Bastian, 2015).

This introductory chapter seeks to problematise the shifting boundaries between the archive and its communities of care, use and representation through the example of the photographic archive. In this respect it sees the archive as an exciting competitive space in which there has been a discernible shift in the balance of ownership and interpretational power from institutions and gatekeepers, from a Derridean sense of *arrested knowledge* to a more open and contested *liberated knowledge* that is the result of polyvocal endeavour (Derrida,1998): an endeavour based on disrupting and disturbing formal traditions of archival practice, notions of the archival space and the position and nature of 'communities' in relation to it; and in actively seeking the collaborative presence of the 'represented' (Kindon et al, 2007). Critically, it seeks to locate the value of these communities in relation to each other and to resist the often tokenistic co-option of communities for the benefit of institutions rather than the collective (Denison and Stillman, 2012; Owens, 2013: Ridge, 2014).

This chapter examines the transition and alignments of communities through a consideration built around the changing role of the community in the photographic archive and the shift from subjecthood to agency. It also examines the use of the photographic archive as a means of exploring the new potentialities of the community archive. It reflects on the sense of the community as pictured within the archive and the increasing potential of self-archiving and curation afforded by new digital technologies, drawing on recent projects funded by the Arts and Humanities Research Council (AHRC) Connected Communities and Digital Transformations schemes. It offers a model in which the disruptive can be privileged and the counterfactual become an essential component of the archivist's armoury.

The surveillant archive: community as 'subject'

Archives have historically been seen as repositories of power, a means by which dominant elites inscribe communities and implement their authority over them (Emerling, 2011: 121). They formed part of an infrastructure controlling memory and access to knowledge, which also included libraries, museums and universities (Merewether, 2006: 10). Archives have traditionally been elite institutions and restricted spaces, open to civil servants, curators and academics but largely closed off to members of the public (Sandell, 2002). In seeking to examine how these traditions have shifted and where they might be leading the photograph, and the photographic archive, we need to accept the photograph as a vital text imbued with the means of *surveillant* and *sousveillant* agency; as a means of looking and being looked at. Photographs, privileged in our ocular-centric culture, have always operated as texts characterised by a series of oppositions; between public and private, official and vernacular, analogue and digital, valued and ephemeral, haptic and formless, real and illusory, stabilising and disruptive, community and institution, citizen and state (Tagg, 2009). The photograph is a text that has been deployed by and imposed upon the whole spectrum of society to record, measure and memorialise lives present and past, forming the skeleton of popular and collective memory (Brink, 2000). The problematisation of competing cultural histories and memories is laid bare through Brink's consideration of the Holocaust and of the composition and control of the photographic record, and the stories that these inanimate texts articulate. The allure of photography is, on the surface, very simple. It promises to preserve lived experiences and, as Bazin noted, 'embalm' them, thus preserving an ongoing memory of the subject against the continuum of time (Bazin and Gray, 1960: 4). The act of photography can be a means of warding off the inevitable decay of memory and our own mortality. Photography offers both to preserve a trace of our brief lives and also 'resurrect' those that have passed before us.

The mnemonic qualities of the photograph act as a guarantee not just for us in the here and now, but allow us to intersect with any historical epoch captured by the camera; and if we accept the ontological promise of authenticity, to relive them. Digital images and digital archives appear to bring that promise within reach. Indeed, the increasingly digital memory of photography, both in terms of storage and access, offers to deconstruct centuries-old practices and disrupt relationships between institutional, commercial and vernacular collections.

> As 'photography' mutates into its digital double (like a sister or brother) whose system operates in a different way and is still in the process of re-definition, what we thought photography was, is and will be remains in flux. Is this why interest in the archive and memory is so current? Or is it also to do with the multitude of archives, whether commercial like Getty and corporate institutions or state-owned collections, museums, public-lending libraries, private family attics, artists' estates and so on, which is creating an unease about archives and potential memories? (Bate, 2010: 243)

In the essay *The Body and the Archive* (1986), Sekula characterised the surveillant archive as a place in which history, politics and power elide in a struggle for ascendancy and authority. His essay sought to illuminate the role that the photographic archive played in the 19th century in constructing and policing working-class communities and in the making of a new class, the bourgeoisie. He described how the bourgeoisie defined themselves in opposition to the criminal and 'beleaguered body' of emergent working-class industrial communities, cementing their new political ascendancy and allowing the archives they helped foster to increasingly hold their 'subjects' subject. The archive not only created a new class in opposition to its subjects, but also classified and inscribed those subjects in the form of new communities of inclusion rather than affinity. At their most extreme, for example in terms of criminal records, the photographic archive constituted the eyes of the state, a surveillant repository in which knowledge and power were concentrated for the benefit of an elite (Foucault, 1991).

In his analysis, Sekula argued that we should always consider the subject community – the people in the archive – rather than those dependent upon its authority and control for their power. We should, he later advocated, approach the archive 'from a position of solidarity with those displaced, deformed, silenced or made invisible' (1986/2003: 451). This analysis surfaced the nature of the 'silenced' within archival collections and much of the ensuing critique focused, often unfairly, on those who have had custodianship of the archive – characterised as hand servants of inequality and maintaining, as gatekeepers, the stability of social and cultural meaning. Tagg, in *The Burden of Representation* (1988), similarly outlined the role that the archive played in the service of state power and in the control of communities and citizens across a range of social contexts.

However, we also have evidence of the contemporary contestation of such practices – and the birth of the use of photography as a corollary to the official representations of 'community'.

For example, photographer John Thomson and radical journalist Adolphe Smith embarked on a project to document and report on the lives of the London poor, making the series of portraits that formed the core of the work a potent series of studies of working-class and underclass life.

> And now we also have sought to portray these harder phases of life, bringing to bear the precision of photography in illustration of our subject. The unquestionable accuracy of this testimony will enable us to present true types of the London Poor and shield us from the accusation of either underrating or exaggerating individual peculiarities of appearance. (Smith and Thomson, 1877: Preface)

The unswerving belief in the accuracy of the photograph to define and inscribe the subject, regardless of the social liberalism of the photographer's approach, still belies a strong paternalistic and reductive use of the archive that Thomson created, mirrored in previous reductionist approaches such as Henry Mayhew's *London Labour and the Poor* (1844). The investigative approach further developed by Jacob Riis in the 1890s similarly saw the poor as unable to help themselves and relied on the images as evidence of their plight and the need for social reform. His influential book *How the Other Half Lives* (1890) relied heavily on photographic images as illustrations, which were latterly used as lantern slides for his comprehensive campaigning talks. However, such use of the archive as a source of social good did not break through the sense of the community being a subject entity. Rather, it marked an ongoing realisation of the ability of the archive to talk back on behalf of its inscribed (Bogre, 2011).

The historic resource they now represent allows us to recognise the factors at play and reveal an archival gaze in which intervention is invited. The revolutionary technology of the Kodak snapshot camera, which first arrived in 1888 and reached mass popularity through the Folding Pocket Camera (1897) and the Box Brownie (1900), began to challenge the institutional gaze, enfranchising those previously excluded from the photographic project. Citizens and communities made their entry through the vernacular snapshot and began to visually represent their own lives for the first time in history (Olivier, 2007). These early 'amateur' photographs demonstrated the potential of oppositional practices; for example, in the memorialisation of family, works outings, holidays, sports and war (Sarvas and Frohlich, 2011). They also offered points of challenge to the official orthodoxies of news management and censorship in events such as the Boer War (1899–1902), during which troops carried cameras onto the battlefield for the first time (Popple, 2010).

These vernacular images now exist as a site of historical instruction and, as such, illustrate our acceptance of the 'historical' archive as a primary site of contestation, reclamation and re-empowerment. They constitute the accidental archive that exists in contrast to the institutional archive. We understand the role such archives have played in history, in the shaping and construction of state and community and, more recently, in their centrality to our sense of 'self'. They signify not just the processes of inscription, but of agency and the potential for disruption. To do so their contents need to be de-ghettoised (Crimp, 1995: 75), on the one hand liberated from the museum and institution, and on the other released from personal or community arrest. Both are, in their own ways, the domain of privilege. Both are ripe for a distributed and evolving conversation.

The *sousveillant* community: the archive as subject

While Foucault and Tagg exposed how formal archives play a fundamental (and often repressive) role in the politics of knowledge, at the same time their work stimulated interest in the examination of existing archives and the formation of new archives by community groups as a means of affirming the identity of previously marginal, excluded and forgotten groups.

The archive has increasingly been subjected to an emancipatory gaze in which communities play a dynamic role: a gaze in which the community, not just the historian, is able to look back (Foster, 2004). The rereading of history through the archive, and the creation of alternative archives, has for example been embraced in relation to the gendered archive and the recovery of suppressed and hidden histories (Wooten and Bly, 2012; Tinkler, 2013; Dever, 2018).

The photographer and historian Joan Fontcuberta, much of whose work is grounded in uncovering the buried archival histories of the Spanish Civil War, clearly seizes on the potential to reread and recover histories – both through traditional archival research and through creative and collaborative practices:

> Institutionalised history is a corset that shapes memory, but at the cost of constricting the experience of the present and the future ... the first critical duty of the historian is to de-institutionalise history, to deconsecrate it – in short, to strip it of its authoritarian discourse. (Fontcuberta, 2014: 172)

Fontcuberta's approach is built on a recognition of the value of the archive and the images that haunt them, and how they can be mobilised through creative interventions in the archive and through the use of the archive as an exploratory terrain. His work emerged out of the final days of Franco's rule and increasingly challenged the enforced political orthodoxy and associated amnesia that characterised Spain in this period. Shimon Attie similarly used the archive as a provocative component of his *The Writing on the Wall* (1991–2) project. Attie projected archival photographs of Jewish street life in Berlin onto the walls of surviving buildings and rephotographed the projects that reunited the original communities with their homes and businesses that were subsequently appropriated by the Nazis:

> Block by block, the specters of a vanished population reappeared – uninvited and unexpected- confronting the city's contemporary residents ... On multiple occasions they provoked denial, anger, or outright denunciation from current residents ... The picture invites reflection on place and displacement, loss and erasure, and photography's role in the making of collective memory, in sustaining the presence of the past. (Reinhardt, 2007: 29–30)

Attie's work, an early example of rephotography, was offered as a provocation on behalf of the archival subject and from a position of solidarity that sought to make the 'realities' of the images tangible within the context of both history and place. It reunited them with their original contexts and took them out of the archive and back into their former community.

Similarly, the recent *Grafters: Industrial Society in Image and Word* (2016–17) exhibition by the social documentary photographer Ian Beesley held at Bradford Industrial Museum placed its subjects into a milieu that would have been familiar to the subjects. Held in concert with heavy industrial machinery and former factory premises, the context made them more poignant and affecting. Beesley's own career has centred on photographing marginalised or at-risk communities – particularly those facing the loss of employment and tradition in terms of industrial decline and changing working practices. His work approaches the subject community from a non-institutional and emplaced perspective that clearly suggests the disruptive potential of archival plurality and the power of the distributed archive in exhibition form. Containing as it does a mixture of institutional record images, the lionising perspective of Soviet photography, and often unregarded vernacular self-representations, the result is a complex and overlapping realisation of a working community. Integrating his own practices with this wholescale historical representation as a form of social and aesthetic commentary and incorporating the work of poet Ian McMillan as a means of vitalising the lives of the communities represented, the exhibition fully reveals the potential of new curatorial approaches.

A recent interview allowed for an exploration of the collaborative creative partnerships involved and of the responsibility of the artist–curator in respect to the historical archive:

What motivated you to make the exhibition?
The motivation came from the long frustration of seeing working people being represented photographically in patronising and objectifying ways, I think the situation has become worse in the last decade as photography and the arts have become more and more dominated by the middle class and affluent, whose interest in the working life of others is at best superficial.

It also came from my experience of having worked in industry (a foundry, a mill and a sewage works) before I became a photographer and the photographs I saw published and exhibited at that time bore no relationship to my experience as an industrial worker.

What duty do photographers/curators have to the communities they represent?

Personally, I think they should have a duty of care and responsibility to the communities they are hoping to represent. Unfortunately in this day and age I think that this attitude is often overlooked by many photographers and curators who see their own opinions/perceptions and prejudices as more important and indeed more valid than those they are representing.

Were any community members/advisors involved in the collation of images?

Yes, I sought the advice from as many individuals as possible who had worked in some of the industries I was representing in the exhibition. Some of these people were able to direct me to a number of local archives/collections which contained work with which I was not familiar, and they proved to be very valuable contributions to the exhibition.

What is your own approach to working with rather than on behalf of communities to make new work?

I always work in close collaboration with the communities, groups or organisations; they have a greater or different knowledge of the subject I am exploring. I like to explain exactly what I am thinking of doing. This will often open a dialogue discussing potential difficulties or sensitivities that I need to be aware of, rather than just steaming straight in.

I have always found that working in a collaborative way produces results that have a greater depth and understanding. It's all about developing trust and having respect for your subjects and more often than not giving them a voice in the representation of their lives. (Beesley, 2018)

Beesley approaches the archival record from a dual perspective – that of his own experience and insight, and as an emplaced observer through his own representational practices; from a perspective that 'appears to open the past whilst simultaneously marking the boundary between the past and living present' (Shurkus, 2014: 67).

Such interventions are about the disordering of the uniform archive, the integration of historical representation with ongoing explorations of countervailing histories that forge new representations, leading to a more open and empathetic re-presentation of the archive by photographic practitioners. The Archive: Imagining the East End project provides another example of this collaborative approach in which professional and community photographers produced their own archival representation of their community space (Andrews et al, 2013). They are about the challenging and rearticulation of the voices of those unable to speak for themselves – of the disruptive intervention on behalf of a social-political cause. But are they merely a proxy voicing of those lives, whatever the intent, and not from that or similar community experience? (Wagner, 2017). How can collaboration and co-voicing impact here? The heart of the question relates to issues of ownership, of authority, of presence and of evaluating who has the right to voice and how that is manifested (Bailey and Popple, 2011; Janes, 2016). The process of reinterpreting the archive on behalf of the historically inscribed – and challenging the integrity of the formally constituted archive – can certainly be mobilised through community action as Flinn has continuously demonstrated (Flinn et al, 2009). The sense of whose voice speaks and whose voice is heard can be made explicit.

The community in the archive: case studies

As in Attie's work, the question of place and the emplaced community was to the fore in two projects (2017–18) that emerged as part of the follow-on funding for the AHRC Connected Communities/ Digital Transformations-funded Pararchive: Open Access Community Storytelling and the Digital Archive (2013–15). York 1905 (http:// yarncommunity.com/projects/17) and Weaving Ossett's History (http://yarncommunity.com/projects/3) explored the potential of self-directed collaborative work with local institutional and community photographic archives around the theme of place and identity. The question of voice was central to both, and the intent of the core project was to explore how digital resources could be used to broaden access and promote archive collections held in their local areas and distribute materials through online storytelling (Lambert, 2013). The aim was to develop local resources, give voice to communities and create digital virtual archives that mixed local materials with anything published online through YARN, one of the outputs of the Pararchive Project.

The platform works on hyperlinks, so does not constitute a repository but a linking and orchestrating site on which users can publish their research while keeping control of their assets by hosting materials on third party sites that they control (Popple and Mutibwa, 2017). Our research team worked to help co-researchers address a series of difficult self-identified issues relating to local history, genealogy, co-working, publishing, working with disadvantaged and hard to reach audiences, and the use of 'hidden' or degraded digital resources (https://digitalcommunity.leeds.ac.uk/).

The York 1905 project involved collaboration between Blueberry Academy (which provides specialist support for adults with learning difficulties) and Explore York (an integrated library, archive and museum). We worked with Blueberry Academy's young trainees to develop activities that allowed them to develop confidence and build skills in working with Explore York's archives and library content around the theme of local identity. Our approach was to support students in an exploration of their own place within the city, and to help give voice to this often marginalised community (Tilley, 2006). Here we wanted to understand how best the digital photographic resources might support our partners through their citizenship programme and how we could develop the resource to make it more accessible. The approach that emerged from workshop and storytelling activities focused on a reimaging of the history of the Melbourne Centre – the training premises of the academy and a working community centre that the Academy runs on behalf of its local community. Students worked directly with an Explore York Archivist and a professional storyteller to research the history of the Melbourne Centre and the local area, using digitised archival materials.

These were then explored through a series of role play exercises, art works and workshops in which images from the city archive were selected to produce timelines and stories that could be shared through YARN. The learners then developed and consolidated their findings through role-play and artwork, which was recorded for adding to YARN. The resulting stories make evident the value of mixing approaches to working with the archive and the ability of the archival content to allow users to express their understandings of their community context and their contribution to the city. One story, 'Natalie and Cameron's working day at Explore York', explored the contribution made by volunteers from the Academy to Explore York Archives where they volunteered, while another showcased images from the archive that could later be used as the inspiration for artworks, new stories and other online sources. The 'Learning about York from Edwardian Archive' story, with its combination of topographic, entertainment and street images, formed the basis for more expressive commentaries devised by the students, and were used as part of the role-play workshops, themselves covered in 'Using role-play and storytelling to engage with Archives'.

> Once the learners felt comfortable with the idea of historical role-play and improvisation, we split into pairs and each chose a character who might have lived in Fishergate at this time. Some chose to be the mother/father/brother/sister of Cath's character, whilst others selected occupations such as 'tram driver' or 'barman'. We took it in turns to ask each other questions and respond in character. (Wilkinson, 2017)

Rather than acting as a 'scene for recollection', as Kuhn suggests, these photographs formed a new site for collective storytelling, invention and experimentation (Kuhn, 2002: 13). This was strongly evidenced both in the work itself and also in the evaluation event held in March 2018, at which learners and staff gave very positive accounts of their experience and discussed how the project could be continued beyond the funding stream. As a consequence, ongoing work is continuing with Blueberry to promote photographically focused digital storytelling to support the small and medium-sized enterprises (SMEs) that the organisation runs; for example, the Blueberry Shop, which sells craft work and recycled furniture, decided to produce a story for each piece of furniture that is renovated so that new owners can continue its history. Other work focused on establishing an SME based on developing representations of spaces that physically and intellectually disabled people might encounter on a visit to York. This stemmed from work that emerged on the project Safety-first @Melbourne, where members photographically mapped fire escape routes. This marked a transition to more autonomous and self-orientated use of the resources, and the creation of a new archive based on self-identified concerns within the community of the Academy.

The second project, Weaving Ossett's History, relied on working with a well-established community of local historians who already had their own developed but precarious photographic archive. The Ossett and Gawthorpe Community Archive (OGCA) are a self-organising group who have a tradition of collecting and publishing historical archival material and an existing digital presence (Terras, 2011). They were part of a now defunct Heritage Lottery Fund Community Archive Network project, which created software specifically for local community and family archiving. This project developed database software to help local communities digitise and preserve digital content (photographs and audio-visual recordings of interest and relevance to them) in an effort to create their own digital archives. The digitised material was stored on hard drives and on CD-ROMs, which are now extremely vulnerable and inaccessible as the parent company went into liquidation and communities lost access to their on-line content that had been painstakingly generated over several years.

The group, in partnership with Wakefield Libraries, worked to use the OGCA and local library collections to develop a range of projects (over 20 to date) 'contributed by local (and ex-pat) people of all ages in the areas of heritage which interest them' (Ossett Archive, 2017). The stories produced range from very personal reminiscences of family and community life that use family archives combined with local archival resources and broader online materials to offer very contemporary reflections on past histories and the changing nature of community identity.

'Uncle Swearer' is indicative of the former type of project, where the focus is on personal family memory that reveals broader notions of community life through its very graphic description of home dentistry and family life.

> I once went with my mother and he was sitting in his usual Windsor chair in front of the fire trying to pull out one of his own teeth. He had a string round the knob of the open oven door with the other end tied around his tooth. He had killed the nerve with a red-hot needle heated in the fire first and then he kicked the oven door closed to pull out his troublesome tooth. Unfortunately it did not work first time so he had to have another go to finish the job off. Unlike my father and other members of my family he swore an awful lot. (O and G Archive, 2017)

It uses the possibilities presented by the digital format to draw together a range of sources including photographs, paintings and interviews to act as 'ritual signs of (re)connection', both with the individual family story and the broader sense of community it evokes (Van Dijck, 2008: 62). The resultant history is more universalist than specific to one family and the appeal of the social history is compelling. There are several similar warm family histories that reveal much about the historical nature of the community as a whole that also mix family photographs and ephemera with a range of contextualising images, films and topographical materials. These stories are all characterised by an evocation of the past, a lost and often lamented passing, and there is a clear sense of nostalgia in the tone of the written components.

'Refugees Arrive' falls into the latter category in its concerns with new arrivals into an established community and has more of a contemporary resonance in the context of Brexit. It is framed around a single group portrait of 66 Belgian refugees who arrived at Ossett station on 17 October 1914. It recounts their reception by the Ossett Brass Band and the subsequent contribution they made to the British war effort by working in a local munitions factory. The 'outsiders' were, as the story recounts, generally welcomed – but 'there were grumbles that they were better fed than some of the townspeople' (Ossett Historical Society, 2017). Someone had commented that they would like to know what happened to these people and whether there were any descendants still living in the area.

A similarly themed 'Ossett – an incomer's view' recounts the experiences of an incomer from London who has lived in the community for 40 years and, as an outsider, has seen a decline in the community over that time:

> Wake up, Ossett, the writing's on the wall! Comparing today's Ossett with the one I moved to all those years ago is a bit like reading that Thomas Hood poem 'November'. No Gas shop, no Electricity shop, no public refuse site, no Sorting Office, no Fire Station, no municipal golf (until earlier this year we had a lovely little 9 hole course), no free car parks and soon, possibly, no Post Office (You get the idea?). (Soo, 2017)

The project has evidenced the power of collective remembering, the sharing of content and expertise within a local community, and the photographic resource 'opens up a terrain of conversation and memory to multiple participants' (MacDonald, 2015: 31). They are self-constructed community histories, often sourced from public heritage events where the communal sharing of memory and experience produce highly individualised and disruptive histories (Lydon, 2010). The group also used (and continue to use) the resource to archive their own public events; for example, 'Weaving Ossett's History at Ossett Gala 2017', from which some of the project stories originated. From the local library perspective, the project worked to enable the OGCA to:

> Share stories and harness digitised archive resources, whilst also demonstrating the crucial role of local libraries and the services and resources they provide. It was felt that the project had achieved impact by helping people who wouldn't normally access library archive resources to do so and to use them to tell their own stories and understandings,

rather than acting as passive consumers of authorised histories. (Wilkinson, 2018)

There were, of course, important limitations revealed by these projects as well. Both depended on the co-option of existing communities with established practices such as social media use and were not autonomous in origin, being the consequence of our research process and approach (Hart et al, 2013). Trying to mitigate against directing the groups was a complex and sometimes conflicting experience, but at the core was the intent to trigger ongoing and post-research activity through the provision of a digital platform for hosting their research and stories, training and the forging of new relationships with local library and archival resources that could be mutually reinforcing (Light and Millen, 2014). The post-project evidence is that these activities are ongoing: both groups continue to use and develop the resource, and the use of photographs remains central to their practices.

Conclusion

Roush argued a decade ago that despite a recognition of the dynamism and agency of the archive, there is still a tendency to regard photographs as 'static identificatory objects' (Roush, 2009: 155). Archival photographs are objects without agency, fixed in an institutional frame. These two case studies, however, mark a positive shift in the ways in which community interventions can open up the archive and advance the positive disruption of collaborative digital approaches, finding new ways of telling stories, combining resources and discovering hidden histories through the use of photographs – both archival and current (Bolick, 2006). The combination of existing and newly formed collections, personal and orphan materials constitute a new form of distributed and shared practice that thrives on the disruptive intervention of multiple partners.

Arguably the archive has, largely as the result of digital publishing technologies, become a pluralist site of exploration (Smith, 2007: 7). The paradigm shift has also marked the community transition from that of subjecthood to playing collaborative, disruptive and proprietorial/ curatorial roles. Such a shift is increasingly marked in the development of approaches that mix institutional collections with private and community assets. Such 'archive fever' so effectively identified by Derrida has also been stimulated by an increasing interest in 'history from below', digital storytelling and co-creation practices. The balance of power may well have shifted in terms of the future of the archive per se, offering important challenges to data longevity, preservation formats and standards, to the professional status of the archivist and curator and accepting a new form of fluid archive in which one has to accept the transience of content (Murray, 2008; Zylinska, 2010). The ceding of archival responsibility to the community has its own implications, for instance threatening sustainability and the danger of swapping one set of attendant orthodoxies and hierarchies for another. But perhaps it is time to consider pushing in that direction. Naturally both traditions need to be central to this process and proceed in partnership (Haskins, 2007; Mutibwa et al, 2018).

This might well be a messy, disruptive and sometimes uncomfortable process in which aspirations and expectations are not always realised, and indeed the process can be negative and disillusioning for some as they struggle with protocols and technologies that fail to deliver on their evident promise. The research process can lead to many dead ends, abandoned projects, moribund websites and caches of images. But this is no reason not to persevere and embrace the process, learning, negotiating and feeling a constant sense of pleasure at the *liberated* knowledge that is the consequence of new collaborative practices. If it is not disruptive for all involved it is, perhaps, not worth undertaking in the first place.

References

Andrews, Susan, Haeffner, Nicholas and Cheatle, Zelda (2013) *Archive: Imagining the East End: A Photographic Discourse*, London: Black Dog Publishing.

Bailey, Michael and Popple, Simon (2011) 'The 1984/5 Miners' Strike: Re-claiming Cultural Heritage', in Smith, L., Shackel, P. and Campbell, G. (eds) *Heritage, Labour and the Working Classes*, London: Routledge, pp 19–33.

Bate, David (2010) 'The memory of photography', *Photographies*, 3(2): 243–57,

Bazin, André and Gray, Hugh (1960) 'The Ontology of the photographic image', *Film Quarterly*, 13(4): 4–9.

Beesley, Ian (2018) Interview, 13 September.

Bogre, Michelle (2011) *Photography as Activism: Images for Social Change*, Abingdon: Focal Press.

Bolick, Cheryl Mason (2006) 'Digital archives: democratising the doing of history', *International Journal of Social Education*, 21(1): 122–34.

Brink, Cornelia (2000) 'Secular icons: Looking at photographs from Nazi concentration camps', *History & Memory*, 12(1): 135–50.

Buchanan, Alexandrina and Bastian, Michelle (2015) 'Activating the archive: Rethinking the role of traditional archives for local activist projects', *Archival Science*, 15(4): 429–51.

Crimp, Douglas (1995) *On the Museum's Ruins*, Cambridge, MA: MIT Press.

Crooke, Elizabeth (2007) *Museums and Community: Ideas, Issues and Challenges*, New York: Routledge.

Denison, Tom and Stillman, Larry (2012) 'Academic and ethical challenges in participatory models of community research', *Information, Communication & Society*, 15(7): 1037–54.

Derrida, Jacques (1998) *Archive Fever: A Freudian Impression*, Chicago: University of Chicago Press.

Dever, Maryanne (ed.) (2018) *Archives and New Modes of Feminist Research*, London: Routledge.

Emerling, Jae (2011) *Photography Theory and History*, London: Routledge.

Facer, Keri and Enright, Bryony (2016) 'Creating living knowledge report: connected communities' [online], Available from: https://connected-communities.org/index.php/creating-living-knowledge-report/ [Accessed 25 July 2018].

Flinn, Andrew (2010) 'Independent community archives and community-generated content "Writing, Saving and Sharing our Histories"', *Convergence: The International Journal of Research into New Media Technologies*, 16(1): 39–51.

Flinn, Andrew, Stevens, Mary and Shepherd, Elizabeth (2009) 'Whose memories, whose archives? Independent community archives, autonomy and the mainstream', *Archival Science*, 9(1): 71–86.

Fontcuberta, Joan (2014) 'Archive Noises', in *Pandora's Camera: Photogr@phy after Photography*, London: MACK books, pp 169–81.

Foster, Hal (2004) 'An archival impulse', *October*, 110: 3–22.

Foucault, Michel (1991 [1975]) *Discipline and Punish: The Birth of Prison*, London: Penguin.

Hacker, Karen (2013) *Community-Based Participatory Research*, Thousand Oaks, CA: SAGE.

Hart, Angie, Davies, Ceri, Aumann, Kim, Wenger, Etienne, Aranda, Kay, Heaver, Becky and Wolff, David (2013) 'Mobilising knowledge in community-university partnerships: what does a community of practice approach contribute?', *Contemporary Social Science: Special Issue*, 8(3): 278–91.

Haskins, Ekaterina (2007) 'Between archive and participation: public memory in a digital age', *Rhetoric Society Quarterly*, 37(4): 401–22.

Janes, Julia E. (2016) 'Democratic encounters? Epistemic privilege, power, and community-based participatory action research', *Action Research*, 14(1): 72–87.

Kindon, Sara, Pain, Rachel and Kesby, Mike (eds) (2007) *Participatory Action Research Approaches and Methods: Connecting People, Participation and Place*, London: Routledge.

Kuhn, Annette (2002) *Family Secrets: Acts of Memory and Imagination*, London: Verso.

Lambert, Joe (2013) *Digital Storytelling: Capturing Lives, Creating Community*, 4th ed., London: Routledge.

Light, Ann and Millen, Tamar (2014) *Making Media with Communities: Guidance for Researchers*, Newcastle: University of Northumbria.

Lydon, Jane (2010) 'Return: The photographic archive and technologies of indigenous memory', *Photographies*, 3(2): 173–87.

MacDonald, Richard Lowell (2015) 'Going back in a heartbeat': collective memory and the online circulation of family photographs', *Photographies*, 8(1): 23–42.

Mayhew, Henry (1985 [1844]) *London Labour and the Poor*, London: Penguin.

Merewether, Charles (2006) *The Archive: Documents of Contemporary Art*, London: Whitechapel Gallery Press.

Moore, Niamh, Salter, Andrea, Stanley, Liz and Tamboukou, Maria (2017) *The Archive Project: Archival Research in the Social Sciences*, Abingdon: Routledge.

Murray, Susan (2008) 'Digital images, photo-sharing and our shifting notions of everyday aesthetics', *Journal of Visual Culture*, 7(2): 147–63.

Mutibwa, Daniel H., Hess, Alison and Jackson, Tom (2018) 'Strokes of serendipity: community co-curation and engagement with digital heritage', *Convergence: The International Journal of Research into New Media Technologies*, Available from: doi: 10.1177/1354856518772030.

O and G Archive (2017) [online], Available from: http://yarncommunity.com/stories/581 [Accessed 5 July 2018].

Olivier, Marc (2007) 'George Eastman's modern Stone-Age family: Snapshot photography and the Brownie', *Technology and Culture*, 48(1): 1–19.

Ossett Archive (2017) [online], Available from: http://yarncommunity.com/projects/3 [Accessed 5 July 2018].

Ossett Historical Society (2017) [online] Available from: http://yarncommunity.com/stories/420 [Accessed 5 July 2018].

Owens, Trevor (2013) 'Digital cultural heritage and the crowd', *Curator: The Museum Journal,* 56(1): 121–30.

Pollock, Griselda (2007) *Encounters in the Virtual Feminist Museum: Time, Space and the Archive*, London: Routledge.

Popple, Simon (2010) 'Fresh from the Front': Performance, war news and popular culture during the Boer War, *Early Popular Visual Culture*, 8(4): 401–18.

Popple, Simon and Mutibwa, Daniel H. (2017). 'Tools You Can Trust? Co-Design in Community Heritage Work', in Borowski, K., Forbes, N. and Fresa, A. (eds) *Cultural Heritage in a Changing World*, Switzerland: Springer, pp 197–214.

Reinhardt, Mark (2007) *Beautiful Suffering: Photography and the Traffic in Pain*, Williamstown, MA: Williams College Museum of Art.

Ridge, Mia (2014) 'Crowdsourcing our Cultural Heritage: Introduction', in Ridge, M. (ed.), *Crowdsourcing our Cultural Heritage*, Farnham: Ashgate, pp 1–14.

Riis, Jacob (1890/1997) *How the Other Half Lives: Studies among the Tenements of New York*, London: Penguin.

Roush, Paula (2009) 'Photography, subcultures and online-offline counter archival strategies', *Photographies*, 2(2): 143–67.

Sandell, Richard (2002) *Museums, Society, Inequality*, London: Routledge.

Sarvas, Risto and David Frohlich (2011) *From Snapshots to Social Media: The Changing Picture of Domestic Photography*, New York: Springer-Verlag New York Inc.

Sekula, Allan (1986). 'The body and the archive', *October*, 39 (Winter): 3–64.

Sekula, Allan (1986/2003) 'Reading an Archive: Photography between Labour and Capital', in Wells, Liz (ed.) *The Photography Reader*, London: Routledge, pp.443–52.

Shurkus, Marie (2014) '*Camera Lucida* and affect: beyond representation', *Photographies*, 7(1): 67–83.

Smith, Abby (2007) 'Valuing preservation', *Library Trends*, 56(1): 7.

Smith, Adolphe and Thomson, John (1877/2009) *Street Life in London: People of Victorian England*, London: Dodo Press.

Soo (2017) [online], Available from: http://yarncommunity.com/stories/446 [Accessed 6 June 2018].

Tagg, John (1988) *The Burden of Representation: Essays on Photographies and Histories*, London: Palgrave Macmillan.

Tagg, John (2009) *Disciplinary Frame: Photographic Truths and the Capture of Meaning*, Minnesota: University of Minnesota Press.

Terras, Melissa (2011) 'The digital Wunderkammer: Flickr as a platform for amateur cultural and heritage content', *Library Trends*, Winter: 686–706.

Tilley, Christopher (2006) 'Identity, place, landscape and heritage', *Journal of Material Culture*, 11(1–2): 7–32.

Tinkler, Penny (2013) *Using Photographs in Social and Historical Research*, London: Sage.

Van Dijck, Jose (2008) 'Digital photography, communication, identity, memory', *Visual Communication*, 7(1): 57–76.

Wagner, Karin (2017) 'The personal versus the institutional voice in an open photographic archive', *Archival Science*, 17(3): 247–66.

Wilkinson, Rosie (2017) [online], Available from: http://yarncommunity.com/stories/562 [Accessed 20 May 2018].

Wilkinson, Rosie (2018) 'Project report', unpublished. Internal report for the AHRC-funded follow-on project 'Digital Community Workspaces: Delivering impact through Public Library and archive networks'.

Wooten, Kelly and Bly, Lyz (2012) *Make Your Own History: Documenting Feminist and Queer Activism in the 21st Century*, Sacramento, CA: Litwin Books, LLC.

Zylinska, Joanna (2010) 'On bad archives, unruly snappers and liquid photographs', *Photographies*, 3(2): 139–53.

PART I

Storytelling, co-curation and community archives

BBC Pebble Mill: issues around collaborative community online archives – a case study of the Pebble Mill Project

Vanessa Jackson

Introduction

It can be tempting to adopt an evangelical view towards collaborative community projects, but reflecting on the challenges, constraints and limitations of projects is as valuable to expanding our understanding as concentrating on the opportunities, rewards and empowerment they provide.

This chapter considers what we can learn that is generalisable from the Pebble Mill project: a multi-media online resource, http://pebblemill.org, with social media interaction on Facebook, where members of an online community build what Dougherty and Schneider (2011) term an 'idiosyncratic archive' of memories and artefacts, including photographs, videos, audio and written text, creating a democratic history of BBC Pebble Mill, which complements the BBC's institutional archive. Some of the tensions and limitations of community archive projects are explored, including moderation, ethics and legal matters, namely defamation and copyright. One of the major challenges for community archives regards the continuing commitment of 'citizen curators', the facilitators of online community projects, whose labour includes devising policies, moderating and encouraging engagement. Issues of longevity and sustainability are considered, along with the vulnerability of online collections in a precarious virtual world, where platforms are subject to evolution, or removal, threatening the survival of small projects.

Background to the Pebble Mill Project

Pebble Mill was the first purpose-built broadcast production centre in Europe (BBC, 1962). It opened in Birmingham in 1971, closing in 2004. At its height it produced around 10 per cent of BBC output (Wood, 2005), boasting a renowned drama department that produced 'Plays for Today' such as *Nuts in May* (1976, BBC2) and series such as *Boys from the Blackstuff* (1982, BBC2). There was a prolific factual unit producing *Top Gear* (1977–2001, BBC2), *Countryfile* (1988–present, BBC1) and *Gardeners' World* (1968–present, BBC2), and live studio programming such as *Pebble Mill at One* (1972–86, BBC1). Much of Pebble Mill's output falls under Frances Bonner's definition of 'ordinary television': frequently factual formatted programming incorporating 'real people' (Bonner, 2003). Such shows included high volume, low budget lifestyle and makeover shows featuring members of the public, such as *Style Challenge* (1996–8, BBC1) and *Real Rooms* (1997–2002, BBC1). These types of programme are often neglected by scholars and critics.

The Pebble Mill Project consists of a WordPress website with an ancillary Facebook page, comprising 1600 members, many of whom were BBC Pebble Mill employees. Blogs are regularly posted on the website and copied to Facebook, where most of the community activity occurs: comments and new artefacts are added by participants, facilitating lively discussion. There is a symbiotic relationship between the website and the Facebook page, with social media driving traffic to the website and individuals commenting via Facebook, with the content being repurposed on the website.

I worked in television production at Pebble Mill for many years, which explains my interest in documenting its unofficial history. I began the Pebble Mill Project in 2010 and have seen it grow to a collection of over 1600 artefacts, resulting from community involvement. However, through establishing and operating the project a number of challenges have been observed, offering lessons for similar projects.

The role of the 'citizen curator'

Projects such as this, creating an online community archive, seldom happen spontaneously; they require an individual or group to shape and deliver them, facilitating the growth of an online community. This requires commitment because fostering online engagement demands sustained effort. If a burgeoning online community suspects that their contributions are not valued, they may cease participating. Therefore, individuals developing similar projects must be realistic about the commitment and appreciate the interdependence between the input of the curator and the community.

Dobreva and Duff describe digital curation as including selecting, maintaining, using, preserving and adding value to digital assets (Dobreva and Duff, 2015: 97). This curation can occur in an institutional setting or, as Costis Dallas has identified, 'in the wild' (Dallas, 2015: 423). Thus the 'citizen curator', an unofficial custodian, gathers content, sometimes 'commissioning' it, repurposing it, checking it for accuracy, ensuring it conforms to the house style, scheduling it and ultimately publishing it online. It is easy to underestimate the complexity, which combines technical operations, creativity and project management with editorial decision-making, researching and communicating with participants. The citizen curator frequently provides the driving force behind the project, bringing together and shaping disparate elements, and directing the community's focus.

Without someone carrying out the curatorial role, a project will lack shape and direction. There must be a contact person for participants when they have material to share, or when a mistake is made and requires correcting. A major challenge for community projects is if the citizen curator is no longer able to devote their time and energy, and the work the community has produced might be lost or become inaccessible. Spreading the burden of curatorship, for instance through a committee or group, rather than one individual, is sensible.

Ethics and moderation

One of the tasks of the citizen curator is to moderate content. This can be challenging, particularly initially, as there is little guidance on how citizen curators should behave or, indeed, what the role encompasses. There are legal considerations to be aware of, particularly defamation or libel, privacy and copyright, which apply to written blog posts, photographs and online comments.

A libel is a 'published false statement that is damaging to a person's reputation; a written defamation' (Oxford Living Dictionaries, accessed 2017). With the Pebble Mill Project, the majority of content is not contentious; however, there are exceptions. I received a long comment in response to a published photograph regarding a makeover show from a former presenter, who had been replaced after an incident allegedly involving racist language. He named the original complainant, the executive producer and the channel controller, making mild threats against them. The presenter felt aggrieved by his treatment. I decided not to approve this comment, because of the allegations and mild threats. While it added insight into how the BBC tackled this kind of incident, the potential repercussions outweighed the positives. However, in not approving this type of comment I am circumscribing the history being told, omitting some unpleasant aspects and presenting a potentially distorted view. This incident highlights some of the responsibilities required in running community projects. It was reassuring that the website required comments from new contributors to be approved before publication. This is a sensible precaution that I would recommend for similar websites.

On another occasion, a personal attack was posted in response to a blog because the blog writer had left their family and started a new relationship. I did not publish the comment as the content was personal and would have been extremely hurtful for the contributor. The incident highlights the need to take decisions pragmatically, guided by ethical principles. Sarah Pink states that ethical decisions are usually made with reference to personal and professional codes and take into account the intentions of other parties (Pink, 2001: 37); although she is writing regarding ethnographers, the same principles apply here. As a citizen curator, I feel a responsibility towards participants in the project who might face unwanted comments because of their contributions and apply similar codes that I adopted in my television production career.

Most of the comments in response to the Pebble Mill website blogs appear on the linked Facebook page. People seem more comfortable posting comments on Facebook than on the website. However, the informal nature of Facebook can lead to unguarded comments. It is often viewed as a platform of the moment, where comments are ephemeral, although they are published publicly and generally remain on the site, albeit in a form that may be difficult to retrieve. My normal practice is to copy comments from Facebook to the website. This preserves the comments, attaching them to the related blog post and making them searchable.

Facebook has changed over the years, and our sense of the site and opinion of what we have written on it can change retrospectively; our historic comments can surprise us now, and we often forget that they have been published and might resurface. Owing to differences in perception and the context of use for Facebook and the website, care has to be taken about the comments copied across. There have been incidents where material on Facebook has invaded privacy. For instance, when I published a blog concerning a drama, one of the make-up designers posted a comment about how sad it was when the lead actress suffered a miscarriage on location. I decided not to copy this comment because of privacy issues, and fortunately the individual realised its inappropriateness and deleted it from Facebook.

There have been other comments posted that I have approved despite the fact that they were highly critical. The following comment, by a current drama director, was in response to photographs from the production *Witchcraft* (1992, BBC2), directed by Peter Sasdy:

> This show was a nightmare. As 1st AD I ended up being the go-between between a 'difficult' director and the crew – many of whom used to be in tears because of something the aforesaid director had said/implied. I went prematurely grey and ... [the designer] left show-business as a result! I hope my own directing career hasn't scarred any of my crews to such an extent. (http://www.pebblemill.org/blog/witchcraft-photos-by-willoughby-gullachsen/)

While the comment was critical, the sentiment was echoed by others, and I judged it fair comment in expressing the commentator's opinion. I therefore approved it, despite Sasdy being alive.

These exchanges highlight some of the challenges faced by moderators. Each blog post and its responses can bring unexpected issues requiring a degree of judgement concerning whether to publish or not; while not wanting to be over cautious and fail to publish interesting comments, you do not want to lay yourself open to legal confrontation or causing offence. It can be a difficult balancing act, where each instance must be judged on competing merits and risks.

Rights protection

The citizen curator is responsible for rights protection on sites they manage. Online platforms have changed our perception regarding copyright protection and access. Axel Bruns argues that current copyright and patent laws favour existing rights holders and discourage the culture of sharing that is at the nexus of produsage communities, where innovation thrives on available knowledge, and that these frameworks are no longer adequate (Bruns, 2008: 396). The assertion that existing copyright laws are inadequate for collaborative networked communities is pertinent to the Pebble Mill Project. The comments that users post add value to the original blogs, and their copyright should remain the intellectual property of the writer, although they may not be able to control their use or alter them after publication. By posting a comment there is a licence implied, allowing its reuse within the original context. The following information is from an Australian advice site:

> If someone makes comments on your blog they are probably giving you an implied licence for at least that display on the comments page, and any other incidental reproduction or associated copying. (Arts Law Centre of Australia, n.d.)

Jurisdiction might be different elsewhere and can be more complex still if what looks like a UK site is hosted in another jurisdiction. With the Pebble Mill Project, I am frequently copying across comments from the Facebook page to the website, but this raises rights and ethical considerations.

There are questions concerning whether a member of the Pebble Mill community commenting via social media is giving consent for their comment to be copied. I have explained in the profile to the Pebble Mill Facebook page that this is my practice, in order to preserve the comments. However, many users might not read the profile page and might comment unaware that I might copy it. The concept of 'informed consent' has been highlighted by academics as an ethical concern. In the guidance given by the Centre for Social Justice and Community Action at Durham University, the advice is to ensure that contributors are given information about the purpose of the research and how their contribution will be used (Banks et al, 2012: 10). This is relatively easy to achieve via a consent form for an interview, but more challenging when the contribution is an online comment.

Different layers of copyright pertain to different activities within the Pebble Mill Project. There are copyright implications around video interviews, photographs, sound clips published on the website and around written blogs. The most challenging copyright issues for the project concern third-party images and audio files where the BBC almost certainly holds the copyright, and a calculated risk of copyright infringement is being made given that no BBC clearance has been sought or given. This material was produced using public funds, is not being exploited commercially on the site and is being used for criticism and review, and therefore I perceive this as a measured risk.

In terms of justifying the use of uncleared copyright material, including photographs, audio or video clips, a fair dealing defence is feasible:

Quoting parts of a work for the purpose of criticism or review is permitted provided that:

- The work has been made available to the public.
- The source of the material is acknowledged.
- The material quoted must be accompanied by some actual discussion or assessment (to warrant the criticism or review classification).
- The amount of the material quoted is no more than is necessary for the purpose of the review. (The UK Copyright Service, 2009)

The Pebble Mill Project would seem to qualify for this defence. The copyrighted material has generally been publicly available, the source is acknowledged, where known, there is discussion around the material and the quantity of material is not excessive.

On one occasion I was asked to take down a photograph or attribute copyright differently. This concerned a photograph, donated by a regular contributor, of a piece of vintage audio equipment. I had assumed, albeit wrongly, that the copyright belonged to the contributor and only realised the mistake when the owner asked me either to remove the image or to credit him and provide a link to his vintage machine business. Once I had ensured the photograph was his, I changed the credit and provided a link to his website. This incident highlights different individuals' perceptions of what is fair use and what constitutes an infringement. The original contributor did not see copying the image as a breach of intellectual property rights, rather as a helpful illustration. In contrast, the owner of the image saw it as infringement and potentially a missed business opportunity.

The intellectual property rights of many photographs on the Pebble Mill site are unknown or unclear. The majority of copyright holders are content for their material to be published on the website, especially when credited, owing to the non-commercial nature of the project. The use of a copyright disclaimer seems sensible, as does a take-down policy when a copyright holder objects. I attribute copyright, when known, adding a descriptor saying that 'copyright resides with the original holder, no reproduction without permission' if copyright is unknown. This statement is unlikely to protect against a breach of copyright, but it makes it clear that I do not own the copyright or licence use of the artefact.

Platform choice

Platform choice is critical to the success of online community projects, with each site having associated positives and negatives. When I initially established the Pebble Mill Project, I wrongly assumed that the focus would be the website rather than social media. However, the Facebook activity is crucial and without it the project would be diminished, securing significantly less community engagement.

By choosing any specific social media platform some potential participants will be excluded; this is particularly the case with older people, who are less likely to use social media – over 65s make up only 3 per cent of Facebook users (Fanalyzer, 2013). Face-to-face events and email groups can be better methods of engaging older members of a community and should be considered as complementary activities.

Aside from user demographics, there are issues over lack of control to be considered with external platforms. The Facebook element of the Pebble Mill Project was set up as a 'group' and I was able to add 'friends' when they requested to join. This worked smoothly until the 1200th 'friend' was recruited. At this point I was emailed by a member of the group, saying that he had tried to access it but a message told him it had been 'deactivated'. When I tried logging in, a message told me that I had infringed Facebook's rules, by having too many 'friends' to be an individual, and that I seemed to be operating as a community or organisation. The only option I was given was to change the 'group' to a 'page', which I did. The 'friends' were transferred, but were termed 'likes'; the photographs that had been posted were carried across, but none of the comments. These had taken years to build, but fortunately I had developed the practice of copying many of the comments to the website. It is not easy to enter into dialogue with such organisations as Facebook. One participant objected to the status being changed, but received an automated response from Facebook stating they would not consult with individuals. It is ironic that an organisation that facilitates meaningful interaction between users chooses not to communicate with them. I can moderate the Pebble Mill Facebook page and interact with users, but I am unable to interact with the host.

The groups and pages established on Facebook are controlled on a micro-level by their administrators, and while that is undoubtedly important for the day-to-day operation, there is a macro-level of decision-making from Facebook that dictates everything from functionality to aesthetics. Changes are regularly made concerning appearance and procedures in order to respond to commercial priorities. Facebook is not a democratic organisation and users have little control over corporate decisions imposed. Changes to platforms such as Facebook might make them less attractive to community groups, and illustrate the precarious nature of some fascinating online content that has been built up.

This episode demonstrates the consequences of lack of control over platforms, as well as the resilience of users and the value that they place on the apparatus that enables engagement. Through their seemingly arbitrary action in deleting the group, Facebook disempowered me and disenfranchised members of the group. This is the price of convenience, of using platforms that the people you wish to reach use, but which are beyond your control.

Sustainability and longevity

The Facebook incident illustrates the vulnerability of online community projects and the benefits of using platforms where there is greater control. However, all online platforms are subject to change as technology develops, companies are bought and sold, and priorities shift. This makes the question of how to preserve the 'work' of the online community a pressing one.

In order to preserve the contributions of the Pebble Mill online community, I have downloaded the posts and comments from the Facebook page to my computer. This practice builds in resilience, and provides a record if the page were to be disbanded. But, while producing back-up copies is a sensible measure, they lack the functionality of live sites.

Perhaps the most challenging issue facing online community projects is the lack of permanence of internet artefacts. Web objects are frequently updated and overwritten, without earlier versions being preserved and searchable (Dougherty and Schneider, 2011: 253). A web object lacks the temporal location and fixed nature of a printed or broadcast text; we often do not know when the artefact was created nor whether it has been updated. This is something I encounter regularly with the Pebble Mill Project as I edit and update existing blog posts, correcting mistakes and adding new information. There is no trace of this editing for the user, although the website administrator can view the edits on their dashboard. As a producer of content this is not a significant concern, but it could be for future historians.

Online projects rely on particular technologies that are liable to change, frequently with no physical artefact to refer back to, only a virtual image, which may become unlinked, disconnected or deleted. Dougherty and Schneider observe that to keep pace with the speed of content production and destruction online, preservation practices tend to amass content and make it technically accessible over archival sensibilities of categorisation and accuracy (2011: 261). The work of online community projects is vulnerable, therefore, not only to technical obsolescence, but to shortcomings in organisation, categorisation and veracity.

There are pressing issues around how we preserve online community archives that fall outside institutional control. The Pebble Mill Project is a vulnerable web object. If I lost interest in the project, it would probably cease to exist and all the historical information gathered would be lost. However, the same fate could befall a similar physical, rather than virtual, project. If WordPress went out of business or was sold to a competitor, in the way that Posterous was to Twitter (Laughlin, 2013), then transferring the website content to a new site would be a mammoth undertaking. Equally the online community could disintegrate if Facebook changed its nature, and it would be challenging to establish a similar group on a different platform. Whilst the Internet Archive's Wayback Machine (http://archive.org/web/web.php) performs a valuable service in preserving and retrieving historic internet pages, it is not an answer to web impermanence. In future, one hopes there will be advances to archive websites more fully, but this is uncertain, and in the meantime valuable historical digital content is likely to be lost.

Owing to the dynamic nature of websites such as the Pebble Mill one, they are difficult to archive effectively, with material hosted on diverse external platforms and gathered on the website. My videos are hosted on Vimeo, for instance, with audio items being embedded from SoundCloud. This makes archiving the archive a challenging task. There are measures that can be taken (for instance, I have downloaded versions of the website using proprietary software), but these are not particularly user-friendly and, while they provide a version of the site that would enable it to be rebuilt, they do not provide a usable static version resembling the original. Personally, I feel an obligation to preserve the digital artefacts that have been donated largely by participants, especially if democratic living histories are to have a currency beyond their founding communities. An element of future-proofing is required to keep these projects accessible.

Linked to the notion of the impermanent web object is the potential impermanence of the networked community and the individual or group of activists at its core. Andrew Flinn et al note the vulnerability of community archives, which are often driven by committed individuals. If these individuals cease to participate for any reason, the continued existence of the archive is in jeopardy (2009: 80). The difficulty of finding a mechanism for continuing these idiosyncratic archives beyond the involvement of their founders should not be underestimated. At present there seems no systematic way of achieving this, and these newly accessible histories risk becoming inaccessible once more.

Conclusion

There is much to learn from the challenges of online community projects, particularly concerning the complex role of the citizen curator and the responsibilities they face regarding legal and ethical considerations, as well as project development, platform choice and community-building. However, the most salutary lesson is around sustainability. We should accept that permanence is not something that can be guaranteed and, while building in resilience is desirable, we should become more relaxed about how long online community projects remain accessible. Members of the community I am working within are writing their history for the future, to explain how they spent their working lives, but that future may be more immediate than envisaged, and we should acknowledge that we are creating these types of project for ourselves and our immediate friends and families, in addition to a potentially nebulous future.

References

Arts Law Centre of Australia (n.d.) [online], Available from http://www.artslaw.com.au/info-sheets/info-sheet/legal-issues-for-bloggers/#headingh35 [Accessed 5 April 2017].

Banks, S., Armstrong, A., Carter, K., Graham, H., Hayward, P., Henry, A., Holland, T., Holmes, C., Lee, A., McNulty, A., Moore, N., Nayling, N., Stokoe, A. and Strachan, A. (2012) 'Community-based participatory research: a guide to ethical principles and practice', Centre for Social Justice and Community Action, Durham University, November, Available from: https://www.dur.ac.uk/resources/beacon/CBPREthicsGuidewebNovember2012.pdf [Accessed 7 November 2014].

BBC (1962) Press release, 12 November, BBC Archives, Caversham, Folder M10/23/10.

Bonner, F. (2003) *Ordinary Television – Analyzing Popular TV*, London: Sage Publications Ltd.

Bruns, A. (2008) *Blogs, Wikipedia, Second Life, and Beyond: From Production to Produsage*, New York: Peter Lang Publishing Inc.

Dallas, C. (2015) 'Digital curation beyond the "wild frontier": a pragmatic approach', *Archival Science*, 16(4): 421–57.

Dobreva, M. and Duff, W. (2015) 'The ever changing face of digital curation: introduction to the special issue on digital curation', *Archival Science*, 15(2): 97–100.

Dougherty, M. and Schneider, S.M. (2011) 'Web Historiography and the Emergence of New Archival Forms', in Park, D.W., Jankowski, N.W. and Jones, S. (eds) *The Long History of New Media, Technology, Historiography, and Contextualising Newness*, New York: Peter Laing Publishing Inc., pp 253–67.

Fanalyzer (2013) [online] Available from: http://www.fanalyzer.co.uk/demographics.html [Accessed 24 April 2016].

Flinn, A., Stevens, M. and Shepherd, E. (2009) 'Whose memories, whose archives? Independent community archives, autonomy and the mainstream', *Archival Science*, 9(1–2): 71–86.

Laughlin, A. (2013) 'Twitter to shut down blogging platform Posterous', *Digital Spy* online], Available from: http://www.digitalspy.co.uk/tech/news/a459538/twitter-to-shut-down-blogging-platform-posterous.html#~oH4LbCYqyvpWFH [Accessed 13 June 2014].

Oxford Living Dictionaries (n.d.) [online], Available from: http://www.oxforddictionaries.com/definition/english/libel [Accessed 4 April 2017].

Pink, S. (2001) *Doing Visual Ethnography*, London: Sage Publications Ltd.

The UK Copyright Service (2009), 'Fact sheet P-27: Using the work of others [online], Available from: http://www.copyrightservice.co.uk/copyright/p27_work_of_others [Accessed 10 April 2017]

Wood, J. (2005) '2005 *Prospero* article by John Wood' [online], Available from: http://www.pebblemill.org/blog/2005-prospero-article-john-wood/ [Accessed 26 June 2017].

4

New island stories: heritage, archives, the digital environment and community regeneration

Paul R.J. Duffy

Introduction

Heritage (hi)stories, digital skills enhancement and community empowerment are frequently cited ingredients in the mix of approaches to promoting community regeneration and development. Between October 2014 and March 2015 two University of Leeds-led projects explored some of these themes with residents of the Isle of Bute, Scotland. Jointly, the projects brought together community, academic, institutional and private sector partners to create new digital tools to support heritage-based community research and creative expression, and to further explore questions about heritage perception and digital engagement.

In this chapter, I reflect on my experiences as the local partner lead for both projects and explore what can be understood from them about the relationship between communities, digital heritage archives, institutions and heritage engagement. I also discuss the meaningful contribution that projects such as Pararchive can make in the wider context of national ambitions for digitally engaged communities, and how project implementation might usefully be aligned with local communities in the future.

Introduction to the Isle of Bute

The Isle of Bute is a small island situated in the Firth of Clyde on the west coast of Scotland. It is 15 miles long and 4 miles wide. The majority of the island's (circa 6500) residents live in an extended urban ribbon along the central east coast, focused around the main town of Rothesay. The remainder are mostly scattered throughout the rural hinterland in small villages, farms and in former farm buildings.

The island is well positioned in respect to the central belt of Scotland and enjoys transport links that allow a journey to/from the centre of Glasgow in 90 minutes. Despite best efforts, however, uncertain island sustainability has had a corresponding negative impact on community resilience. Economic changes in the second half of the 20th century, particularly a collapse in tourist numbers and an increasingly technologised agricultural economy, led to a loss of around 35 per cent of residents between 1951 and 1971, and by 2011 it was estimated that Bute had only around 50 per cent of the 1951 population level. Social and local employment statistics mirror this decline, highlighting the weak performance of the Bute economy compared to both regional and national averages (Ekos, 2010; HIE, 2014).

In recent years, efforts to address these issues have mobilised the island's rich heritage as a keystone for economic regeneration. Heritage is increasingly cited as a critical part of the regeneration mix (see Scottish Government, 2014a; CHCfE, 2015; Heritage Lottery Fund, 2015) but, despite a central place in several national heritage narratives (for example, a power centre in the 6th-century Southern Dalriadic kingdom; a key ecclesiastical centre in early Christian monastic expansion; a royal power base of the Stuart kings in the 14th and 15th centuries), island heritage stories have been relatively underarticulated in recent times and tend to be dominated by narratives relating to Bute's role as a seaside tourist mecca of the 19th and early 20th-centuries (see Duffy, 2012a).

More recently, however, projects such as the £2.8 million multi-partner Heritage Lottery Funded Discover Bute Landscape Partnership Scheme (DBLPS), which ran between 2008 and 2012, and the £2.6 million Rothesay Townscape Heritage Initiative, which ran between 2011 and 2016, have sought to stimulate a more nuanced understanding of, and engagement with, the island's past (Geddes and Hale, 2010; Duffy, 2012b), and a widening of public heritage activism beyond the membership of the 'traditional' local society (see Thomas, 2014 for further discussion). This in turn has enabled more clearly articulated roles to emerge for local residents as knowledgeable activists and co-collaborators (Moshenska, 2008) in heritage-based explorations on the island.

In 2014 and 2015 the local community was invited to participate in two University of Leeds-led projects. The first, the Pararchive Project, was an 18-month Arts and Humanities Research Council Connected Communities collaboration, which brought together community partners (active heritage groups in Bute, Stoke-on-Trent and Manchester), academic partners (University of Leeds, University of York), institutional partners (the BBC and the Science Museum Group) and private sector partners (Carbon Imagineering), with the ambition of translating community driven research on rural heritage into web-based digital stories (Duffy and Popple, 2017). The second, Island Stories, was funded under the Research Councils UK Sustainable Societies Network and sought to understand better the hyper-local context of attitudes to heritage and the digital environment encountered during the Pararchive Project (Popple et al, 2015). Intrinsic to both of these projects was the exploration of four core issues: how would local communities utilise the digital realm to retell stories relating to local heritage; how enabled were local participants to be able to tell these stories digitally; how supported were local communities in telling their stories, both by digital infrastructure and archive institutions; and what role could this process play in enhancing regeneration efforts for the island.

Archives as experiences, collections as authority

At the heart of the Pararchive project was an ambition to unlock the creative heritage potential of interest communities through the collaborative creation of a new open platform (YARN), which would allow users to harvest and orchestrate existing online archival sources and share their own collections and research (see Popple and Mutibwa, 2016; Duffy and Popple, 2017). Importantly, the involvement of collaborative partners such as the National Science Museums Group (NSMG) and the BBC also offered the opportunity to explore how, and if, publicly funded archive institutions could respond to the ambition of community groups through the digital environment as part of this process.

From a local community viewpoint, a key attraction of the project was the opportunity to access significant institutional archive resources through collaborative work with significant partners who shared the same ambition to challenge traditional 'expert' boundaries (see, for example, Schofield, 2014) as had been pursued through the DBLPS project (Duffy and Paterson, 2011) and 'cut through the rhetoric of custodianship' (Smith and Waterton, 2009: 11). In this respect, the most interesting archive engagement came through collaborative work with the NSMG. For Bute residents, this London-based institution was perhaps the most remote of all the Pararchive partners at the start of the project, both geographically and intellectually, with only a small percentage of participants reporting any previous engagement with it at the project start.

The Bute group's interest was predominantly focused around constructing rural heritage stories inspired through the recording of empty 19th-century farmsteads on the island. Although the evolution of technological aspects of farming practice had been noted and recorded at Bute sites, much of the focus of interest was on how building architecture could be understood as a consequence of political decisions (such as the impact of European Union policy in the 1970s) or economic demands (such as the demands of the expanding tourism industry in the late 19th-century). Engagement with practitioners from the Research and Public History department of the NSMG, however, provoked alternative thinking and actions that recognised the place of science and technology in the (hi)stories that were being created, such as during the subsequent archaeological excavation of a preserved 19th-century horse engine on the island

That institutional engagement provokes this sort of positive public response is, of course, the ambition that underpins much public facing work. Success, however, demands an effective strategy that enables a positive experience with the archive. As a remote community, the main engagement barriers facing the Bute group were distance/travel time to the NSMG archive (cited as a main factor in the lack of uptake for an expenses-paid guided visit to the archives) and, critically, any incidental knowledge about the institution holdings. Although the digitisation of interesting archive material helped bridge the former, it was the proactive human engagement between NSMG staff, project researchers and the group within the Pararchive framework that was perhaps the most important aspect of this relationship, signposting the potential of available archive resources and enabling digital reproductions. In an increasingly competitive, overcrowded and anarchistic information landscape, successful digital engagement strategies perhaps therefore need to consider not only how to make archive resources better available through the web, but also how better communication can be achieved between archive institutions and communities to lead people towards these resources.

Although there was common agreement that publicly funded archive collections should be more widely available for public use, one of the central challenges encountered in creating digital artefacts for use during the project revolved around issues of ownership and copyright. Although digitised images of material culture were relatively straightforward to produce, for the Bute group it was photographs, films and documents that were of particular interest for use in their digital storytelling. Despite institutional enthusiasm to make this material available, historical collection protocols and the complexity of unpicking copyright permissions relating to material collected over several decades dictated that this was a slow and resource intensive process for both the BBC and the NSMG. What became clear was that, despite mutual enthusiasm for the democratisation of archive material through digital release, the complexities of this process are likely to remain a frustration for institutional ambitions in this sphere. It might, therefore, be important that public expectations are appropriately managed through clear dialogue around archive resources of this type in the future.

Similar concerns around copyright and ownership were interestingly also encountered at a community level. Concerns were frequently voiced about the appropriation of content by third party organisations and fear about copyright infringements and the loss of ownership of heritage items, such as family photographs and personally gathered ephemera. To some extent the design strategy addressed some of these concerns; by hosting links through YARN rather than embedding digital content in it, users could choose where and how their digital assets should be hosted. However, for dedicated local collectors, who have often invested considerable time and money to amass collections that would otherwise have been lost, the balance between creating free content on the YARN site and maintaining an authority over digitised resources often influenced choices.

One local collector illustrated this tension through sharing a previous experience of finding in which an advertisement jpeg of a rare original image purchased online had been copied from the online site and reproduced digitally elsewhere. That the clear frustration this created came not from a desire to be the sole possessor of the image, but rather from the perceived undermining of legitimate efforts to curate the local past was a valuable lesson. Project encouragement to share such resources also demanded a clear explanation of the potential consequences of that sharing and the protective role of initiatives such as Creative Commons, not only in order to maintain trust between project and participants, but also to avoid eroding the dedicated human enthusiasms we aimed to celebrate.

Of similar interest was understanding the translation of enthusiasm for the concept of a democratisation of knowledge collection processes play out in a practical setting. In total six local heritage stories were identified and explored during the Pararchive Project, creating a series of 'classical' narratives or stories (Chatman, 1978; Herman, 2009). Three became digital 'Yarns' of varying lengths, one was never fully realised in any output form, while, surprisingly, two . substantive pieces of individual research were only disseminated through local society lectures and traditional journal-based papers, despite an active participation in the digital design process over a number of months.

These outcomes provoked interesting questions about community motivations, attitudes and skills. While at first glance the uptake for YARN stories appeared to be evidence of the oft-cited digital divide, this did not seem to account for our experiences during the project. These questions encouraged a wider appraisal of the digital and heritage context in which the project took place.

Engagement, enablement, empowerment and choice

Islands and island communities are increasingly becoming a focus for political, economic and academic attention. Research such as the ESPON 2013 EURO ISLANDS Programme (www.espon.eu) has put forward a number of common island challenges, including: lower economic performances than regions of the connected mainland; the presence of a technology gap, resulting in lack of the information and knowledge necessary to achieve social equity and economic competitiveness; and an unavailability of data at island level, which restricts analytical approaches to research and prevents the development of a nuanced understanding of the environment (ESPON, 2013).

One response to these challenges has been the identification of the need for 'smart growth' as a key priority through the active promotion of a digital society that utilises information and communication technologies (ec.europa.eu/europe2020/europe-2020-in-a-nutshell/priorities/smart-growth/). In Scotland, this ambition has been rearticulated through Scotland's Digital Future Strategy (Scottish Government, 2011) and a series of framework documents at regional and national level (see, for example: Argyll and Bute Council, 2012; Scottish Government, 2014b). The importance of digital connectivity for rural populations has also recently been highlighted in the Scottish Rural Parliament's six-point action plan, arising from a programme of collaborative consultation with local communities across rural Scotland (www.scottishruralparliament.org.uk/rural-issues-and-actions/).

Our work through Island Stories took place at the end of 2014 and looked at connectivity as a key part of the project remit, addressing issues of both the availability of hyperlocal island data and the contribution of islands to research and design. Although a number of infrastructure barriers and frustrations were identified, including slow non-fibre internet access, limited open Wi-Fi access and limited 3G mobile phone coverage, nearly all of the 95 respondents to the community survey we undertook were regularly digitally engaged, most usually via a personal or family computer. Just over two thirds of respondents recorded online channels as one of their primary information resources, with most of these people reporting social media use as their most frequent digital interaction. Ambitions for the future were more concerned about how engagement with the world through the digital environment could be made more reliable and stable through infrastructure advances, rather than how engagement could be achieved (Popple et al, 2015).

Although people were, therefore, clearly familiar with the digital environment, for many Pararchive participants experience of new web interfaces had been described as frustrating and confusing as participants struggled with (and against) a top-down (Thomas, 2014) imposition of unfamiliar concepts through non-intuitive interfaces. Perhaps unsurprisingly, Island Stories identified that much of the community's digital practice was a replication of existing non-digital communication methods familiar to any small community; so, word of mouth culture was imitated and supplemented through shared stories on Facebook pages, local interest newspaper stories from the local paper were accessed and circulated through web-based platforms as much as print copy, and so on. At the same time however, broader knowledge about how what this shift in engagement media meant in terms of issues such as personal copyright, data harvesting or content manipulation through algorithms was less clearly evident in what people told the project.

Co-creation was eagerly anticipated by the Bute group as a route to offsetting some of the previous web interface frustrations, and this enthusiasm was carefully nurtured through a supported navigation of the digital design process, design choice concepts and iterative testing of the functionality and appearance of the tool by the design team and research facilitators. This process took place over 18 months, a patient approach to learning and design that reduced participant frustrations by allowing room for enquiry and adoption of new concepts and allowed trust to become established between designers, participants and research facilitators through the affectionately appropriated concept of 'deep hanging out' (Geertz, 1998: 69). This intentional pace allowed upskilling of participants to happen more naturally than in a more classroom-based skills learning environment, and it also allowed detailed understanding of the implications of sharing personal data and material on the web. The success of this process also matched community demands identified in our Island Stories work, which recognised trust as a key component for future digital training and clarified local preferences for training to be delivered through face-to-face learning with peers.

The Pararchive project had a measurable impact in terms of skills and confidence in, and understandings of, the context in which digital choices are made. Subsequent activity by participants included the spontaneous digitisation of several thousand items from a private collection of Bute memorabilia, and informed consideration of and contribution to other digital archives projects (such as the Imperial War Museums 'Lives of the First World War'). This impact was achieved through a 'soft' learning process that encouraged ease and familiarity with the wider digital environment through supported iterative experience rather than hard training around digital tool functionality. In this regard, projects such as Pararchive provide a valuable model for how collaborative and longer-term approaches to digital engagement with archives offer wider social benefit.

However, as previously described, only half of the research topics studied as part of the project became digital YARNs, with other participants choosing to disseminate their stories through traditional formats and forums. Despite improved digital skills, better digital understanding and a physical and emotional ownership of, and satisfaction with, the YARN platform, the medium through which local stories were shared did not automatically become digital. For at least some participants, ownership of that research, and dissemination through lecture and journal publication venues, was judged to be more appropriate than the YARN platform. Clearly, individual decisions about how new skills, learning and knowledge are utilised are driven by the complexity of factors implicit in individual human choice (see, for example, Bonacchi and Moshenska, 2015). That this was unanticipated is perhaps the result of projection of our own expectations of altruism on the community 'actors' within the performative space created by the project (see, for example, Brown et al, 2017), rather than recognising that individual volunteers would define their own roles in the project over time.

Conclusions

Both the Pararchive and Island Stories projects offer useful learning in unpicking something of the relationships between heritage archives, remote communities, regeneration and the digital environment. Bute is, in many ways, a typical European island with typical island challenges, and at the start of these projects it had a population that was socially connected, digitally enabled but digitally naïve. Residents were informed and engaged as a result of previous heritage initiatives, ambitious for heritage to become a key component in improving island fortunes and enthusiastic to understand how wider archive holdings could contribute to locally generated research.

Despite the digital nature of the project, human interaction was a vital methodological component, and undoubtedly a central part of project success. Direct engagement between project partners, researchers and Bute participants enabled the successful signposting of previously unrecognised institutional heritage archive resources, while the use of those digitised resources as a basis for a co-design process not only made these resources available but also offered crucial 'soft' engagement with, and learning about, the digital environment. That this was the 'right' engagement for the local community, even in the face of tricky and complex issues, was reinforced through wider community survey that identified 'trust' and 'face-to-face instruction' as vital components for future digital learning projects.

In an age of ever increasing archive profusion (see, for example, https://heritage-futures.org/profusion/), concepts of value and relevance are increasing recognised as extending to local and individual archives (Prescott, 2015). Although Pararchive identified new challenges in understanding how the gap between these and institutional archives could be bridged to allow new stories to be created and knowledge to be shared, there was common agreement between participants at all levels that efforts to construct a digital venue in which this could happen was both important and valuable. For communities such as Bute, digital initiatives are perhaps one of the key ways that the relevance of institutional archives can be reinforced in the future.

In seeking to utilise the digital environment for the project, what became clear was that digital engagement was less of an issue for the Bute community members than a lack of confidence and knowledge about the terms on which they were engaging. The knowledge gap between understanding the front-facing architecture of web platforms and the motivations and processes that lie behind the creation of the platforms was of far more significance than the skills gap about how to use the Web. Although platforms that mask these issues through successful replication of familiar and comfortable communication patterns are locally well used, open conversations around copyright and data harvesting provoked initial suspicions about web user motivations and hesitations around sharing of personal archive material on the Web. It was only through the collaborative, longer-term approaches offered by the project that these concerns were overcome.

In this respect, the Pararchive project perhaps offers an alternative way to think about how communities are supported through heritage projects. Whilst opportunities to digitally participate in heritage projects have grown significantly in recent years, often the focus of this participation is as content providers for predesigned platforms in the form of informal blogs, digital artefact submission, participation in film capture of memories and so on. Far less attention is paid to encouraging participation from the outset in the actual design process of the web platform to be filled and this, I would argue, means that an important opportunity to fulfil strategic digital ambitions is being consistently missed. If our collective national ambition is to achieve 'smart growth' for our communities, then embracing end users as active and valuable contributors to the design process, as well as important content generators, offers exciting and underexplored ways in which to achieve a shared aim.

References

Argyll and Bute Council (2012) 'Economic development draft action plan – 2013 to 2018' [online], Available at: http://www.argyll-bute. gov.uk/moderngov/mgConvert2PDF.aspx?ID=71401 [Accessed 3 July 2015].

Bonacchi, C. and Moshenska, G. (2015) 'Critical reflections on digital public archaeology', *Internet Archaeology*, 40 [online], Available at https://intarch.ac.uk/journal/issue40/7/1/index.html

Brown, H., Reed, A. and Yarrow, T. (2017) 'Introduction: towards an ethnography of meeting', *Journal of the Royal Anthropological Institute*, 23: 10–26.

Chatman, S. (1978) *Story and Discourse: Narrative Structure in Fiction and Film*, Ithaca, NY: Cornell University Press.

CHCfE (Cultural Heritage Counts for Europe) (2015) 'Cultural heritage counts for Europe full report' [online], Available at: http://www.encatc.org/culturalheritagecountsforeurope/wp-content/uploads/2015/06/CHCfE_FULL-REPORT_v2.pdf [Accessed 7 July 2015].

Duffy, P.R.J. (ed.) (2012a) *One Island, Many Voices: Bute, Archaeology and the Discover Bute Landscape Partnership Scheme*, Donnington: Shaun Tyas.

Duffy, P.R.J. (2012b) 'An archaeological research framework for Bute', unpublished DBLPS booklet.

Duffy, P.R.J. and Paterson, B. (2011) 'Discovering Bute's archaeology', *History Scotland*, March–April: 14–15.

Duffy, P.R.J. and Popple, S. (2017) 'Pararchive and Island Stories: collaborative co-design and community digital heritage on the Isle of Bute', *Internet Archaeology*, 46 [online], Available at https://intarch.ac.uk/journal/issue46/4/index.html

Ekos Ltd (2010) 'CHORD programme socio–economic baseline, Rothesay locality', Report for Argyll and Bute Council [online], Available at: http://www.argyll-bute.gov.uk/sites/default/files/Rothesay%20Socio-Economic%20Baseline.pdf [Accessed 20 May 2015].

ESPON (2013) 'The development of the islands – European islands and cohesion policy (EUROISLANDS)', Interim Report (version 3) [online], Available at: http://www.espon.eu/main/ [Accessed 3 July 2015].

Geddes, G and Hale, A. (2010) *The Archaeological Landscapes of Bute*, Edinburgh: RCAHMS.

Geertz, C., (1998) 'Deep hanging out', *The New York Review of Books*, 45(16): 69.

Heritage Lottery Fund (2015) '20 years in 12 places' [online], Available at: http://www.hlf.org.uk/about-us/research-evaluation/20-years-heritage#.VV485EZe8gY [Accessed 12 May 2015].

Herman, D. (2009) *The Basic Elements of Narrative*, London: Wiley-Blackwell.

HIE (Highlands and Islands Enterprise) (2014) 'Rothesay profile' [online], Available at: http://www.hie.co.uk/common/handlers/download-document.ashx?id=b6543fc8-8c98-4cbd-8e06-8529704ba324 [Accessed 3 July 2015].

Moshenska, G. (2008) 'Community archaeology from below: a response to Tully', *Public Archaeology*, 7(1): 52–3.

Popple, S., Duffy, P., Phillip, F., Rivlin, P. and Turner, A. (2015) 'Island stories: growing digital heritage', Pilot Study Final Report and Policy Recommendations.

Popple, S. and Mutibwa, D.H (2016) 'Tools You Can Trust? Co-design in Community Heritage Work', in Borowiecki, K.J., Forbes, N. and Fresa, A. (eds) *Cultural Heritage in a Changing World*, New York: Springer Verlag, pp 197–214. Ebook available at: https://link.springer.com/book/10.1007%2F978-3-319-29544-2

Prescott, A. (2015) 'Being Local and Connected', in Papadimitriou, I., Prescott, A. and Rogers, J. (eds) *Crafting our Digital Futures*, London: Uniform Communications Ltd.

Schofield, J. (2014) *Who Needs Experts? Counter-mapping Cultural Heritage.* New York: Routledge.

Scottish Government (2011) 'Scotland's digital future strategy' [online], Available at: http://www.gov.scot/Topics/Economy/digital/ Publications [Accessed 15 May 2015].

Scottish Government (2014a) 'Our place in time: the historic environment strategy for Scotland' [online], Available at: https://beta. gov.scot/publications/place-time-historic-environment-strategy-scotland/ [Accessed 12 August 2017].

Scottish Government (2014b) 'Digital participation: a national framework for local action' [online], Available at: http://www.gov. scot/Publications/2014/04/6821 [Accessed 3 July 2015].

Smith, L. and Waterton, E. (2009) *Heritage, Communities and Archaeology*, Duckworth Debates in Archaeology, London: Bloomsbury.

Thomas, S. (2014) 'Making Archaeological Heritage Accessible in Great Britain: Enter Community Archaeology', in Thomas, S. and Woodbridge, J. (eds) *Participation in Archaeology*, Woodbridge: The Boydell Press, pp 23–33.

5

Memories on film: public archive images and participatory film-making with people with dementia

Andrea Capstick and Katherine Ludwin

Introduction

This chapter explores the use of images from local history archives in the co-construction of short individual films with people with dementia. The study on which the chapter is based was carried out with two men and eight women living in a housing-with-care facility in the northern UK.[1,2] Although we did not set out to draw on archive images, we found that they quickly took on a central role in the film narratives of several of the participants. In the process, the archive materials themselves were also transformed, memorialising the everyday spaces and places in which the participants had lived. In this study, archive images were often used to elicit memories of people, or places that no longer look the same in the present day. We found that such images were often more recognisable to the participants than were contemporary photographs. This corresponds with research into the 'reminiscence bump' (Thomsen and Bernsten, 2008), which suggests that autobiographical memory for the period between about five and 30 years of age remains well preserved in people living with dementia.

The archive images we used stood in for a past that was simultaneously personal and shared with others who had grown up and come of age in the same geographical area. Using such images often helped to establish the accuracy of historical accounts offered by people with dementia, who are prone to being unheard or disbelieved. The films work to trouble binary distinctions between the personal and the social, remembering and forgetting. They also historicise the experience of those men and women who now live with dementia.

Many of the co-created films, therefore, have a dual role, both as personal life story narrative and as visual folklore. The latter term has traditionally been used by anthropologists to refer to the non-professional use of popular imagery, artefacts, implements and icons to create and perpetuate group identity (Goodman et al, 2005). In recent studies, visual anthropologists have turned increasingly to the role played by photography and film in folklore and popular culture (Joubert, 2004). In the work discussed below, we found that using archive images helped to re-connect the participants with a sense of community and cultural history. More unexpectedly, however, we also found that in the process of moving from static to moving image, and from non-narrative to narrative form, the archives images were also reinscribed with new forms of meaning.

Background

The participants in our study had an average age of 87 years and all were living, at the time of the study, in the same housing with care facility. They spent the majority of their time in a relatively closed environment, with few links to either the surrounding area – a large housing estate in Leeds – or the neighbourhoods and communities where they had lived before moving into long-term care. The film-making process chosen for the study was an intentionally participatory one, intended to promote social inclusion and participation. We hoped to work in partnership with the participants to co-create films about their lives, experiences, interests and concerns. In doing so, we were consciously trying to resist some notable tendencies in mainstream social research on dementia. These include a focus on deficits in short-term memory and other cognitive skills, rather than what remains intact, such as longer term and procedural memory, humour and self-expression. We also wanted to avoid the reliance on family members as proxies that still characterises much research carried out in this field. Instead we wanted to hear the voices of the people with dementia themselves, and indeed to 'amplify' them as Frank (1995) advocates. This was achieved by including the participants' voices as soundtrack and ensuring that they had full editorial control over the content of their films.

The principles underpinning the research were taken specifically from participatory video (Milne et al, 2012), an approach that gives people who are socially marginalised or excluded an opportunity to tell their own story on film. The methods traditionally adopted by participatory video are not entirely suitable for people who have dementia, however, as they require the participants to take part in all stages of the film-making process, including the technicalities of image capture, lighting and sound (Capstick, 2012). These were not the aspects of making a film that were of greatest interest to our participants. We quickly found that the aspects they most enjoyed were storytelling, selecting images to accompany their stories and watching the unfolding film-in-progress as it was played back to them. For a number of participants we found that this enjoyment was enhanced when they watched each other's films together.

Although based on principles of participatory video, therefore, the process employed to co-construct the films had more in common with digital storytelling. This is a method for creating and editing a slideshow from still images, so that complicated film-making equipment and editing techniques are not required. Digital storytelling has been widely used in social research on diversity and disability and a variety of health-related subjects. Writers such as Burgess (2006) have noted its potential for unleashing a more democratic and vernacular creativity, and this was also a goal of our study.

It is important to stress that at the beginning of the research we did not know whether it would be possible to make films with this group of participants. Several had difficulties with verbal expression in everyday contexts and others typically spent large parts of the day in withdrawn or anxious states. What was most needed to establish a connection was something that sparked genuine personal interest for the participant in question. Sometimes this was a particular song (for example, Joyce loved 'Daisy, Daisy' and 'If you were the only girl in the world') or sometimes an object (Eileen's old cycling jersey) and sometimes it was an image. A breakthrough came with Nora, one of the earliest participants, when we followed up her reference to having lived in Tynemouth as a girl by finding images of the seafront and beach there from the website of a local history group from the area. Later we added archive images of the primary school she went to and the Pitman's secretarial college she attended. This became a model for the process later used with other participants.

Ethical issues and the limits of the visual

Formal ethics approval was granted by the Social Care Research Ethics Committee, under Sections 30–3 of the Mental Capacity Act (Department of Health, 2005). This states that people who lack capacity may still take part in research if there is evidence that they wish to do so and also if in the opinion of a consultee they would have wished to do so when they still had capacity. Of the ten participants in the study, we judged three to have capacity to consent for themselves, while personal consultees were nominated for the remaining seven. We followed the approach to process consent advocated by Dewing (2007) for research involving people with dementia, checking regularly at each new stage that they were happy to continue.

Consent to take part in research is often sought very early in the process, at a first or second meeting between researchers and potential participants. However, our approach was somewhat different as we sought to engage in a process of relationship-building with potential participants through several months of immersive work prior to the film-making process. Our initial relationship-building visits to the fieldwork site were often enlightening in terms of thinking about capacity assessments. We came to understand more fully that capacity was context-specific and that the procedures for assessing capacity with people with dementia often, in themselves, exacerbate the problems with memory and language typically experienced by people with dementia. This can create excess disability in people who have such a diagnosis (Yury and Fisher, 2007; Ludwin and Capstick, 2017).

There were, of course, some limitations and tensions in using archive images. Generally these were of three types: issues arising from monochrome photography, those related to visual impairment in participants and those related to traumatic memory. Older black and white images were less recognisable than more recent colour images for some participants; a useful reminder that the past was not actually lived in black and white. It was also not always easy to tell if a participant's less than enthusiastic reaction to an image was due to the content of the image itself or to a lack of the visual acuity needed to decipher its meaning. Finally, there was the possibility of unwittingly showing a participant an image that triggered a painful memory. One participant, for example, had associations with images of a housing estate where she had once lived because of media coverage related to a high-profile murder that took place many years later. This cautions us to remember that images of people and places may reactivate social shame or historical trauma.

The co-construction process; using archive images in film narrative

Most films were composed partly of generic images drawn from online sources such as Google Image and Flickr. Many also included existing family photographs, from albums the participants or their families already had. As time went on, though, it became increasingly clear that the participants' consistent focus on early life and significant places would require us to draw on public archive images to fill in gaps in visual narrative. Frank, the oldest of our participants, was born in Northern Ireland in 1922, and Eileen, the youngest, in Leeds in 1938. Historically, therefore, their peak 'reminiscence bump' years spanned the period between the late 1920s and the late 1960s. Few of their homes had been well off enough to own a camera, and in those that did the tendency would have been only to take photographs of such rites of passage as baptisms, weddings and departures on military service. We turned to public archives and local history sites to find the more mundane images to accompany the stories our participants told us about the communities they belonged to, and the places they frequented as children and young adults.

The central film-making process involved working with each participant for at least an hour a week over a period of six weeks. The long lead-in time spent familiarising ourselves with the environment, participants and staff meant, however, that by the time we started work with any individual we were already well known to them. We began with image searches related to things people talked about spontaneously, and spent time looking at them together as part of an iterative storyboarding process. Images that people showed little interest in were discarded, while those a participant was excited by, or clearly related to, were retained. Often the introduction of a new image would lead to further revelations, suggesting further subjects to research for the next visit. The storyboards we gradually built up together in this way were sometimes kept in a folder that the participant could look through independently between our visits. In other cases we used collaging to capture the unfolding narrative. Conversations were also audio-recorded and later edited onto the slideshow as a soundtrack. Finished slideshows could be made more or less sophisticated by the inclusion of sound effects, music, panning within images and other visual effects.

'Spaces and places' quickly emerged as a key theme in the film narratives, with every participant spontaneously locating his or her narrative in a particular geographical environment (Capstick and Ludwin, 2015). Most often this was somewhere the person had lived or visited as a child, and particular qualities or characteristics would often be associated with this place. Lilian, for example, associated the neighbourhood where she grew up in the 1930s – despite its material poverty – with a certain set of moral codes (see Figure 5.1).[3]

Figure 5.1: Back-to back houses, Leeds, 1930s

From the Leodis Photographic Archive, Leeds

> There's a lovely atmosphere – it's homely. Doors are all'us open. If they hear anyone chattering, or talking or laughing and they're in't house doing nothing, they'll come out and join you…

It was rare for participants or their families to have photographs of the buildings that had become such key parts of their stories. Images of places such as former schools, workplaces, cinemas or dance halls rarely featured in a family photograph album, but it was precisely these locations that tended to be foregrounded in participants' accounts. For Rita, a lot of memories centred on the sewing room in the clothing factory where she went to work aged 14 (see Figure 5.2). Sheila made frequent reference to the children's home where she grew up, and Hope often spoke about the print works where her father worked. Although all three buildings still exist, none of them now have the same function, and in present-day photographs the surroundings, vehicles and other features of the built environment also appear confusingly different. Archive images from the relevant time period were, in contrast, ideal for validating the participants' memories and reconnecting them with social history.

Figure 5.2: Former Heaton's clothing factory

From the Leodis Photographic Archive, Leeds

Many of the images we used came from local history sites such as Leodis, a photographic archive of Leeds delivered by the Leeds Library and Information Service, which consists of over 60,000 images. East Leeds Memories, a user-led site curating memories of people who lived in the area between the 1930s and 1950s, was another valuable source. These sites were almost always happy to provide permission for us to use images, and they often demonstrated genuine interest in the project.

Images were most evocative when they were from the right historical era. For example, we were able to show Henry, who was evacuated to a village in Cambridgeshire during the Second World War, archive images of the village from that time period. When he saw them he became very animated, pointing off to the sides of the image to explain where the different roads led to. We could not, however, find any images to correspond with another event he told us about, an unexpected reunion with his mother who had been billeted to a different nearby village. Although this incident clearly had great emotional significance for Henry, his reaction to photographs of the village taken in the later post-war period, was more muted. In these images, the village was significantly changed, with modern cars and shop-fronts, and people dressed quite differently from the 1940s.

The transformation of archive images

The digital storytelling approach we employed allowed still images to be strung together to create a film sequence. Individual images no longer stood alone, as they were joined together in order to create a narrative sequence. Archive images used as part of this process became part of a biographical narrative, connecting individual experiences back to the broader temporal and social contexts in which they originally occurred.

The process was a hermeneutic one in which the finished films could not be understood without consideration of each individual image while, simultaneously, the individual images became part of a whole and could no longer be understood in isolation. While images held in public archives have frequently been used to develop and illustrate our understanding of different sociopolitical moments in time, the images drawn on in this study had never previously been used to articulate the individual life stories of the study participants. In their finished form these stories hold potential to become part of a wider landscape of witnessing and accounting about historical moments. For example, Nora, born in 1928, lived in Jarrow as a young girl, and remembered the hunger marches of the 1930s ('Those poor men,' she said on one occasion, 'they had to go and beg for everything. It was awful; well *I* think it was.'). The films, therefore, weave together the personal and the social, reminding us of the turbulent decades that people now in their 80s and 90s have lived through.

Images transformed: two examples

Florence's entire story was located in a very particular neighbourhood and one specific railway bridge on the outskirts of Liverpool, close to where she had lived as a child. We were able to locate, and gain permission to use, an archive image of the bridge. Taken during the period Florence was recounting, the image of the bridge corresponded closely to her visual and emotional memory. During the storyboarding process, which in this case involved collaging, the bridge was placed at the centre of the piece. As Florence looked over the collage, her hands repeatedly returned to the bridge at its centre as she explained about the area, her relationship to it and the deeply rooted ties of family and community. On its own, the photograph of the bridge may not have told us much about Florence's life, but together with other neighbourhood images and her own narration it became part of a larger story about the extended family, class divisions and social mobility.

Lilian enjoyed talking about her life, frequently recounting the same stories, which we took as an indication of their importance. She also sang a great deal, performing the same three or four songs every time we visited. These songs were linked into her narrative (for example, 'My husband always used to sing the same song to me; it went like this...'), and they came to form a large part of the audio track to her film. While Lilian showed no real objection to looking at still images, she rarely showed great enthusiasm either. At times she indicated that she thought looking at pictures might be a childish activity. Instead she was keen to tell us about her husband, parents, children and the area where she had grown up and lived most of her adult life. Lillian's reaction to the completed film, made up of family photos and archive images, told in her voice and punctuated by her singing, was notably different. She instantly became highly animated and emotional, reacting positively to the film and wanting others to watch it too. In Lillian's case, the transformation from individual image to film sequence appeared to make a significant difference.

As with Lilian, the pride several participants took in their completed slideshows may have had something to do with the glamour they associated with being in films. Just as picture palaces and 'cinemadromes' featured strongly in the narratives of their youth, appearing on film and owning copies of a film they had made appeared to contribute strongly to the increase in social participation that we noted during the study. For example, participants not only developed new friendships with each other, they also discovered shared memories with people without dementia who lived in the same facility. It would not have been possible to achieve this without the use of archive images.

The historicisation of personal memory

In keeping with research into the 'reminiscence bump' in dementia (see, for example, Thomsen and Berntsen, 2008) historically-appropriate archive images were often more recognisable to the participants than contemporary photographs would be. It was not unusual for participants to introduce themselves to each other with reference to the area of the city they grew up in; for example, 'I'm Meanwood' (Hope) and 'I'm not Moortown; I'm Richmond Hill' (Rita). These memories were validated by showing participants corresponding images, such as Richmond Hill School (which Rita attended, bombed during the Second World War) and a derelict folly called St Alfred's Castle where Hope had played as a child. Beyond this, however, as Keightley (2008: 181) notes, 'the elicitation of everyday working class memory [can provide] unique access to accounts of the past marginalised in conventional history [and] dominant memories can be contested by vernacular memory'. Through generating alternative, democratised narratives of the past we may also resist the cultural amnesia that writers such as Jameson (1991) have deemed inevitable.

Rita's use of the now unfamiliar term 'tingalaries' may, for example, have been explained away simply as 'dementia talking', an explanation frequently used to explain away cultural references that are not understood by younger generations of caregivers. In fact we found that it was an old term first used for street barrel organ players and later to refer to ice-cream sellers (Capstick and Chatwin, 2016). Similarly, Rita's use of the term 'The Berthas' to refer to the long ago-demolished back-to-back streets where she grew up was often not recognised by others as a valid cultural reference, although it was not difficult to find archive evidence of the area where Bertha Street, Bertha Terrace and Bertha Place had once been (see Figure 5.3). This tendency to assume that people with dementia are unreliable narrators is an example of what has been described by Fricker (2007) as 'epistemic injustice'.

Figure 5.3: 'The Berthas' in 1947, before demolition

From the Leodis Photographic Archive, Leeds

Conclusion: visual folklore

Our participants seemed to relate to their films not just as passive remembrance or reminiscence, but as active testimony and commemoration of events, places and people. This became evident when the films were disseminated through internal screenings in the care environment and in public. At one of the screenings, for example, Eileen talked about her hope that showing her film more widely might help to prevent children today having the same experience of growing up in care that she did herself. 'I hope it doesn't still go on,' she said, 'but if it does I want people to know.'

The completed films ranged from three to 12 minutes in length. All focused on experiences during early life, predominantly between the ages of five and 30 years. All had a strong focus on place, neighbourhood and community, and all elicited findings about the participants that had not previously been known by the staff who were responsible for the participants' day-to-day care. Using archive images helped to fill in what would otherwise have been visual blanks in the narratives, thereby synthesising personal and social memory to create something new and remaking the archive in the process of making each film.

The films operate as visual folklore, by creating and perpetuating group identity (Goodman et al, 2005), as evident from their reception at public screenings, arts festivals and conferences. They cut across the traditional 'them and us' divide between those who do and do not have a diagnosis of dementia by opening up a space to explore shared memories of places and events. Weaving together images from local history archives and the narratives of older people who are prone to social exclusion and epistemic injustice, therefore, has value for both the archive and those whose contested memories are placed on film.

Notes

[1] As some years have now elapsed since this study, the chapter has not been written in collaboration with the people with dementia concerned. Instead we have tried to give a flavour of the co-constructive process used at the time and the important role that archive images played within this.

[2] This chapter presents independent research commissioned by the National Institute for Health Research School for Social Care Research (NIHR-SSCR). The views expressed are those of the authors and not necessarily those of the NIHR-SSCR, the Department of Health, NIHR or National Health Service.

[3] All images in this chapter are used by kind permission of Leeds Library and Information Service, www.leodis.net.

References

Burgess, J. (2006) 'Hearing ordinary voices: cultural studies, vernacular creativity and digital storytelling', *Journal of Media and Cultural Studies*, 20(2): 201–14.

Capstick, A. (2012) 'Participatory video and situated ethics: avoiding disablism', in Milne, E.-J., Mitchell, C. and de Lange N. (eds) *A Handbook of Participatory Video*, New York: Alta Mira.

Capstick, A. and Chatwin, J. (2016) 'The carnival is not over: cultural resistance in dementia care environments', *Pragmatics and Society*, 7(2): 169–95.

Capstick, A. and Ludwin, K. (2015) 'Place memory and dementia: findings from participatory film-making in long-term care', *Health and Place*, 34: 157–63.

Department of Health (2005) *The Mental Capacity Act*, London: The Stationery Office.

Dewing, J. (2007) 'Participatory research: a method for process consent with persons who have dementia', *Dementia*, 6(1): 3–25.

Frank, A.W. (1995) *The Wounded Storyteller: Body, Illness and Ethics*, London: University of Chicago Press.

Fricker, M. (2007): *Epistemic Injustice: Power and the Ethics of Knowing*, Oxford: Oxford University Press.

Goodman, M., Cohen, J. and Sorkin, D. (eds) (2005) *The Oxford Handbook of Jewish Studies*, Oxford: Oxford University Press.

Jameson, F. (1991) *Postmodernism, or the Cultural Logic of Late Capitalism*, London: Verso.

Joubert, A. (2004) *The Power of Performance: Linking Past and Present in Hananwa and Lobedu Oral Literature*, Berlin: De Gruyter.

Keightley, E. (2008) 'Engaging with Memory', in Pickering, M. (ed.) *Research Methods for Cultural Studies*, Edinburgh: Edinburgh University Press, pp 175–92.

Ludwin, K. and Capstick, A. (2017) 'Ethnography in Dementia Care Research: Observations on Ability and Capacity' in Flett, B. (ed.) *SAGE Research Methods Cases – Health*, London: SAGE. http://methods.sagepub.com/case/ethnography-dementia-care-research-observations-ability-capacity

Milne, E.-J., Mitchell, C. and de Lange, N. (eds) (2012) *A Handbook of Participatory Video*, New York: Alta Mira.

Thomsen, D.K. and Berntsen, D. (2008) 'The cultural life script and life story chapters contribute to the reminiscence bump', *Memory*, 16(4): 420–35.

Yury, C.A. and Fisher, J.E. (2007) 'Preventing excess disability in elderly persons with Alzheimer's disease', *Clinical Case Studies*, 6(4): 295–306.

6

Doing-It-Together: citizen archivists and the online environment

Jez Collins

Introduction

In *Global Music Report 2017: Annual State of the Industry*, the International Federation of the Phonographic Industry commented on the substantial growth in revenue for digital sales of recorded music and noted the shift in the recorded music industry of the last two decades as 'one of transformation: from physical to digital; downloads to streaming; ownership to access' (International Federation of the Phonographic Industry, 2017: 6). As the access and consumption of music has increasingly moved into the online environment, the number of individuals, communities and organisations who have come together to capture, share, preserve and celebrate a broad range of popular music histories, heritage and culture in participatory online archives has also proliferated.

Taking advantage of bespoke platforms such as Wordpress and Blogger are sites dedicated to a diverse range of music histories and heritage. Some are focused on specific places, such as Pompey Pop (the city of Portsmouth in the UK), Archive of Southeast Asian Music or the Manchester Digital Music Archive. Others focus on broader music culture. For example, 45 Sleeves, hosted by Big Boopa, is concerned with documenting and matching 45rpm records to their sleeves and the labels they were issued on. Kill Your Pet Puppies was created in order to document and make available the fanzine of the same name and has developed into a cultural archive of the UK anarcho–punk milieu; and Tape Attack is dedicated to German cassette culture of the 1980s and 1990s. Perhaps even more prolific are the actions of individuals who utilise social media, crowdsourcing and user-generated platforms such as Facebook, Twitter, Pinterest, Tumblr, YouTube and Historypin to capture and celebrate popular music culture and memory in unintentional archives (Baker and Collins, 2015). Estimated to number into the thousands, if not tens of thousands, of groups, engaging hundreds of thousands, if not millions, of individuals in communities of interest, these activities produce prodigious amounts of digital artefacts alongside the vernacular knowledge and memories of their participants. Topics range from the Texas music scene (for example, Texas Music History), to The Smiths posters (for example, The Smiths in posters), to more general music history (for example, Classic Alternative @altclassic).

In this chapter, I first explore the motivations behind the creation of what Roberts and Cohen (2014) class as self-authorised sites of popular music heritage, those created and curated by citizen and activist archivists that are devoted to the archiving, preservation and sharing of popular music heritage.

I then turn to the use of social media platforms and the communities of interest that form online and who take a 'Doing-It-Together' (Collins, 2015) approach to harvesting vast amounts of popular music materials and memories. While such platforms offer the opportunity for the celebration and sharing of obscure or niche music cultures, they also pose issues for their creators and those who may have an interest in participating or studying them. The loss of materials in the rapid 'churn'; the lack of search, navigation and retrieval functionality; the potential of technologies becoming redundant; and founders, owners and administrators losing interest in their sites, all resulting in the loss of substantial numbers of musical memories, are just some of the issues that need to be addressed.

Citizen archivists Doing-It-Together

Although still in its relative infancy, the internet and its associated digital technologies have developed rapidly since the early 1990s, shifting from the World Wide Web (Web 1.0) to the Social Web (Web 2.0) and now the Semantic Web (Web 3.0) (Serge, 2015). Each stage has brought new applications and uses for users that have impacted on our understanding of the archive and the possibilities for those with an interest in history and heritage. First, Web 2.0 saw the rise of connectivity and social media platforms that allowed individuals to connect with one another and to form communities of shared interests. Web 3.0, although still (2019) in its early stages, seeks to connect knowledge by developing devices and applications that 'speak' to each other and humans, and offers the potential to radically alter how we access and engage with archives and their collections.

Archivists and institutions have found themselves in the middle of the shifting modes of access and consumption that the internet has afforded to users seeking to engage with or create their own archives and collections in the online environment. Seeking to position these changes to the archival profession as the next stage in its progression, Terry Cook (2013: 105) presented a framework for thinking about the evolution of archives and wrote of the 'four shifting archival paradigms'. Cook named these shifts and ascribed their individual characteristics as Evidence; Memory; Identity and Community and stated that the fourth and most current archival period, Community, was associated with the rapid growth in digital technologies and the advancement of the internet. Cook goes on to write that the internet is democratising archival practices, empowering a broad range of individuals, communities and organisations to come together in order to document, preserve, share and promote community identity through shared histories and heritage. Cook (2013: 113) highlights the countless 'lobbying groups, community archives and "ordinary" citizens joining together' in online communities of practice (Wenger, 1999) and interest (Castells, 2002).

Mary Stevens, Andrew Flinn and Elizabeth Shepherd's definition of community in the context of the archive is useful here in thinking through what we mean by online communities and how such spaces are inhabited by individuals that coalesce in and around online sites that are devoted to music history and heritage, and how the originators of, and contributors to, such sites and activities define and identify themselves. For Stevens et al, 'By community archives we mean any collection of material that documents one or many aspects of a community's heritage, collected in, by and for that community and looked after by its members' (Stevens et al, 2008). The participation of the community as an active agent in creating and sustaining virtual sites of popular music heritage and memory is therefore a key factor in understanding the motivations behind these endeavours.

Archivist Kate Theimer, in exploring the meaning of participatory archives and their role in the wider archive field, has written that technology has blurred the barriers of the archive profession. As a consequence of this, individuals and communities have moved from being passive consumers to active agents in archival activities; whether in institutional archives or in the creation of their own archive sites. Theimer (2013) defines a participatory archive as 'An organization, site or collection in which people other than the archive professionals contribute knowledge or resources resulting in increased appreciation and understanding of archival materials and archives, usually in an online environment'. Theimer's work therefore complements Terry Cook's suggestion that technology is enabling citizen archivists to come together to create and sustain communities of interest through active participation in activities that I suggest can be seen as a Doing-It-Together approach to the archiving of popular music's past.

Virtual sites of popular music heritage, preservation and memory

In response to a perceived absence of an authorised and systematic approach to documenting, collecting, preserving and sharing of their popular music history and heritage, individuals and communities of interest have taken a proactive and activist approach to popular music history, heritage and archive practices (see Collins and Long, 2014; Collins, 2015; Baker and Collins, 2015, 2016; Long and Collins, 2017). One such example of these practices, and the motivations and actions of the founders of virtual sites of music heritage, preservation and memory, is the UK Rock Festival archive.

The archive: a history of over 30 years of UK festivals

Ranging from globally famous festivals such as Glastonbury to the more obscure Tiree Music Festival held in the Outer Hebrides, the United Kingdom has a long history of music festival activity, with an estimated 1076 events taking place in 2016 (Dean, 2016). In 2014 the Victoria and Albert Museum acquired the Glastonbury archive (Bailey, 2014), but aside from this, and in spite of a rich legacy, there has not been a systematic attempt to document or preserve this important contribution to British popular culture. In response to this, in 1998 founder Dave created *The Archive: UK Rock festivals 1960–90 & UK Free festival 1965–1990* in 1998 (http://ukrockfestivals.com).[1]

As stated on their website, UK Rock Festivals is 'a social and musical history (of sorts) of commercial Rock festivals of the United Kingdom, from 1960 to 2000 – and of the Free Festivals and related traveller scene of the United Kingdom, from 1965–2000'. The site has over 20,000 items and is organised into decades, this structure consisting of a series of links that take the user to specific festival pages, Festival Of Flower Children .Woburn 67 or National Jazz and Blues Festival (Reading) 70–75, for example. The site also has a Feature Artists sections, a Wanted section and promotes other 'festival related products and projects'.

The motivations of Dave in creating and sustaining this archive is evident in his mission statement, which supports Andrew Flinn's (2007) suggestion that citizen archivists and community archives are motivated by the failure of the formal archive sector to collect and preserve popular cultural heritage. Dave makes a claim for its importance by highlighting the sociological relationship between music and culture, and he explicitly rejects that his work is purely nostalgic or belonging to the 'retromania' that commentator Simon Reynolds has said is an addiction to popular culture's past (2011).

> This is NOT a nostalgia site! Yes, we celebrate the past, but this is as much a sociological project as it is a musical odyssey. The Archive aims to eventually provide as much information as possible about all aspects of the major UK festivals, Free festivals and outdoor concerts from 1960 to 1990 and scrutinise them from sociological and musical perspectives. Festivals are not divorced from society and they usually mirror changes in our general culture as well as in musical tastes. As music fans we also provide information on many of the groups who performed at the festivals, well, we do have to have some fun! (Dave, n.d.)

Throughout the site the community is encouraged to actively engage and become involved in building the archive by uploading their own personal materials and memories 'we need more info on these events...', 'Please note – this site grows by donations of material by its viewers...' and 'Wanted ... everything!' are just some of the calls made by Dave.

This participatory approach is taken up by the community, members of whom send and upload an array of artefacts and memories relating to UK festivals. One example of this can be seen on the Great Western Express Festival. Bardney. Lincolnshire. May 26th–29th 1972, a page dedicated to the festival of the same name. Despite featuring a line-up that included internationally renowned bands such as Sly & the Family Stone, Beach Boys, Faces, Genesis and others, the festival has largely been forgotten.

A report of the festival has been written, giving context to the event that is accompanied by reviews of each day of the event and the bands that played. Photographs from the event have been uploaded and partial set lists compiled. Contributor John S. has written an entry informing viewers that he taped some of the bands and that 'The quality of these varies depending on how heavy the rain was falling, how drunk we were at that time, how many tinnies were being thrown at the can dump beside us etc.' (John S., n.d.). There are also links to sections such as Press Articles, Publicity and Program, which contain a prodigious amount of material and number of digital images. There is even a section dedicated to Festival Toilet Paper, which has a scan that reveals Virgin Records produced the toilet paper as something both to read and to promote their business.

Taking advantage of the participatory approach to the history and archiving of popular music, there are a substantial number of posts generated by users of the site who attended the festival. Members share their memories and photographs and reveal the role music has, and does, play in their everyday lives. One such example serves as an illustration. For poster Chris Found, the discovery of the UK Rock Festival site, and the Great Western Express page in particular, prompted 'wonderful memories'. Chris then goes on to write how the festival gave him a sense of purpose following the death of his mother, and he details the experience of attending the festival and the music he heard there. For Chris, though, the festival was also a significant event in his life 'Over the three days I moved from a boy to a man…'; 'without this festival I may have not chosen my career and all the things that followed' (Found, n.d.). Chris goes on to state that he is a recording engineer. Other posters recall similar memories: attending with friends, partners and future spouses, of the terrible weather, of the good and bad music on offer and of the Hell's Angels security personnel. Posts are accompanied with photographs of the crowd and bands that played, providing a visual documentation of the event. Taken together, the community has provided a detailed account of a music festival that is not part of the dominant narrative constructed around other more celebrated music festivals: a festival that in some cases was life changing, but that would remain hidden and potentially lost to history forever were it not for the actions of citizen archivists such as Dave.

Social media and the harvesting of memory

Communities of interest on social media platforms such as Twitter, Pinterest, Historypin, YouTube and Facebook attest to what Andreas Huyssen (2003) has termed the 'memory boom'. Anchored around popular music culture, Facebook alone is home to a vast number of groups and pages that allow 'people to share their common interests and express their opinion. Groups allow people to come together around a common cause, issue or activity to organize, express objectives, discuss issues, post photos and share related content' (Hicks, 2010). Taking advantage of this facility, tens of thousands, if not hundreds of thousands, of individuals upload digital materials, share memories and exchange knowledge, celebrating the known and not so well-known histories of popular music's past. As Long (2015: 65) has noted, groups mirror the organising structures of popular music cohered around individual musicians, bands, spaces, places, events and particular periods of time in music history. Furthermore, he suggests that online music history, heritage, archive and memory activities are in part responses to 'the conventions of popular music as culture and as industry that are imbued with a sense of history, memory, curatorial and archival practice…' (Long, 2015: 67).

The broad range of Facebook Group subjects include those dedicated to the celebration of venues and club nights, often associated with a particular period in music history. Discussion in these communities of who did what or what bands played and what it meant to *them* can evoke personal recollections in some and more generic responses in others. Members of the group recall friends and acquaintances, bands who played there and speak of the affective qualities of the club and its meaning to them.

JBs Dudley – King Street back of the Pathfinder

One such example is the group named JBs Dudley – King Street back of the Pathfinder, a group dedicated to a live music venue situated in the Black Country town of Dudley in the UK that operated for 41 years between 1969 and 2010. As described on Facebook, JBs played host to 'Almost every band worth a chart single' and makes a call to those who may have attended the venue 'Why not share a few of your memories with us by uploading a few photos or just post us some of your stories' ('JBs Dudley – King Street back of the Pathfinder', Facebook, https://www.facebook.com/groups/16648688206/, n.d.).

In response to the call to 'share a few memories', members of the group upload digitised photographs, flyers, ticket stubs and other artefacts associated with the club. Contributors also add memories and enter into discussion with one another, revealing the role that JBs played in helping to foster a sense of community. In response to the death of a regular JB attendee, one poster likens the loss to losing a family member.

> Tonight I'm not thinking about brexit, I'm not thinking about what's happening to the country. I'm not even thinking about movies (which I'm sure you all know I love), no, tonight I'm remembering the friends I had 25 years ago. In a tiny little club in a shithole called Dudley, we found

ourselves. We also found each other. We were in bands, or we followed bands. Some of us just went to get pissed. We started relationships because the place was so small, you had no choice but to talk to each other … We've lost one of our own today, and it's hurt but we will always be family, we will always be … JB's. (Tonks, Facebook https://www. facebook.com/groups/16648688206/, 26 June 2016a)

Other members of the group respond to this post, mostly by adding comments such as 'R.I.P.' or posting xxxxx's to symbolise kisses. Some recall more personal connections: 'sleep tight angel will miss our crazy cat lady conversations' or remember a particular piece of clothing associated with the person: 'Stripy topped red stripe smiler…'. These online tributes and reminisces manifest into the organisation of a physical celebration held in close proximity to where JBs once stood in order that the community can come together and 'celebrate Maz's life and her impact on all of us…' (Tonks, Facebook, 26 June 2016b).

Other questions posed to the group include topics such as a call to those who played at the club to name their band and the dates they played and what the audience was like, a thread about who were the favourite local bands to play at the club and a thread specifically for those who met their partners at the venue. Each thread produced a copious amount of responses recounting long forgotten bands, memories of playing to near empty rooms for some and packed rooms for others, and tales of lifelong relationships.

In 2014 author Geoff Tristram posted a message to the group asking for members to supply him with anecdotes, photos, stories, bands, ticket stubs, posters and other materials associated with the club for a book he was writing, offering to credit everyone who contributed. Over the following months he would continue to seek the collective knowledge of the community on specific aspects of the club history such as the punk years of 1975–80. Members responded with detailed anecdotes and materials from their personal archives for the book, and such was the collective knowledge that the authors compiled a comprehensive list of bands and gigs that took place at JBs (an estimated 14,000 gigs and 8000 bands).

As Long has written, members of Facebook groups 'produce a form of community archive' (2015: 67) through the uploading and sharing of a range of digital images that in turn stimulate the posting of personal memories and histories. Members then respond to prompts by commenting and adding further memories and materials. For Long (2015: 67), it is the memories of the members that are the most characteristic and prodigious features of these communities, highlighting 'what such things [have] meant to individual lives, in both private and public events' that prompt further questions about the nature of history, heritage and archives and their relationship with popular music and society.

Conclusion

Online sites dedicated to popular music heritage such as those explored in this chapter support Jose van Dijck's (2006) suggestion that the practices and associations of popular music culture present frameworks for recollection. Van Dijck states that remembrance is always embedded in the individual, but our wider social contexts stimulate memories of the past through frameworks in the present. Here, then, we can see how the internet, and in particular sites related to popular music's past and its collective histories, memories and recollections, can be seen as 'cultural frames for recollection' that 'do not simply invoke but actually help construct collective memory' (van Dijck, 2006: 358) through the exchange of personal histories, memories and artefacts that reveal and celebrate previously hidden histories of popular music culture.

This chapter has focused on the practices of citizen archivists in the online environment and the opportunity this affords individuals and communities of interest to come together to capture, share and celebrate a broad range of music history, activity and culture. The memory exchanges that are described here and are replicated across many sites and platforms attest to the importance of music and music culture in the everyday lives of individuals and communities. While I have accentuated the positive characteristics of the practices I have explored in this chapter, I want to briefly acknowledge some of the issues and challenges faced by the online archiving of popular music's past. Despite the rhetoric around the transformative and democratising power of social media, a growing body of literature has begun to question such claims.

Garde-Hansen's (2009: 136) work, for example, discusses how the architecture, algorithms and corporate interests of companies such as Facebook or Twitter may 'not be liberating personal memory at all but rather enslaving it within a corporate collective'. Sarah Baker and I have drawn attention to the fragility, risk and loss of a number of online music archive sites, their collections and the vernacular knowledge contained within them. Issues such as copyright infringement, the sheer volume of content uploaded to sites and the poor metadata assigned to them, content creators removing their materials, and technologies and platforms becoming redundant all threaten the materials of popular music's past posted to sites of virtual musical memory (Baker and Collins, 2016).

Baker and Huber have written of how do-it-yourself institutions, 'Despite an "amateur" status … often mirror the mission statements and internal structures of national institutions, and endeavour to replicate similar standards of preservation' (2014: 112). When read alongside Roberts and Cohen's critical framework that 'explores the ways in which popular music heritage in the UK (or in England more specifically) is variously understood, discussed, critiqued, practiced or performed' (2014: 241), it is clear there are different approaches and methodologies employed, but there are also shared values and aspirations in the actions of those involved in the preservation of popular music histories and heritage.

Andrew Flinn (2007) has commented that mainstream archives are mainly concerned with conservation and preservation while community archives are mainly concerned with practice, access and engagement, and it is in this nexus, this embryonic ecology of practices, that more collaborative research and work should take place between citizen and community archivists, mainstream institutions and scholars so we can better understand and learn from one another. Only through active participation and collaborative approaches between these groups will we fully realise the possibilities that the internet offers us all for creating and sustaining genuine participatory archives of popular music histories and heritage, infused with memory-making, affective discussions and rich personal materials that enhance our understanding of popular music and the role it plays in the lives of so many people.

Note
[1] Personal correspondence with Dave established how he wished to be cited as founder.

References
Bailey, K. (2014) 'V&A acquires the Glastonbury archive' [online], Available from: http://www.vam.ac.uk/blog/network/va-acquires-glastonbury-archive [Accessed 1 December 17].

Baker, S. and Collins, J. (2016) 'Popular music heritage, community archives and the challenge of sustainability', *International Journal of Cultural Studies*, 20(5): 476–91.

Baker, S. and Collins, J. (2015). 'Sustaining popular music's material culture in community archives and museums', *International Journal of Heritage Studies*, 21(10) [online], Available from: http://www.tandfonline.com/doi/full/10.1080/13527258.2015.1041414 [Accessed 13 May 2015].

Baker, S. and Huber, A. (2014) 'Saving "Rubbish". Preserving Popular Music's Material Culture in Amateur Archives and Museums', in Cohen, S., Knifton, R., Leonard, M. and Roberts, L. (eds) *Sites of Popular Music Heritage*, London and New York: Routledge, pp 112–24.

Castells, M. (2002) *The Internet Galaxy. Reflections on the Internet, Business, and Society*, Oxford: Oxford University Press.

Collins, J. (2015) 'Doing-it-together: public history-making and activist archivism in online popular music archives', in Baker, S. (ed.) *Preserving Popular Music Heritage: Do-It-Yourself, Do-Itt- Together*, New York: Routledge, pp 77–90.

Collins, J. and Long, P. (2014) 'Online Archival Practice and Virtual Sites of Musical Memory', in Cohen, S., Knifton, R., Leonard, M. and Roberts, L. (eds) *Sites of Popular Music Heritage*, London and New York: Routledge, pp 81–96.

Cook, T. (2013) 'Evidence, memory, identity, and community: four shifting archival paradigms', *Archival Science*, 13(2–3): 95–120.

Dave (n.d.) 'About the archive [online], Available from: http://www.ukrockfestivals.com/index.html [Accessed 16 November 2017].

Dean, S. (2016) 'Do the growing number of music festivals actually make any money?', *Daily Telegraph* [online], Available from: http://www.telegraph.co.uk/business/2016/07/02/do-the-growing-number-of-music-festivals-actually-make-any-money/ [Accessed 1 December 2017].

Flinn, A. (2007) 'Community histories, community archives: some opportunities and challenges', *Journal of the Society of Archivists*, 28(2): 151–76.

Facebook (n.d.) 'JBs Dudley – King Street back of the Pathfinder' [online]. Available from: https://www.facebook.com/groups/16648688206/ [Accessed 20 October 2017].

Found, C. (n.d.) 'The Great Western Express Festival. Recollections' [online], Available from http://www.ukrockfestivals.com/gwrecollections-2.html [Accessed 16 November 2017].

Garde-Hansen, J. (2009) 'My Memories? Personal Digital Archive Fever and Facebook', in Garde-Hansen, J., Hoskins, A. and Reading, A. (eds) *Save As … Digital Memories*, Basingstoke: Palgrave Macmillan, pp 135–50.

Hicks, M. (2010). 'Facebook tips: what's the difference between a Facebook page and group? [online], Available from: https://www.facebook.com/notes/facebook/facebook-tips-whats-the-difference-between-a-facebook-page-and-group/324706977130 [Accessed 9 June 2014].

Huyssen, A. (2003) *Present Pasts: Urban Palimpsests and the Politics of Memory*, Palo Alto, CA: Stanford University Press.

International Federation of the Phonographic Industry (2017) *Global Music Report 2017: Annual State of the Industry* [online], Available from: http://www.ifpi.org/news/IFPI-GLOBAL-MUSIC-REPORT-2017 [Accessed 21 April 2017].

Long, P. (2015) '"Really Saying Something?" What Do We Talk about When We Talk about Popular Music Heritage, Memory, Archives and the Digital?', in Baker, S. (ed.) *Preserving Popular Music Heritage: Do-It-Yourself, Do-It-Together*, New York: Routledge, pp 62–76.

Long, P. and Collins, J. (2017) '"my god i loved this tune:)RESPECT 4 POSTING!!!!" Affective Memories of Music in Online Heritage Practice', in Brusila, Johannes, Johnson, Bruce, Richardson, John (eds) *Music, Memory and Space*, Bristol, UK/Chicago, USA: Intellect, pp 85–101.

Reynolds, S. (2011) *Retromania, Pop Culture's Addiction to Its Own Past*, London. Faber & Faber.

Roberts, L. and Cohen, S. (2014) 'Unauthorising popular music heritage: outline of a critical framework', *International Journal of Heritage Studies*, 20(3): 241–61.

S., John (n.d.) 'The Great Western Express Festival' [online], Available from: http://www.ukrockfestivals.com/Great-Westernlineup.html [Accessed 16 November 2017].

Serge (2015) 'Web technologies: now and tomorrow' [online], Available from: https://atomate.net/blog/web-technologies-now-and-tomorrow/# [Accessed 24 July 2017].

Stevens, M., Flinn, A. and Shepherd, E. (2008) 'Archives and identities' [online], Available from: https://archivesandidentities.wordpress.com/about-2/ [Accessed 16 November 2017].

'The Archive: UK Rock festivals 1960–90 & UK Free festival 1965–1990' (n.d.) [online], Available from: http://www.ukrockfestivals.com [Accessed 1 December 2017].

Theimer, K. (2013) *The future of archives is participatory: archives as platform, or a new mission for archives* [online]. Available from: http://www.archivesnext.com/?p=3700 [Accessed 27 May 2014].

Tonks, S. (2016a) Facebook [online] Available from https://www.facebook.com/groups/16648688206/?fref=gs&dti=16648688206&hc_location=group_dialog [Accessed 10 November 2017].

Tonks, S. (2016b) Facebook [online] Available from https://www.facebook.com/groups/16648688206/search/?query=tonks [Accessed 10 November 2017].

van Dijck, J. (2006) 'Record and hold: popular music between personal and collective memory', *Critical Studies in Media Communications*, 23(5): 357–74.

Wenger. E. (1999) *Communities of Practice: Learning Meaning and Identity*, Cambridge: Cambridge University Press.

7

'I've never told anybody that before': the virtual archive and collaborative spaces of knowledge production

Tom Jackson

The creation of 'virtual archives' of community spaces has the potential to engage community members who inhabit (or, through some other form of lived experience, identify with) those spaces as active participants in the collaborative construction of knowledge regarding their cultural, historical and social significance. In the representation of community spaces using 'immersive' and 'embodied' technologies and the open dissemination of the resulting archival materials through online platforms, new ways of accessing, experiencing and reflecting upon the quotidian reality of such spaces are facilitated. With the addition of participatory features, the virtual archive is reconfigured not simply as a method of representing data, but as a dialogic platform with the potential to democratise the processes through which situated knowledge is produced. In this chapter, each of these arguments will be evaluated and problematised using a specific virtual archive project, developed by the author, and a specific community as an illustrative case study. The overarching intention is to explicate how new forms of virtual archive might challenge the power relationships historically associated with archives as privileged spaces of knowledge production, while simultaneously avoiding the many pitfalls associated with digitally mediated forms of experience and participation, both of which are well documented within the academic disciplines of new and digital media.

Experience Temple Works (Jackson, 2016) is a multisensory and participatory virtual archive of a Grade I listed building in South Leeds. The building, known as Temple Works, was originally constructed as a flax mill in 1840 and represents a significant stage in the development of the textile industries in the North of England and the wider industrialisation of the region (Elton, 1993). Possessing a stone facade inspired by the architecture of Egyptian temples and reputedly containing the largest single room in the world (at the time of construction), the building embodies a complex and contested history of economic, social and architectural problems. During the creation of Experience Temple Works, the building was no longer a site of manufacturing but rather the residence of a community of artists, makers and performers. This community, hereafter Temple. Works.Leeds, aimed to provide a space for creative and cultural activity within the city (and in particular, to facilitate exhibitions and events that might not find a place within 'traditional' cultural venues) while concurrently maintaining, promoting and advocating for the building itself. *Experience Temple Works* was conceived as part of a 30-month 'sensory ethnography' (see Pink, 2012 and Jackson, 2018) with the Temple.Works.Leeds community and was originally designed to communicate aspects of the sensory experience of the building through standard web browser technology. This new form of virtual archive was intended to facilitate an analysis of the relationships between the vivid sensory experience of the building and the creative and cultural activities taking place within it, answering anthropological questions about why a community of creative practitioners were so drawn to such a challenging and unconventional space in which to operate and how that space might have informed the artistic works resulting from their residency. However, as this chapter will attest, the project came to attain much greater social and academic impact through its later reconfiguration as a community-orientated platform for collaborative knowledge production.

The first version of Experience Temple Works (released in 2015) integrated a range of features intended to facilitate the ethnographic analysis outlined above. These included interactive 360-degree photography (communicating aspects of the visual experience of being within the building), a navigation system of 'spatial hyperlinks' (facilitating movement and interaction), high-resolution macro-photographs of objects within the building (not only allowing those objects to be interrogated in great detail but also engaging the haptic sense through a process of artificial synaesthesia), interactive 360-degree binaural audio recordings (communicating aspects of the auditory experience of being within the building through an embodied and 'spatialised' type of sound recording) and a temporal navigation system (revealing how the sensory experience of the building changes over time and the extent to which the building was reconfigured for different purposes). The affordances of each of these features and, in particular, the cumulative impact of their integration into a single unified platform, achieved the intended aim of opening up new ways of studying the sensory experience of the building. However, it also brought about two unexpected, but very welcome, outcomes: a method of engaging the members of the Temple.Works.Leeds community as active collaborators in the research and, in conjunction with the participatory features added in the second version of the virtual archive, a significant shift in the authorial processes associated with the study, allowing the community members to construct their own research materials and findings.

The production of the audio-visual materials that would later form the 'records' within the virtual archive necessitated working closely with the members of the Temple.Works.Leeds community, explaining the intentions of the study, gaining the permissions required to access private studio spaces, planning when the recordings could take place and so on. Although this was a lengthy process, it quickly became apparent that the methods being employed were highly effective in co-opting the community members as engaged and enthusiastic collaborators. Throughout the fieldwork, the creation of the virtual archive was commonly referred to as something 'important'; and when this pattern was investigated it became clear that a large number of the community members felt that something of cultural significance was happening at Temple Works during this time, and it was therefore important to document what was taking place. In collaborating with the artists, makers and performers in the creation of an archive that they felt represented their community, their achievements and the significance of the space in which these achievements had been made, it was not only possible to produce a range of research materials of great value to the academic study, but also for the community to establish and maintain a positive identification with the project. Members of Temple.Works.Leeds were eager to be 'present' within the archive and, following their inclusion, proudly utilised it to evidence and exhibit their association with the building. This demonstrates the efficacy of the project's approach in encouraging community engagement.

Experience Temple Works demonstrated the capacity to co-opt community members as active collaborators and this can, at least in part, be attributed to the way in which the academic knowledge it represents is communicated. One of the recurring challenges of research with communities is finding a way to communicate the resulting findings in a way that is meaningful to the people they are intended to represent. The translation of fieldwork encounters into language and writing (and particularly into the 'academic' diction often necessary for publication) has the potential to represent those encounters in a format that members of the community are unable to fully appreciate (Levack Drever, 2002). Similarly, the translation of fieldwork encounters into 'conventional' archival records might not engage the community or encourage them to utilise the materials that are produced. Both of these 'translations' also commonly reside behind the 'paywalls' associated with academic journals and digital archives. Experience Temple Works differs greatly with regard to these issues. From its inception, this form of virtual archive was intended to represent academic knowledge in a 'humanised' format, relatable to audiences outside academia. Utilising embodied forms of audio-visual media (such as binaural audio), customary types of interactive functionality (such as interactive 360-degree photography, popularised by Google Street View) and standards-compliant web technologies (such as HTML, CSS and JavaScript), the intention was to make the archive accessible, comprehensible and meaningful to as wide an audience as possible. Through its exhibition at a wide range of public engagement activities (including the Digital Design Weekend at the Victoria and Albert Museum), the capacity of Experience Temple Works to present an academic research project in a relatable format, engaging the public in debates regarding 'immersive' technologies, the virtual archive and cultural heritage has been extensively evaluated.

Virtual archives such as Experience Temple Works do not simply possess the capacity to co-opt community members; they also have the potential to facilitate new ways of collaborating with communities in accessing, experiencing and reflecting upon the quotidian reality of the spaces they represent. What follows is an evaluation of four different affordances of Experience Temple Works and the impact they had on the power relationships associated with the academic study. Quite distinctive from 'conventional' forms of archive, these affordances engendered a different kind of 'researcher-researched' relationship, disrupting long-established assumptions regarding ownership, expertise and authorial voice.

While a conventional image archive is likely to contain photographs that represent a 'framed' abstraction created by a single, lens-based composition, the interactive 360-degree photography contained within Experience Temple Works encompasses a 360 degree field of view. This is significant as it represents a shift in authorial control over the visual records contained within the archive. Viewers are afforded the ability to reframe the environment in accordance with their own interests and intentions, rather than those of the photographer. The potential obviously exists to include a broader range of visual data within this type of image, but it is of much greater significance that this data is communicated in a format that is more 'pre-reflective' in nature. Interactive 360-degree photography also has the potential to aid in communicating research comprehensibly to non-academic audiences. Not only does this mode of representation offer an engagingly 'immersive' and meditative visual experience, it might require less 'decoding' and interpretation regarding the intentionality of the photographer and 'the predicament of the frame' (Favero, 2014). However, it is important to note that the photographer is still 'present' in this type of photography. Intentions that would typically be manifested in compositional decisions made through the lens are not removed; they are reconfigured into concerns regarding the positioning of the 'fulcrums' from which the image will be experienced, which necessitates a different kind of spatial awareness.

The high-resolution macro-photographs of objects within the building are far more comparable to the visual records that might exist within a 'conventional' image archive as they are the result of single, lens-based compositions. However, the way in which these images are accessed is of great significance. Presented as records within a searchable database, the context and locality of the object might be lost. Within Experience Temple Works, objects are accessed from a representation of the environment in which they were originally encountered, not only providing locative data, but maintaining the spatial narratives created by their relationships with other aspects of the space. Accessing the archival records through an environment familiar to the community members might also make them more relatable.

The types of movement and interaction that Experience Temple Works facilitates might also be of significance, depending upon the intentions for which the virtual archive is being utilised. The 'spatial hyperlinks' included within the interactive 360-degree photography offer a sense of traversing a space, creating ways of exploring the archive that are reflective of embodied perceptual behaviour. Not only are movement and perception inextricably linked (Gibson, 1986), but movement and interaction also encourage engagement. Where a static, framed image might have the effect of 'distancing' the observer, the movement and interaction that Experience Temple Works facilitates goes some way towards recreating the active and exploratory nature of visual perception in which 'the subject derives information about the environment by continuously engaging it through attention, multisensory stimulation and behaviour' (Grasseni, 2004: 46). Accessing the data contained within this type of virtual archive *necessitates* movement and interaction, in contrast to more 'passive' forms of media such as film, and it is through active and exploratory processes such as this that places become meaningful. All of these affordances could be very meaningful for any project that intends to use archival materials as a form of sensory elicitation, or in the context of any research methods in which the biographical encounters of place need to be recreated, or at least reimagined, away from the field of study.

The interactive 360-degree binaural audio recordings included within Experience Temple Works also represent an important shift in authorial control and another form of sensory elicitation for use with the collaborators. The hardware and software solution designed to acquire and present these recordings (created specifically for this virtual archive but now integrable within any other) allows for the 'immersive', embodied and spatial qualities of binaural listening to be experienced within a navigable 360-degree visual environment. This means that although the listener will hear a predetermined sequence of sonic events from a predetermined position within the environment, the act of listening to the recording is no longer a singular, unified experience. The listener can direct their attention through the spatial orientation they select, in contrast to 'standard' stereo recordings that typically embody a perspective dictated by the recordist. Furthermore, while visual media have the potential to result in a sense of 'distancing', listening is a haptic and auditory experience that both surrounds and penetrates, creating a sense of 'closeness'. Audio recordings therefore have the potential to be a highly effective aid in the context of sensory elicitation, achieving a 'reintegration of the listener with the environment in a balanced ecological relationship' (Truax, 2008: 106).

As compelling as the inclusion of auditory media within any form of virtual archive might be, it introduces the necessity to maintain a critical awareness regarding issues of 'presence', intention and editing. While photography and film-making clearly index the presence of the person behind the camera and are widely recognised to embody the compositional impulses of that person, there is 'a common presumption … that field recordings represent authentic, impartial and neutral documents' (Anderson and Rennie, 2016: 222). Failing to acknowledge that compositional, selective, technological and intuitive processes (determined by the recordist) are present in every audio recording has the potential to mask the subjective and personal nature of the resulting files. Also commonly overlooked in the analysis of audio recordings is the issue of intent. The processes described above are all informed by the recordist's desire to communicate specific meanings and inevitably embody the ways in which they have approached these intentions. However, the 'directness' of listening and the personal, intimate and embodied nature of auditory experience has the potential to obscure these processes. Finally, while the concepts of 'presence' and 'intention' have direct correlates in visual media and can be interrogated in very similar ways, the editing of a sound recording must be conceptualised differently. In the seminal audio recording project The Vancouver Soundscape, Schafer (1973) equates the selection of sounds to placing 'a frame around them ... [j]ust as a photograph frames a visual environment'. This contention suggests that the editing of sound recordings might not be any more problematic than the framing of a composition within visual forms of media; the process of abstraction simply takes place in the temporal, rather than spatial, domain. However, the temporal compression that this process introduces requires the listener to be made aware that the auditory experience offered by these edited recordings does not reflect the rhythm and pacing of the lived experience it is intended to represent.

The affordances of Experience Temple Works addressed above all illustrate the capacity for virtual archives to change the relationships between community members and archival collections. However, there are problems associated with using technological modes of representation as a method of co-opting and collaborating with communities. Digitally mediated forms of experience, such as those that might be presented by a virtual archive, can introduce troubling effects that must be acknowledged during the study and the analysis of the results. Virtual technologies have the potential to 'reify' aspects of experience, making them appear more explicit and concrete than the original ephemeral encounter, to obscure the significance of those aspects of sensory experience that current technology is not capable of communicating (such as olfactory and gustatory stimuli) and to create problems in identifying whether the meanings and emotions elicited by a digitally mediated experience are a response to the original encounter or to the mode of representation. Failing to acknowledge the possibility of these effects occurring has the potential to introduce misinterpretations, or even, of much greater concern, for the concept of using virtual archives in the context of community research to be misappropriated. The solution is simply to ensure that when using any form of virtual or 'immersive' technology in dialogue with communities, both the researcher(s) and collaborators consider them a 'third space' through which knowledge might be produced, not as a simulacrum of experienced reality.

Virtual archives also implicate a number of debates regarding the concept of 'immersion'. Many of the technologies integrated into Experience Temple Works (including 360-degree photography, binaural audio recording, interactive environments) are commonly proclaimed to offer an 'immersive' experience in popular vernacular, journalistic media and academic publications. However, the use of this term should be rigorously examined, not only because it should not be assumed that a sense of immersion has been achieved but also because the concept of immersion is itself problematic, implying types of human computer interaction that are potentially misleading. Although the creation of any virtual space 'implies the possibility of immersion', describing the experience as such without qualification has the 'ability to articulate what are often fictional scenarios' (Dyson, 2009: 1–2). With regard to the concept of using virtual archives in research with communities, arguing that the experience of accessing the archive is 'immersive' has the potential to mask the impact of analysing the materials away from the field of study and to imply that they have a direct evidentiary power, rather than simply bringing the sites of observation and interpretation closer together (see Poole, 2005 and Pink, 2012).

While the first version of Experience Temple Works proved effective in instigating notable changes in the processes associated with using archives in the context of community research, the second version (released in 2016) introduced new functionality with even greater potential to impact upon preconceptions of archives as privileged spaces of knowledge production, disconnected from the communities they are intended to represent. A participatory system was integrated allowing members of the Temple.Works.Leeds community (and, in fact, anyone from around the world with access to standard web browser technology and an internet connection) to contribute to the archive. Within any of the interactive 360-degree environments, or the high-resolution macro-photographs of objects, users were now afforded the ability to post text, images and (via third-party hosting platforms) audio recordings and videos of their own creation. With this system in place, the ownership of the archive was disrupted, and it was reconfigured not simply as a source of primary data, but as a collaborative platform through which knowledge might be co-created.

The impact of this development in the virtual archive will now be illustrated through the analysis of a number of contributions by one specific member of the Temple.Works.Leeds community: stained-glass artist Zoë Eady. Zoë enthusiastically embraced the participatory functionality implemented in the second version of Experience Temple Works, and her contributions reveal a number of ways in which new collaborative practices were instigated by it, all with the potential to generate new knowledge within the archive.

Atop a display cabinet in the main reception of Temple Works, a photographic portrait of a man was presented in a plastic leaflet holder. Unaware of his identity, I often considered asking a member of the Temple.Works.Leeds community about his relationship to the site, but the opportunity never seemed to present itself. Following the introduction of the participatory features into the virtual archive, Zoë quickly revealed that his name was Brian and that he used to help with the maintenance of the building. This textual contribution took the form of a deeply personal narrative in which Zoë described a day spent with Brian, engineering a new door for her studio space:

> We spent a fun day together scavenging round the site trying to find a door that might fit my toilet-studio … Brian came to this project with an endearing ferocity. The most terrifying part culminating with an axe and some rusty hinges that he refused to be defeated by. I had fun that day, I was so pleased with my new door! He left his safety goggles and some tools in my room because we were going to finish it off later in the week, but I never saw him again. A few days later we heard how he'd died. No-one ever claimed his things and I wasn't sure who to give them back to, so I kept using them. I still wear his goggles most days and I often think about him. I've never told anybody that before.

This contribution illustrates the capacity for the participatory virtual archive to become a space for collaborative knowledge production with community members. However, potentially of even greater interest, is the concluding sentence: 'I've never told anybody that before.' Experience Temple Works had motivated Zoë to share something that she had never previously communicated in any other form, revealing the extent to which it had induced an unconventional relationship with the archive, opening up in a space in which intimate and previously unspoken information might be shared.

The inclusion of participatory functionality within the virtual archive also has the potential to alter the dynamics of power associated with the creation of archival records. During her residency at Temple Works, Zoë regularly produced timelapse videos in her studio, utilising the temporal compression of this format to reveal how a stained-glass project comes together over a long period of time. During the production of the 360-degree photography and binaural sound recordings of her studio, Zoë also created these videos and then contributed them to the archive. This act not only illustrated how engaged she was in the co-creation of the archival records related to her space, it also revealed a significant change in the balance of power. By indexing my presence within the virtual archive through the creation of her own materials, I was no longer the 'author' and she was no longer the 'subject'. We were both implicated in the authorial processes and present within the resulting archival records.

Conceptualised as part of a 'sensory ethnography', Experience Temple Works was also intended to open up discussions with the members of the Temple.Works.Leeds community regarding the sensory experience of the building. A number of the contributions submitted by Zoë are reflective of this intention, suggesting that the participatory virtual archive has the capacity to facilitate particular types of discussion and analysis. Textual contributions such as the following illustrate that Zoë was actively reflecting upon the vivid sensory experience of particular locations within the building and connecting the sense memories formed by those experiences with specific meanings:

> In the springtime tiny fluffy flakes from the decaying ceiling plaster in the Top Floor Canteen would drift down like snow. The damp would damage it during the winter and then it would peel off as it dried out. It was both disgusting and beautiful. Sometimes I would sit and watch it. During Brian's memorial service in spring 2012 it snowed constantly for an hour.

A particularly poignant example of these 'sensory reflections' came about when the virtual archive was later used for the purposes of sensory elicitation. Zoë vacated the building during the creation of Experience Temple Works, relocating to a new studio space. This presented the opportunity to produce 360-degree photography and binaural audio recordings during her residency and after she had departed. The temporal navigation system built into the virtual archive made it possible to quickly 'transition' between these two different configurations of the same space. While most people accessing this transition commented on how interesting and engaging it was to so vividly interrogate the impact of Zoë's presence and absence on the sensory experience of the space, I was surprised to discover that Zoë found it emotional. Witnessing her disappearance from Temple Works in such a temporally compressed format brought back evocative memories regarding how difficult a decision it was for her to leave. Through this discovery, another way in which Experience Temple Works has the potential to generate intimate and subjective knowledge was identified.

While the illustrations above demonstrate the collaborative potential of virtual archives, technologically mediated forms of participation also present a number of problems regarding power and control and the 'digital divide', the significance of which must be acknowledged during the analysis of the community-generated content. Rather than democratising the production of knowledge, participatory media platforms might replicate the systems of power and control present within the community. Although these technologies might be 'used across lines of gender, class and other differences, the way they are used continues to reflect socioeconomic disparities' (Zoettl, 2012: 210). The researcher must therefore avoid any assumptions regarding online participation as a 'great equaliser', providing a 'voice' to all members of the community, and maintain a critical awareness of its potential to mirror the inequalities present offline. It is also important to note that the virtual archive platform itself will exert power and control, imposing 'structures [that] enable and constrain the actions of media actors' (Sandoval and Fuchs, 2010: 145). Consequently, while participatory media might be 'an agent for social change, culture development and democratization' (Servaes, 1999: 269), the contributions that users are able to make are restricted by, presented within and potentially reflective of the frameworks dictated by the archive. Owing to potential issues regarding access to technology, it should also be noted that using participatory media in the context of community research might not be an effective way of co-opting and building relationships with community members, but rather introduce another barrier by which they are excluded from, or misrepresented by, the study.

In conclusion, Experience Temple Works illustrates the capacity of virtual archives to engage community members in the production and utilisation of archival materials. In the creation of an archive that communicates academic knowledge in a format meaningful to the communities it is intended to represent, members of that community can be co-opted as active collaborators in the research, shifting preconceptions of the archive as inaccessible, 'distant' or disconnected from everyday experience. Even before the participatory functionality was implemented, the affordances of this virtual archive proved effective in engendering a sense of identification and ownership amongst the Temple.Works.Leeds community, evidenced by the extent to which many members wished to be 'present' within the archive. With the addition of participatory functionality, the relationships between the community and the archive were changed to an even greater extent. The production of the archival materials was opened up to a much wider audience, shifting the dynamics of power commonly associated with archives as privileged spaces of knowledge production. However, all of these claims must be tempered by a critical awareness of the problems associated with technological modes of representation and digitally mediated forms of participation. Of particular concern are the extent to which engaging and meditative forms of sensory media might mask the issues of 'presence', intention and editing associated with their production, the potential for 'immersive' technologies to be incorrectly situated as having a direct evidentiary power and for participatory platforms to replicate the systems of power and control present within the community.

The future of this research lies in two key areas: the implementation of the methods within other community contexts, further testing the efficacy and impact of their use, and a commitment to continually revisit and update the theoretical and methodological arguments that have been presented here, not simply in response to developments in virtual archive technologies, but with the intention of informing them. In interdisciplinary collaborations between communities, archivists and scholars engaged in critical debates regarding virtual and 'immersive' technologies, the potential exists to contribute to a number of emerging debates regarding the place of archives in community research.

References

Anderson, I. and Rennie, T. (2016) 'Thoughts in the field: "self-reflexive narrative" in field recording', *Organised Sound*, 21(3): 222–32.

Dyson, F. (2009) *Sounding New Media: Immersion and Embodiment in the Arts and Culture*, 1st ed., Berkeley: University of California Press.

Elton, A. (1993) *The House that Jack built: The Story of Marshall & Co. of Leeds Flax Spinners and School Managers 1788–1886*, Leeds: Thoresby Society.

Favero, P. (2014) 'Photography, new technologies and the predicament of the frame: Theoretical and methodological reflections', panel discussion at 'Anthropology and Photography' conference held at The British Museum, 31 May.

Gibson, J.J. (1986) *The Ecological Approach to Visual Perception*, new edition, Hillsdale, New Jersey: Lawrence Erlbaum Associates.

Grasseni, C. (2004) 'Skilled vision: an apprenticeship in breeding aesthetics', *Social Anthropology*, 12(1): 41–55.

Jackson, T. (2016) 'Experience Temple Works' [online], Available from: http://tomjackson.photography/interactive/templeworks/ [Accessed 2 February 2017].

Jackson, T. (2018) 'Multisensory ethnography: sensory experience, the sentient body and cultural phenomena', PhD thesis, University of Leeds.

Levack Drever, J. (2002) 'Soundscape composition: the convergence of ethnography and acousmatic music', *Organised Sound*, 7(1): 21–7.

Pink, S. (2012) *Doing Sensory Ethnography*, London: SAGE.

Poole, D. (2005) 'An excess of description: ethnography, race, and visual technologies', *Annual Review of Anthropology*, 34(1): 159–79.

Sandoval, M. and Fuchs, C. (2010) 'Towards a critical theory of alternative media', *Telematics and Informatics*, 27(2): 141–50.

Schafer, R.M. (1973) 'The Vancouver Soundscape', *Discogs* [online]. Available from: http://www.discogs.com/R-Murray-Schafer-The-Vancouver-Soundscape/release/1810808 [Accessed 15 June 2013].

Servaes, J. (1999) *Communication for Development: One World, Multiple Cultures*, Cresskill, NJ: Hampton Press.

Truax, B. (2008) 'Soundscape composition as global music: electroacoustic music as soundscape', *Organised Sound*, 13(02): 103–9.

Zoettl, P.A. (2012) 'Images of culture: participatory video, identity and empowerment', *International Journal of Cultural Studies*, 16(2): 209–24.

PART II

Citizens, archives and the institution

8

Rising beyond museological practice and use: a model for community and museum partnerships working towards modern curatorship in this day and age

Daniel H. Mutibwa

Introduction

This chapter discusses effective ways to develop relationships between communities and museums around shared cultural agendas, practice and knowledge exchange. Through the lens of an eight-month pilot that emerged from the Pararchive project (http://www.pararchive. com) and was partnered by the National Media Museum (NMeM), Bradford, the chapter addresses what it means to access a dormant but invaluable national archive and associative collections from the position of differently situated community groups. The chapter not only highlights how the Pararchive-National Media Museum partnership (PNMeM) promoted opportunities for community groups to select, document and creatively exploit archival resources in ways in which conventional museological practice and use do not allow, but also outlines the key challenges encountered.[1] In doing so, it draws on detailed notes generated through participant observation, on the study of relevant documents and artefacts, and on important insights gained from audio recordings of relevant project meetings and an evaluative end-of-project workshop.

Conventional museological practice and use

Museums have been described as arbiters of history and associated developments that chart the extent of human knowledge, achievement and expression in nearly every field of human endeavour including art, craft, science, agriculture, rural life, childhood, fisheries, antiquities and automobiles among many others (The National Museums, 1988; Vergo, 1989). As such, museums have historically been designated as institutions for education and research and for exhibition of collections to provide the widest public benefit. This understanding of museums as places of study and places of display (also increasingly as places of diversion) has engendered the sustenance of museum collections with the overarching intention to promote learning by informing thinking and by shaping attitudes and views of learners – scholarly and lay alike – as they make sense of their shared heritage (Vergo, 1989). Smith (1989: 8) helpfully outlines four principal features of museology:

> the first is that the collections ... should in some way contribute to the advancement of knowledge through study of them; the second, which is closely related, is that the collections should not be arbitrarily arranged, but should be organised according to some systematic and recognizable scheme of classification; the third is that they should be owned and administered not by a private individual, but by more than one person on behalf of the public; the fourth is that they should be reasonably accessible to the public, if necessary by special arrangement and on payment of a fee.

It is useful to unpack each of these characteristics before then showing how they informed the work undertaken in the context of the PNMeM. The first feature speaks to the educational and research function that museums have been said to perform. Historically, learning and researching in museums was a preserve of academics – particularly archaeologists and historians – who took considerable interest in the artefacts and collections amassed in order to attain as well rounded a picture as possible of the development of humankind over time (Hooper–Greenhill, 2000). As such, academics – along with curators and conservators – assigned meanings to collections, something that imbued such collections with superior authority, as did the safe and neutral environment that museum spaces were believed to provide (Smith, 1989). Whereas this ensured that important information was gathered about the circumstances within which collections originated, this tended to be from a predominantly singular and authoritative perspective that was dictated by a range of structural factors, including institutional acquisition and disposal policies, documentation, storage and preservation conventions, and ideological leanings among others (Vergo, 1989). The consequence of this has been twofold: first, multiple perspectives have rarely – if at all – been accommodated in the construction, representation, and interpretation of a shared past, and secondly, conventional museology has not always concerned itself with facilitating investigations into the nature of the relationship between collections and communities and/or the public in an effort to ensure the ongoing relevance of such collections.

The second feature is concerned with the ways in which museums collect, identify, describe and document artefacts in a taxonomic order that ensures the origins, names and detailed descriptions of those artefacts are arranged, organised and presented in a manner based on a system that is centuries old (The National Museums, 1988; Jordanova, 1989; Crooke, 2007). To some critics, the presentation of collections in such a system that is believed to be consistent, unitary and linear inhibits a more democratic approach that allows for agency whereby a much more conscious sense of the role of different publics in interpretation is accommodated alongside formal accounts (Phillips, 2003; Ridge, 2014). The third and fourth features highlight the importance of engaging with artefacts and objects away from their original context of (private) ownership and (restricted) use and into museum settings where wider access can be provided. However, the issue of access has proven problematic. Even where museums are 'reasonably accessible to the public', attempts by community heritage activists, community researchers and many members of the public to reach them will always be hampered by a number of logistical and practical factors – structural constraints (in the form of insufficient opening times as well as opportunities and permission to use collections) and geographical distance (including long travel times and associated arrangements) being two crucial ones among many others (Mutibwa et al, 2018). Moreover, access has tended to be understood as a scenario where communities and 'an undifferentiated, so-called public' (Smith, 1989: 18) have been invited to 'enjoy' objects on display normally through the lens of museum curatorial teams without giving consideration to the possibility that these constituencies bring along their own and varied attitudes, experiences and perceptions of engaging with and reading collections (Jordanova, 1989; Karp, 1992; Samis, 2008).

Community/museum collaborations: the Pararchive– National Media Museum partnership (PNMeM)

At a time of 'existential scrutiny' during which museums are being challenged to demonstrate the value and wider benefit of the multitude of objects and associative canons of knowledge under their stewardship

(Karp, 1992), museological practice and use are being rethought. One outcome of this has been opening up to communities and the public within the context of truly collaborative ventures aimed at democratising engagement with shared heritage (Walker, 2008; Ridge, 2014). This has signalled a move towards a two-way process of engagement whereby communities and the wider public are being invited to record their perspectives on the meanings of collections not only on their own terms, but also on the basis that these constituencies may be viewed as authorities on their own cultures and material heritage by virtue of their experiential knowledge of and relationship with artefacts and objects (Peers and Brown, 2003; Crooke, 2007). A central tenet of this two-way engagement process is that it is built on trust, confidence and respect – all of which are essential ingredients for establishing a meaningful and reciprocal working relationship that has huge potential for developing into a collaborative curatorial praxis geared towards addressing the needs and interests of all stakeholders (Phillips, 2003; Samis, 2008).

It is against this backdrop that PNMeM was formed – 'by special arrangement' (Smith, 1989: 8). The Pararchive project explored how individuals and communities took ownership of cultural and historical materials in which they are represented, combined these with their own media (film, photographs and other ephemera) and made use of archival resources to give voice to their own stories, contributed to a shared collective memory and constructed their own identities (Popple, 2015). To this end, Pararchive established collaborative working relationships between various community groups (orientated towards heritage and creative practice) and relevant public cultural institutions.

Pararchive constituted four differently situated community groups, namely Ceramic City Stories (CCS), Arduino MCR (AMCR), Bokeh Yeah! (BY!) and Brandanii Archaeology and Heritage (BAaH). CCS is based in Stoke-on-Trent, Staffordshire (West Midlands of England) – and is focused on documenting and telling local, national and international shared heritage stories particularly around glass, ceramic and heavy clay production relating to the city's pottery industry. AMCR is based in Manchester and brings together a diverse range of practitioners including electrical engineers, web developers, artists and musicians around knowledge and skill-sharing activities involving open-source technology with a particular focus on physical computing and digital heritage. Similarly located in Manchester, BY! engages in digital film production, featuring work that documents aspects of the city's cultural heritage. By contrast, BAaH is situated on the Isle of Bute (west coast of Scotland) and is committed to documenting and capturing the vanished culture of crofting, small agriculture and the unique archaeological landscape around which the identity and popularity of the Isle of Bute has been built over time.

The differently positioned community groups enriched the partnership in a threefold sense: (a) they represent regions that were famed for their economic prosperity owing to distinct heritage in their heyday (post-Second World War to the 1980s) followed by considerable decay, (b) they are committed to seizing the initiative in actively shaping the construction, representation, and interpretation of museum collections and related (hi)stories that define the identity of their regions, and (c) they not only possess extensive local knowledge of their cultural and material heritage, but they also engage with and transmit this in different but interesting ways (Mutibwa, 2016). NMeM, on the other hand, was keen to partner the Pararchive community groups because it saw an opportunity to add value to its collections through different forms of exploration and engagement. Of this, Paul remarked:

> there's no point having collections unless you're going to actually do something with them. There's no point them lying there dormant and unused and I think that's hugely important, so I think modern curatorship is all about getting those collections out there for people to enjoy and engage with. (Paul Goodman, Head of Collections Projects, NMeM)

A 'dormant and unused' archival collection that was identified as being of great value to PNMeM was the *Daily Herald* Archive (DHA) – a resource that contains more than 3 million images taken between 1911 and the late 1960s when the *Daily Herald* newspaper was in operation. Founded as a strike sheet for the London printing unions, the *Daily Herald* grew into an influential newspaper that documented local, regional, national and international news events that covered important personalities, politicians, royalty and celebrities, sports (especially horse racing), arts, science, industry and entertainment (Philippou, 2013). It was interesting to learn that DHA was uncatalogued, meaning it remained arranged in the same way as NMeM had acquired it, namely along categories of places, events and people. The fact that these had not been really explored before meant that NMeM was keen to develop an accessible taxonomic system in collaboration with the community groups. In essence, staff at NMeM wanted to understand the process of how communities went about mining the archive in search for what they were looking for and/or were interested in. This was part of a strategy to try and restructure museological practice and use by experimenting with a more collaborative curatorial model, as the following comments highlight:

> So approach [the mining of DHA in your own style] and how you would go about that and I think that will give us a greater insight. Because at the moment someone says to us, right I want to come in and see whatever photographs you've got of Stoke. So we just get the stuff out and that is it. It is like a supermarket. What I would much rather understand are the links and possible kind of other opportunities there are. (Paul Goodman, Head of Collections Projects, NMeM)

I now discuss the collaborative curatorial model at the centre of PNMeM in detail.

A model for modern curatorship: mining the *Daily Herald* Archive (DHA)

In order to make the most of the opportunity to mine the DHA for the benefit of the Pararchive community groups, a procedure was devised to work around a number of structural constraints. For example, all the members of the Pararchive community groups had day jobs, which meant that they could not engage directly with DHA, however exciting and enticing they found the opportunity. This was further compounded by the geographical distance between the locations of the community group members and NMeM. Furthermore, the relevant Collections Section was accessible for research activities only on an afternoon each week. A detailed list was compiled with a particular focus on places, events, people and specific industries in Stoke-on-Trent, Manchester and the Isle of Bute. For instance, members of CCS were interested in objects that documented (hi)stories of the ceramic industry. These comprised key places in which iconic infrastructure relating to the pottery industry across Stoke-on-Trent is situated. People of interest to CCS members included a number of 20th-century local ceramic industrialist families: Wedgwood, Minton, Spode, Doulton, Twyford and H&R Johnson among others. There was also interest in crucial events such as the Festival of Britain, which featured exhibitions and shows of what was considered to be the finest pottery, sanitary ware and tiles among other ceramic ware.

The Manchester-based groups – AMCR and BY! – expressed interest in material about Manchester and its cultural, industrial and digital heritage. Places of interest included Ardwick and Hulme – both renowned for their industrial heritage. Prominent music venues included The Haçienda, the Free Trade Hall and the Astoria Ballroom among others. Artefacts and images that recorded the University of Manchester as a venue for computing research were also of paramount significance to some community heritage research projects. Historical personalities of interest to the Manchester-based groups were celebrities associated with bebop or bop (a style of jazz music), such as Tony Stuart, as well as the many musicians, bands and facilitators active in the Madchester scene from the late 1980s onwards. Alan Turing, considered to be the pioneer of modern computing and artificial intelligence, was of great interest, as was textile industrialist Richard Arkwright whose numerous inventions, including the first steam-driven textile mill, were seen to have revolutionised (cotton) manufacturing. Overall, the history of Manchester as an international hub of the textile industry and cotton trade – coined 'Cottonopolis' – was an attractive draw for local community heritage researchers.

The overarching (hi)story themes under which members of BAaH carried out their research projects were the archaeological landscape of and agriculture on the Isle of Bute. Elsewhere, I have discussed the ways in which the distinctive archaeology has had a significant impact on the social, cultural and economic fabric of the island, especially its agricultural rural economy – the identity of which has been encapsulated in dairy farming (Mutibwa, 2016: 19). Objects that associated with the following aspects were generally desired: places in Bute and Argyll, including dairy farm settlements in places such as Rothesay, Port Bannatyne, Kilchattan Bay, Ambrismore and Scalpsie as well as the seat of Bute royalty (Mount Stuart House). People of interest were the Bute royalty and prominent dairy farmers who are associated with the enhancement of the iconic Ayrshire cattle stock – a cow breed that is renowned for its high milk yields and commercial viability owing to its adaptability and resilience, among other characteristics (Mutibwa, 2016: 19). Also of great interest were artefacts that recorded displays of dairy cows at dairy exhibitions and fairs both on the island and beyond, especially the London Dairy Show held at Olympia in London (Mutibwa, 2016: 19).

Because DHA has a multitude of artefacts and images, one challenge encountered early on was the danger that searches would expand too much; they needed to be contained somewhat but in a manner that did not stifle exploration and intuition. In order not to get drawn off into a cul-de-sac, while resisting the temptation to follow all potentially interesting leads that opened up during searches, a reflective journal was maintained throughout. In the journal, the artefacts and images that piqued interest, and why, were documented. Notes were taken that explained how those selected corresponded to the interests and research themes of the Pararchive community groups, with a particular emphasis on places, events and people as well as key dates wherever applicable. 'Gut instinct' utilised to select material that was judged to provide useful contextual and background information of one kind or another was recorded. The journal record became a useful resource in providing intimate insights into how the pilot team viewed, thought and acted on behalf of the community groups.

Whereas the documentation of the selected images was undertaken in accordance with established taxonomic protocols that prescribe how NMeM should record and look after its collections, such protocols explicitly acknowledged the partnership between the Pararchive community groups and NMeM. For instance, the electronic 'Capture Form' on which units of information pertaining to the images selected were entered, was titled 'NMeM/University of Leeds Pararchive Project'. All the selected images were accessioned using batch numbers specifically allocated to PNMeM. In addition to the unique accession numbers, a range of other units of information were entered on the 'Capture Form'. The most pertinent for this discussion included:

1. the name of the object (whether a photograph or any other artefact) and its title;
2. name of the photographer or maker;
3. place photographed or place where object was made (including date);
4. process (how objects were prepared and/or treated; for example, the gelatine silver process for photographs);
5. condition rating (whether good, fair, poor or unacceptable and any associated notes);
6. any other notes (including copyright holder, details of signatures, inscriptions, labels and so on);
7. name of cataloguer and catalogue date;
8. any additional information

New possibilities for learning, interpretation, discovery and making connections

This information was entered into the NMeM database and was invaluable in many ways beyond mere documentation. For example, commentaries on the condition of the selected objects provided important details of the state in which those objects were found. Where this was becoming progressively worse, this was highlighted for action to be taken. In the case of images, this was particularly the case where the quality of processing was poor or where there was a lot of silvering. Discoveries were made of images that were stapled together or held together with paper clips, not to mention those with labels stuck on the back with rubber cement glue. It was important for NMeM to know the condition of its material as a kind of internal management tool. Commentaries on the material selected in the 'notes' and 'additional information' sections proved useful. In these sections, the rationale for selection provided, and personal opinions and perspectives on the material were noted down. This not only signalled a real intent on the part of NMeM to facilitate other ways of looking at objects, but it also seemed to imply an acknowledgement of the fact that the same objects can be viewed to stand for different ideas, experiences and (hi)stories over time (Karp, 1992).

Herein lie the 'links and possible kind of other opportunities' that Paul Goodman made reference to. By taking particular note of the kind of material that drew interest from the differently situated Pararchive community groups – including the motivations behind such interest, NMeM became aware of the exact nature of material sought after and why. Most importantly during our interactions, staff at NMeM continually reflected on how various communities and the public more generally could be made aware of DHA and its wider collections as resources that provided opportunities for storytelling, for research into local histories and for supporting activities and endeavours geared towards enhancing creative practice and artistic expression. A number of links across various objects were made that not only helped to add useful dimensions to some research projects of the Pararchive community groups, but also provided an indication of how seemingly disparate artefacts and objects can help make broader and fascinating connections that may not appear obvious at first sight. For instance, what started out as disparate interests in music heritage and the textile industry in Manchester turned out to benefit from the inclusion of a fashion dimension. This was the case with clothing that played an important role in the city's music scene, especially within the Madchester music community. Here, artefacts depicting fashion became a thread that connected images of music heritage and the cotton industry. Similarly, photographs documenting 'Cottonopolis' revealed how Manchester's cotton traditions shaped the architecture of the city, and how the cotton industry dictated the patterns of urban settlement, ordinary working life, and industrial and labour disputes, particularly during slumps. Such connections not only triggered some very stimulating discussions around the construction, interpretation and representation of a shared past – and what that says about the present (Mutibwa, 2016) – but they also greatly enriched community members' (hi)storytelling and research projects (Philip and Mutibwa, 2015).

All in all, over 200 images were selected and documented, and many of them were made available to community members to preview virtually. A record of commentaries made was kept and use was monitored. However, real challenges set in at this stage. Many of the images were not marked as *Daily Herald* copyright. Clearing copyright would have proven prohibitively expensive and time-consuming, considering the modest budget and tight time frame at the project's disposal. A decision was made to work only with the *Daily Herald* copyrighted images, something that substantially limited the selection made publicly available. Moreover, NMeM had a strong preference to host the images on its website and not elsewhere. All in all, only a fraction of images were hosted online, given that a large volume could have slowed down public access during loading, a situation that necessitated balancing volume and performance and/or access. Despite these challenges, PNMeM revealed a strong sense of accomplishment overall from both community and institutional vantage points. For example, Paul Duffy – facilitator of BAaH – noted that:

> the very fact the *Daily Herald* archive was getting opened up [for investigation] was enough. That was satisfaction in itself for that point because we'd already started to explore the difficulties in some of this stuff in terms of copyright and access and all those bits and pieces. So the very fact that the door was being pushed … was great. (Paul Duffy, BAaH)[2]

From an institutional perspective, Paul Goodman observed how PNMeM elicited 'satisfaction and validation' in being a part of an instructive and seminal process that facilitated the generation of 'output [that] is strong and meaningful and impactful'.[3]

Conclusion

The PNMeM was an experimental project that utilised an innovative approach to work with a national museum with a view to engaging with an uncatalogued national archive in as open and collaborative a style as possible. Critics of experiments such as PNMeM may argue that the existential threat posed to museums by gradual successive cuts to public funding and related substantial reductions in staff numbers is increasingly compelling museums to embrace collaborative ventures with different publics around various aspects of museum work – among other strategies – to justify institutional relevance for their own ends (Karp, 1992). Whereas there is some truth in this, opening up appears to offer so many opportunities beyond mere attempts to support and/ or restructure museological practice and use on the terms of museums. Adding crucial insights and experiences to the growing literature on community/museum partnerships around contemporary museological work, PNMeM demonstrated a model for modern curatorship in this day and age that:

> involves a new form of power sharing in which museum and community partners co-manage a broad range of the activities that ... include the initial identification of themes, the design of the research methodology, object selection [and] the integration of training and capacity building for community members and community input into [the meaning-making process]. (Phillips, 2003: 157)

Borrowing the words of Peers and Brown (2003: 6), one might argue that PNMeM exhibited important features of modern curatorship by:

> provid[ing] opportunities to piece together fragmented historical narratives [drawing on new and multiple accounts using] [p]hotographs, whether of people or of artefacts ... to evoke knowledge, spark lively debates on the identity and stories of the people or makers involved, and the cultural knowledge and intention encoded in them, and [to] function as links between past and present.

Ultimately, such curatorship 'revivifie[s] museum collections' by 're-attach[ing] information to artefacts', thereby giving them 'fresh meanings' that might arouse broader interest when viewed through the eyes of source community members (Peers and Brown, 2003: 7).

Notes

[1] The project comprised Niamh O'Donnell (an undergraduate student), Simon Popple (PI, Pararchive), Fiona Philip and Daniel H. Mutibwa (Pararchive project Research Fellows) from the University of Leeds as well as Paul Goodman (Head of Collections Projects), Pete Edwards (Web Producer) and Simon Braithwaite (Collections Information Officer) from NMeM. PNMeM took place between July 2014 and February 2015.

[2] Remarks made by Paul Duffy during an evaluation workshop at the end of the project in March 2015.

[3] Remarks made by Paul Goodman during an evaluation workshop at the end of the project in March 2015.

References

Crooke, Elizabeth (2007) *Museums and Community: Ideas, Issues and Challenges*, New York: Routledge.

Hooper-Greenhill, Eilean (2000) *Museums and the Interpretation of Visual Culture*, London: Routledge.

Jordanova, Ludmilla (1989) 'Objects of Knowledge: A Historical Perspective on Museums', in Vergo, P. (ed.) *The New Museology*, London: Reaktion Books, pp 22–40.

Karp, Ivan (1992) 'Introduction: Museums and Communities: The Politics of Public Culture', in Karp, I., Kreamer, C.M. and Lavine, S.D. (eds) *Museums and Communities: The Politics of Public Culture*, Washington: Smithsonian Institution Press, pp 1–17.

Mutibwa, Daniel H. (2016) 'Memory, storytelling and the digital archive: revitalising community and regional identities in the virtual age', Special Issue: 'Studies in Cultural Memory', *International Journal of Media and Cultural Politics*, 12(1): 7–26.

Mutibwa, Daniel H., Hess, Alison and Jackson, Tom (2018) 'Strokes of serendipity: community co-curation and engagement with digital heritage', *Convergence: The International Journal of Research into New Media Technologies*: 1–21.

Peers, Laura, L. and Brown, Alison, K. (2003) *Museums and Source Communities*, London: Routledge.

Philip, Fiona and Mutibwa, Daniel H. (2015) 'Yarn from the Potteries and Cottonopolis: The Pararchive project in the Daily Herald archive [online], Available from: https://blog.scienceandmediamuseum.org.uk/yarns-from-the-potteries-and-cottonopolis/ [Accessed 7 September 2015].

Philippou, Emily (2013) 'The Daily Herald archive: a historic collection from the world of print journalism [online], Available from: https://blog.scienceandmediamuseum.org.uk/daily-herald-photograph-collection-30th-birthday-countdown/ [Accessed 12 November 2014].

Phillips, Ruth, B. (2003) 'Community Collaboration in Exhibition: Introduction', in Peers, L.L. and Brown, Alison K. (eds) *Museums and Source Communities*, London: Routledge, pp 155–70.

Popple, Simon (2015) 'The new Reithians: pararchive and citizen animateurs in the BBC digital archive', *Convergence: The International Journal of Research into New Media Technologies*, 21(1): 132–44.

Ridge, Mia (2014) 'Crowdsourcing our Cultural Heritage: Introduction', in Ridge, M. (ed.), *Crowdsourcing our Cultural Heritage*, Farnham: Ashgate, pp 1–14.

Samis, Peter (2008) 'The Exploded Museum', in Tallon, L. and Walker, K. (eds) *Digital Technologies and the Museum Experience: Handheld Guides and Other Media*, Lanham: MD: AltaMira Press, pp 3–17.

Smith, Charles Saumarez (1989) 'Museums, Artefacts, and Meanings', in Vergo, P. (ed.) *The New Museology*, London: Reaktion Books, pp 6–21.

The National Museums (1988) *The National Museums and Galleries of the United Kingdom*, London: Her Majesty's Stationery Office.

Vergo, Peter (ed.) (1989) *The New Museology*, London: Reaktion Books.

Walker, Kevin (2008). 'Structuring Visitor Participation', in L. Tallon and K. Walker (eds.) *Digital Technologies and the Museum Experience: Handheld Guides and Other Media*, Lanham: MD: AltaMira Press, pp 109–24.

9

Enhancing museum visits through the creation of data visualisation to support the recording and sharing of experiences

Ian Gwilt, Patrick McEntaggart, Melanie Levick-Parkin and Jonathan Wood

Introduction

This project explores the use of a practice-led research methodology in the design of generative data visualisations that can be used to record and reveal the details of an empiric museum visit. The object of capturing this visitor information is to assist in the future design and development of tools for the creation of interactive museum experiences that can be improved by connecting the physical dimension of museums and exhibitions with digital information in new and novel ways. In this research we were specifically concerned with how user engagement in the museum can be captured, visualised and represented back to a visitor, museum curator or the broader community in a way that might bring added value or insight. Moreover, the capturing of the visitor experience becomes an archival process and practice that can be used in the design of future exhibitions, and more fundamentally to inform thinking around the ongoing ontological and epistemological position of the museum.

This research was initiated through a European Union-funded project entitled Material Encounters with Digital Cultural Heritage (meSch), which had the goal of exploring possibilities for the creation of tangible interactive experiences that connect the physical dimension of museum exhibitions with relevant digital cross-media information. The meSch consortium consists of 12 partners from six European countries and was coordinated by Sheffield Hallam University. The project started in February 2013 and lasted for four years. It was funded by the European Community's Seventh Framework Programme ICT for access to cultural resources (meSch, 2017).

The design research outlined in this chapter is based on exploring the premise that data collected from a museum visit detailing personal profiles; time spent at exhibits, choice and sequence of viewing and so on can be used to explore how data can be generatively visualised to allow visitors to make informed decisions about what they have seen, to help plan return visits, or acquire additional knowledge, and to help curators to organise future displays based on an improved understanding of visitor interests.

In this chapter we introduce a range of novel concepts and ideas developed by Visual Communication academics and students at Sheffield Hallam University to expand and enhance visitor experience in museums and other sociocultural settings. These are discussed through two case studies: proprietary design ideation for the meSch project and a spinout project entitled Sheffield Says, which applies some of the same thinking and technological application in a different sociocultural context (the city market). These two case studies are used first to discuss the creation of prototype interfaces designed to investigate how the potential of digital networks can augment the user and community experience by connecting museums and cultural artefacts to digital archives and related materials at other venues; and second to discuss visual strategies and languages that capture the empiric experience in a dynamic user interface. How the accompanying interaction with digital interfaces might prefigure and extend the experience of a visit before and after the event, in different personal and sociocultural settings is also investigated. Difficulties around digital inclusion and in encouraging people to interact with technologies and share personal information are also highlighted in the Sheffield Says community market work. Other considerations include the development of generic interfaces, transferable designs to different types of sociocultural contexts and the design of context-specific physical 'experience mementoes'.

How we interacted with cultural content as traditionally experienced in the museum is rapidly going through a paradigm shift in response to pervasive digital technologies and 'everything all the time' thinking, which suggests we can have exactly what we want, when and where we want it. Moreover, the very idea of the museum and what this constitutes in itself is also coming under scrutiny in a digitally networked society (Falk and Dierking, 2013). The traditional authority constructs that are associated with the museum, buildings, collections and the curation/selection of artefacts made available to structure visitor experiences, are called into question as the notion of the museum and the museum experience shifts to accommodate digital technologies and the framing of cultural content in contemporary culture (Bremner and Bernadet, 2017).

At the same time, we are seeing a rethinking of the role of design and the designer as a member of a complex team wherein design plays a more facilitatory role and designers work in tandem with end-users to construct product, service solutions (Sangiorgi and Prendiville, 2017). Terms such as co-design, service design and design thinking are becoming commonplace, and speak to a new emphasis on design and designers working in participatory teams that involve a range of stakeholders in the creation of ideas and outcomes.

The research also explores how the empiric encounter of physically visiting a museum can be augmented by the introduction of digital content, not only during the actual visit but also pre- and post-visit through the connection to digital content and information. Finally, the potential of the Internet of Things (IOT), smart environments and sensor-based data gathering, which allow for the collection and representation of visitor choices that can be used by curators and visitors alike, to presage further experiences is explored.

Case Study One: meSch

Overview

As mentioned, the meSch project was a European funded project, which had the goal of designing and developing tools for the creation of interactive experiences that connect the physical dimension of museums and exhibitions with associated digital media information. The broad aims of the project were concerned with the creation of strategies that would facilitate more meaningful, novel and diverse visitor experiences with the museum. The project rolled out experimental methods and technologies through a number of case studies with partner organisations across Europe (meSch, 2017).

As part of this process, academic staff worked with Visual Communication Design students at Sheffield Hallam University to generate design ideas that addressed these concepts in a variety of creative ways. The students were given the brief of visually interpreting data representing an exhibition visit by designing personalised graphic interfaces and memory objects in the form of 'data souvenirs', which could be used to expand on the visiting experience for the individual in a personal and social context and facilitate a deeper and repeated engagement with past and future visits. A souvenir, according to Gordon (1986), can be a tangible and physical artefact that satisfies a desire to 'hold on' to an experience more remarkable than everyday life, allowing a visitor to remember and prove their experience. If the souvenir could be personalised with a visitor's experiential data, it could provide a unique artefact for a unique experience. The data souvenir concept in this case involved the real-time creation of a takeaway artefact that would be personalised by the choices made by an individual during a visit to a museum. The data souvenir acts as a reminder of things seen and experienced and can also be used to point to content missed or additional related content that can be found in other locations or online. For example, experiments in personalised printed postcards that were made available at the end of the museum visit with individually tailored messages and designs were explored. The meSch project envisages a cultural space filled with smart objects, each with their own (adaptive) stories embedded therein, that will be revealed if and when conditions are right; for example, if visitors have reached the right time in the storyline, or a group of them are acting in a certain way, or another smart object is close by. One of the goals of meSch was to create smart exhibits to connect visitors with a rich experience on top of the 'traditional' museum visit. There are many repositories and archives for cultural heritage, but these are typically only partially accessible and often presented in ways that can be quite static. The meSch project was also partly a response to this problem of limited access to heritage content.

The student brief

Students were asked to focus on the idea generation phase of the design process to build a resource for the project and to consider how the design concepts might be applied independent of content across a range of different museums. Working in teams, each team had to present a number of designs for the visual representation of a visiting experience. They were asked to consider a range of tones and voices related to different potential target audience groups. We also asked that visual representation should range from the visually abstract to some options exploring a more metaphorical representation of the visit; and that the visual style and format of the ideas should offer a variety of forms and media, including graphics, illustrative approaches, collaging and three-dimensional (3D) spatial constructs.

Guidelines for the ideas generation were as follows:

1. To design a wide range of visual representation options for data collected.

2. To develop a media strategy planning for audience touch-points in personal, social and professional contexts.
3. To map visual representations of the different possibilities of the individual visit in relation to an exhibition.
4. To design ideas for data souvenirs that materialise the visiting experience and facilitate deeper and repeated engagement with an exhibition.

Each team developed a variety of concepts for data souvenir designs to complement a range of visual data representation outputs. Students recorded their research and development using a blog that would later be used to form a booklet of ideas. The resultant work could be divided into design ideas that looked at creating a unique personal visual identifier for a visitor; recording and visualising the visitor's museum experience; and creating a data souvenir that prolongs the visit experience or could be used as a sharing memento.

Figure 9.1 shows some examples of the work from this phase of the project, starting with quite literally a visitor making a mark by visiting a museum, through the metaphor of the footprint, which moved from a very literal visual image to more abstracted visual interpretations as a means of recording visitor presence and shaping of the museum environment by the documentation and visualisation of this presence.

Figure 9.1: Ideation design exploring different ways to represent visitor presence in a museum

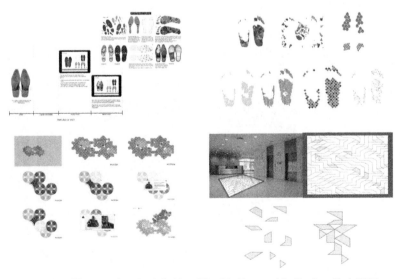

Generated by Abbie Gostelow, Danielle Hart, Nina Markham and Radika Ramdihal, 2014

A number of the other design concepts explored the idea of using visitor pathway choices and viewing data to drive the design of user avatars. In Figure 9.2 geometric shapes, colours and patterns were used to create a representative composite design of visitors' preferences; viewing choices, time spent at exhibits, viewing sequence and so on. In this concept these were used as parametrics to configure the shape and composition of an original avatar design. It was also proposed that these avatar personas could be visualised within the museum environment to share visitor experience with other visitors and in the form of a social media app where comments could be logged and shared. The design concept attempts to give a sense to the visitor of their unique version of the experience, which could be compared and contrasted with the experience of others. According to Boothby, et al (2014), to have some sense of a shared experience can amplify and positively enhance an individual's perception of their own experience, while the use of a digital platform to share these experiences could make them more memorable (Wang et al, 2017).

In Figures 9.3 to 9.6 four different ways of visualising visitor data are explored. The aim of these visual experiments was to explore what might be an appropriate method to represent the data to help curators see emerging patterns of use and to make relevant comparisons with subsets of visitor preferences. These four ways were incorporated into an experimental software tool. The first versions of the software

Figure 9.2: Ideation design of different ways to show visitor choices during a museum visit, and using these choices to shape a personal profile icon

Generated by Alex Fergusson, Lauren Hall, Gemma Milne and Antonia Reale, 2014

were designed for use with minimal or no training and limited the interaction beyond simple parameters such as altering the length of time represented in each visualisation (Figure 9.3). The visualisations were also designed to show simple metadata such as revealing dates or exhibit titles as the mouse approaches, while some interactions allowed the visuals to contort; for example, in Figure 9.4 the spirals unfold to

Figure 9.3: Experimental way of viewing and visualising visitor driven data for curator usage

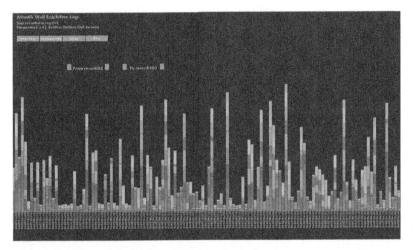

Generated by the project team

Figure 9.4: Experimental way of viewing and visualising visitor driven data for curator usage

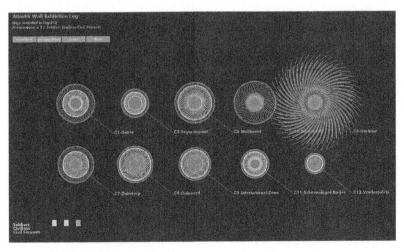

Generated by the project team

give a new perspective on the data around each object. The emphasis at this stage was on curator feedback to inform further iterations of the tool.

The experimental interface designs use a dashboard to allow access to four different ways to view the visitor data. The interface comprises a mix of spatial and spatial-chronological visualisations designed to explore the overall data set and subsets based on predetermined perspectives. To help the curator relate the representations to the physical exhibits it was felt that initial designs should concentrate on two-dimensional (2D) representation of the exhibition space (Figure 9.3 to 9.6); 3D representation was not ruled out at this stage – but 2D projections are not unfamiliar to curators and are typical of most of the exhibition plans and schematics used in the design phase of exhibitions. The use of a 'Treemap' (Shneiderman, 2002) (Figure 9.5) as the overview visualisation allows the representation of small or expansive exhibitions to be algorithmically organised into a fixed size. It also seeks to make comment on the digital footprint that visitors leave. The same algorithm is used to organise data on computer hard disks in a physical way. In a neat reversal of this it is used as a metaphor to digitally represent the physically reality of the visitors' experience recorded in the dataset. (Figure 9.5).

Beyond the overview screen (Figure 9.5), each subsequent visualisation has both spatial and chronological dimensions; the chronological is represented as a line. Although this varies in each

Figure 9.5: Experimental way of viewing and visualising visitor driven data for curator usage

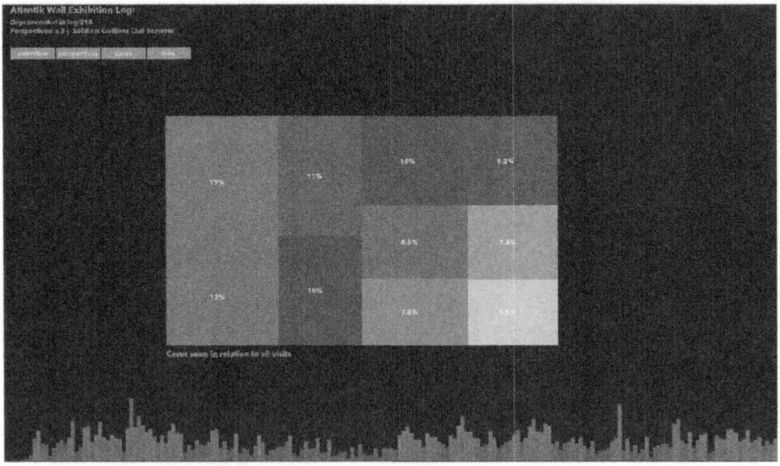

Generated by the project team

screen from straight to curved to spiral, there is no deviation from the use of a line to map time. As Rosenberg and Grafton (2010: 13) suggest, 'Our idea of time is so wrapped up with the metaphor of the line' that our concept of time is hardwired to this way of thinking. However, the visualisations explore how the line might be interacted with, or positioned against, other versions of it (the visualisation of time) to contrast with other aspects of the data as seen in (Figure 9.4 and 9.6).

Figure 9.6: Experimental way of viewing and visualising visitor driven data for curator usage

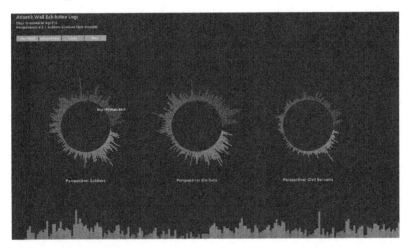

Generated by the project team

Case study two: Sheffield Says

The second case study builds on the prototyping design activities as illustrated in the first case study, with the intention of connecting communities through the use of a visual artefact and a physical keepsake. This project originated from work undertaken for a festival called Catalyst, Sheffield Hallam University's contribution to the 2016 Year of Making, a city-wide project that brought together a number of organisations to promote and celebrate Sheffield's makers and artists, and connect creative activities to the broader Sheffield community. Successful projects were awarded a small amount of funding and some other structural support by the university. Sheffield Says was one of these projects.

The aim of the project was to develop a strategy for connecting the Sheffield City Moor Market with the art and design community in Sheffield. The city market had recently been rehoused in a new purpose-built venue and was still shaping its identity and user community in this new space. The project developed an interactive installation located at the heart of the market. In the form of a giant letter 'S' sculpture (for Sheffield Says), the installation dispenses illustrations from new and emerging voices in the creative arts (Figures 9.7 to 9.9). The installation houses and presents publicly accessible low cost and low-fi printing methods, running on a bespoke setup and software, and also links to an online sharing platform that was initially explored in the creation of the meSch museum visit data souvenirs. The intention of the interaction in this case is to use the illustrative keepsakes that can be generated free of charge by any visitor to the market as a visual provocation in an attempt to link the market trading community with local creative voices.

The text in Box 9.1 is a sample from the Sheffield Says blog, which documents the process, describes how the interactive sculpture works and explains the thinking behind the project:

Box 9.1: Sheffield Says

From roasted coffee beans to burgers to bottles of ale, the Moor Market brings together some of the finest Sheffield-made produce. Now, you can add work by local artists to your shopping list, thanks to the installation of "public art dispenser" Sheffield Says.

Sheffield Says is the result of a project involving Sheffield Hallam University students and graduates, as part of the Catalyst: Festival of Creativity. They wanted to give the city's creative community chance to say something, whether through images or words.

It's not hard to find the *Sheffield Says* dispenser: it stands in the form of a big yellow S in the market, next to The Nut Bar. For its launch in January 2017 the dispenser is stocked with around ten different pieces by illustration students and graduates, all of which respond to the theme of the market. Push the button and the S will print one of these pieces at random for you to take home – all for free.

The plan is for the next round of artworks to respond more generally to Sheffield, and following that there'll be a food specific theme, with potential to print some recipes.

Figure 9.7, 9.8, 9.9: Sheffield Says installation images

Generated by Patrick McEntaggart, Antonia Hall and Naomi Tinker, 2017

Keep an eye on the *Sheffield Says* blog for announcements and to find out how to submit your own work to be dispensed by this shiny new S.

https://moormarketblog.wordpress.com/ (2018).

(Antonia Hall and Naomi Tinker)

The project sought to connect communities through the dispensing of free art to members of the market community, the market traders, marketgoers and creative community visitors. The mechanism through which this project engaged with the stakeholder communities had a number of different parts. The project curated visual work produced through a programme of events/calls that were used to engage members of the creative community, with each call built around a theme that related to the market or wider community in Sheffield. These events were either advertised as open calls or calls inviting creatives to content creation events. The former (open calls) accepted existing work connected to the theme or new works connected to the theme. Themes were generally open to interpretation and were intended to allow for a variety of different perspectives to be explored in the creative interpretations. Each theme was based on a statement such as 'market life…' or 'Sheffield is…'. The content creation events were used to kickstart content creation under a theme, and these varied in nature from walk-rounds of spaces such as the market, where 'quick draw' sessions tried to capture the essence of the space and community, to 'drink and draw' sessions in pubs around the city (before and during the Sheffield Beer Festival). The spirit of these events borrowed much from the concept of street photography, transposing Bresson's (1952) notions of how an image is made in the mind and heart into practices of illustration: drawing and sketching. What Sheffield Says 'said' (when printed) was often a fleeting feeling captured in a drawing that often goes unsaid or is difficult to capture in words.

Printing the creative community's impressions of the market and city in the space that inspired them was intended to bridge the gap between the creative community and the market community (Figure 9.10). The work would always have to pass through the critical viewing of the community it represented, shared in situ and under the gaze of the market vendors and users. The images/impressions the creatives made would be seen and discussed within the market. This was an important point of the project as it was intended to connect these communities through the art in the space rather than in the works found in the more usual, formal spaces frequented by the creative community.

Figure 9.10: Sheffield Says details of illustrations and installation

Photo by Antonia Barraclough, courtesy of Sheffield Says

From the moment the Sheffield Says installation was installed, the project seemed to elicit two types of responses from traders and marketgoers; these could be described broadly as positive or perplexed. The perplexed often fixated on questions around why the work was in this space and not a retail environment such as Meadowhall (a local shopping mall populated with the usual high street outlets). Many traders asked the questions "who is paying for it?", "why is it free?" and "what is it for?". At the time of writing the project has been in the market for over a year (2016–17), with the total amount of printed material somewhere over 3 kilometres (printed illustration tickets), putting individual prints at a figure of around 20,000. Through direct observation from the project team alongside reports from market staff, the evidence suggests that children and parents of children are the largest users. For children, the opportunity to press a button that causes something to happen seems to have an irresistible appeal, which is magnified by the excitement of receiving a printed image. Although this user base has presented some reliability challenges of the physical installation through the unexpected ways in which it has been used (pulling the paper out, posting coins into it, climbing on it and so on), interacting with the project and the visual content appears to elicit a memorable and engaging experience and topic of conversation.

The installation is currently having a technical refit and the aim is to relaunch with a new schedule of content during the second half of 2018. This relaunch will introduce some new themes that will facilitate new creative works to make comment on current and newsworthy events in Sheffield (for example, the Council's controversial felling of some of the city trees), and connect Sheffield to a wider conversation about current national and international events. Funding permitting, the project has ambitions to develop sister installations in other cities with the aim of connecting these in a creative conversation through the printed art works and form an archive of these creative responses to everyday places and activities.

Reflections

As we move towards ever more pervasive digitally informed spaces and experiences through the roll out of IOT technologies, how we interact with cultural content and the places where these interactions occur is undergoing a radical rethinking. Digitally inflected culture that presupposes we can have access to anything at any time, in the form that we want it, sets the agenda for future museums and the experiences and services they might offer. They can also begin to impact on more prosaic shared experiences, such as a visit to the local market. The projects described in this chapter begin to investigate how the integration of digital technologies and the capturing of visitor preferences and experiences can be harnessed to augment these contemporary sociocultural experiences and invite communities of users to take part in the realisation and shaping of those experiences.

As discussed, the implementation of a simple digital printing service connected to user experience and choice (as in the first case study), and as a means to engage disconnected communities (in the second instance), begins to take advantage of the potential to create hybrid digital/physical artefacts and experiences that can draw on the qualities and potentials of both the digitally facilitated and tangible experienced paradigms. What is important is that these combined digital/physical objects and experiences do not attempt to replace the qualities and strengths of one element with the other; that is, by using digital media to simulate real-world experiences or replacing the empiric, located occurrence with digital content. However, the capturing of visitor information to inform data visualisations for use by different groups of service user communities and service providers begins to harness the potential of the digital to help people to make informed choices and enter into conversation about their sociocultural interactions.

Moreover, this approach to the consumption of cultural content in social contexts allows people with different needs and desires to begin to shape and preference their own activities and values through their lived experience of culture.

References

Bremner, C. and Bernadet, L. (2017) 'The museum of the future: a sedimentary cloud', *The Design Journal*, 20,:sup. 1: S3560–8 [online], Available from: doi: 10.1080/14606925.2017.1352858

Bresson, H. (1952) *The Decisive Moment*, New York: Simon & Schuster.

Boothby, E., Clark, M. and Bargh, J. (2014) 'Shared experiences are amplified', *Psychological Science*, 25(12): 2209–16.

Falk, J.H. and Dierking, L.D. (2013) *Museum Experience Revisited*, Walnut Creek, CA: Left Coast Press.

Hall, A. and Tinker, N. (2018, Feb 5) 'Sheffield Says' @ Moor Market. Retrieved from https://moormarketblog.wordpress.com/

meSch (Material Encounters with Digital Cultural Heritage) (2017) [online], Available at: https://www.mesch-project.eu [Accessed 5 February 2018].

Rosenberg, Daniel and Grafton, Anthony (2010) *Cartographies of Time*, New York: Princeton Architectural Press.

Sangiorgi D., Prendiville, A. (eds) (2017) *Designing for Service. Key Issues and New Directions*, London, Bloomsbury Academic.

Shneiderman, B. (2002) 'Tree visualization with tree-maps: 2-d space-filling approach', *ACM Transactions on Graphics*, 11(1): 92–9.

Wang, Q., Lee, D. and Hou, Y. (2017) 'Externalising the autobiographical self: sharing personal memories online facilitated memory retention', *Memory*, 25(6): 772–6.

10

The digital citizen: working upstream of digital and broadcast archive developments

Kim Hammond, George Revill and Joe Smith

Introduction

This chapter explores the potential and significance of digital broadcast archives (DBAs) and associated tools for supporting civic engagement with complex topics. It draws on a three-year Arts and Humanities Research Council-funded project, Earth in Vision, which worked with a sample of 50 hours of environment themed broadcasts drawn from over five decades of BBC television and radio archives. The project critically examines the potential of such broadcast archive content as a resource for the making and debating of environmental histories in the context of imagining and planning for environmental futures. It builds on the principles of co-production and social learning and aims to support more plural and dynamic accounts of environmental change. The overarching question the project addresses is: How can digital broadcast archives inform environmental history and support public understanding of, and learning about, environmental change issues?

To answer this question the team – a mix of cultural, historical and environmental geographers – addressed two aims. The first was to draw on a sample BBC archive content to write our own environmental histories (with broadcasting written into the script). Alongside the standard academic currency of academic journal articles (for example, Revill et al, 2018; Smith et al, 2018), the project resulted in the production of over 30 video interviews with media producers and presenters, and three multimedia interactive e-books.[1] These e-books tell three environmental history stories using BBC digital and paper archives, looking at different aspects of the BBC's place and role as itself a maker of environmental histories. In turn the books examine: the iconic role of Sir David Attenborough in BBC environmental programming; the ways in which BBC programming produces and reproduces ideas of British landscape; and TV's role in shaping global environmental imaginations. These three stories illustrate the potential of DBAs (here the BBC broadcast archives) for telling new histories. These have been published as free e-books. The e-books link to a website holding a sample of cleared content and some resources aimed at encouraging visitors to play with this content, with the goal of supporting them as they tell and share their own environmental histories. We conclude that there is a whole range of exciting possibilities, especially for teachers, students, and academics, to work creatively with the releases of DBAs for public use. However, that potential is currently hampered primarily by the institutional and legal contexts of DBAs.

Our second aim, and the focus of this chapter, was to draw on the pilot BBC broadcast archive content to engage a significant and broad partner group – an array of prospective 'digital citizens' – in a collaborative 'upstream' discussion of the practices, needs and expectations of current and potential DBA users. For this we ran a range of workshops aimed at attracting key constituencies, from academic researchers, university- and school-based teachers and learners, to media and information technology professionals and the general public. In addition, we conducted interviews with media professionals (mainly environmental film-makers) and gauged opinion via feedback forms at certain events. This 'bottom up' approach is in contrast to a model of citizens/consumers as predominantly passive end users of digital media, and its success relies on communication with DBA developers about making their archives accessible in the ways users would like/need them to be, and with the tools to meet those anticipated needs and uses. Could user–developer collaboration, based around an early blueprint of 'what we'd like' and what is technically, legally and financially possible facilitate a new state-of-the-art DBA model and a new standard for digital development?

The chapter outlines the project methodology, from accessing and preparing a selection of BBC broadcast archive content, and adding layers of metadata, through to developing activities for engaging with our workshop participants. It then presents some of what we are learning from these collaborations, including the co-creation with citizens of guidance for DBA developers.

Online digital broadcast archives

Online DBAs have emerged as some of the most popular online media resources. In just 12 years, YouTube has become the second most popular website in the world, with a staggering 1 billion hours of content watched every day and 400 hours of content uploaded each minute.[2] YouTube is considered the gold standard example of DBAs (Burgess and Green, 2009). Other notable DBA releases include British Pathé, which uploaded its entire archive, a collection of 85,000 historic films, on its own YouTube channel in 2014, and those from the British Film Institute and the Prelinger, Shell, BP and British Council film archives. DBAs are fast following in the footsteps of digitised archives of text, image and music, and we can anticipate continued large-scale releases in coming years. These will generate new practices, opportunities and responsibilities for both media organisations and digital citizens. They also represent a substantial extension of the material available on a range of topics and create new opportunities for research, teaching and public engagement.

BBC broadcast archives

This fast-developing digital media landscape presents a particular set of opportunities and challenges for established media organisations such as the BBC. First, it changes how they produce and present broadcasts and associated (digital) content, and second, it changes how they manage their vast archives. The BBC holds over a million hours of programmes, dating back to the 1930s (radio) and 1940s (television), along with the paper archives that tell the story of how these programmes were made. This represents one of the great contemporary cultural and historical treasure houses, and with the emergence of large-scale releases of online digital broadcast and film archives, it is not surprising that the BBC are exploring different ways of releasing archive content. A small amount has been formally released for public viewing, for example, via BBC iPlayer, some dedicated BBC YouTube channels (such as BBC Earth) and via their own BBC archive pages. Yet the vast proportion of this archive remains substantially unavailable. The current barriers to access are not technical but financial, legal and institutional. It sits behind a well-padlocked door, with access limited to broadcasters or other media producers searching for clips. What are the consequences of throwing the door open?

Digital citizens

As digital technologies blur the boundaries between media producers and consumers, the previously established role of the broadcaster (for example, the BBC) is changed: on YouTube we can broadcast ourselves. John Hartley (2012) champions the transformative potential of networked digital technology in entertainment and education. Most importantly, he sees the creative and emancipatory possibility of blurring boundaries in a world in which more and more people can take an active participatory role in the making and remaking of knowledges. He says: 'Now, with every improvement in digital interactive technology ... The possibilities for lay people to engage directly but informally in social *learning*, knowledge *production*, and creative *innovation* continue to grow' (Hartley, 2012: 114).

Hartley argues that the possibilities to extend the social base of creative productivity through the internet enables potentially *everybody* to be producers of 'public thought'. This egalitarian 'shock of inclusion' is, he suggests, most disruptive for existing interests (Hartley, 2012: 208). While cautious of techno-utopianism, the Earth in Vision project is in step with Hartley's positive account of democratic digital citizens freely and creatively making, discussing and critiquing knowledge in the public fora of the internet and carrying this modality into off-screen realms of life, including thinking and acting on environmental change issues and environmental futures.

Earth in Vision: exploring the practices and expectations of 'digital citizens'

If the BBC releases their archives for public use, how would we use them? We designed processes that explored what people want to do with content, the tools and metadata they would need to achieve their objectives, and the problems and solutions they envisage.

To identify a body of content to work with, we selected 50 hours of archive environment themed television and radio broadcasts, amounting to 100 programmes, from a BBC database that contained only scant programme information. We had to choose items before they could be watched or listened to. Selected items were then delivered in a digital format. Seven search categories were used for selecting our sample: climate change, energy, population, pollution, endangered species, lifestyle and a catch-all category of 'general environment' (the results are shown in Table 10.1).

Adding metadata: contextualising the archives

Even our modest 50-hour sample of content of broadcast represents a mass of raw data. One of the team watched/listened to all the programmes and built a table of metadata that held summaries about

Table 10.1: Earth in Vision selection of BBC broadcast archive of environment programmes by theme, medium and decade of broadcast

| Themes | Number of programmes | | Total hours | Decade programme first broadcast | | | | |
	TV	Radio		1950s 1960s	1970s	1980s	1990s	2000s
Climate change	25	5	12.7	1	0	6	13	10
Energy	3	0	1.8	0	1	1	1	0
Endangered species	15	0	7.9	3	3	5	1	3
Pollution	15	4	5.9	4	6	0	8	1
Population	9	1	4.6	4	3	1	1	1
Lifestyle	6	0	2.7	0	5	0	0	1
General environment	8	8	10.9	5	2	2	5	2
	81	18	46.4	17	20	15	29	18

Generated by project team

each one. This added layer of meaning did more than supplement the standard data related to dates of making and transmission, names of programme, channel, programme contributors and presenters. It spliced in all locations in the programmes, key words, themes and ideas or concepts, as well as clearance status (see Figures 10.1 and 10.2).

In addition, we recorded (to broadcast standards) interviews with programme-makers and presenters, and drew on the BBC written archives for a range of paper-based materials (including scripts, scenarios, shooting schedules, letters, accounts, ephemera and reviews). Our aim in bringing these elements together was both to historically contextualise the making of programmes and to reveal them as complex, compromised, composite and heterogeneous. We see this as a

Figure 10.1: Sample from the Earth in Vision database

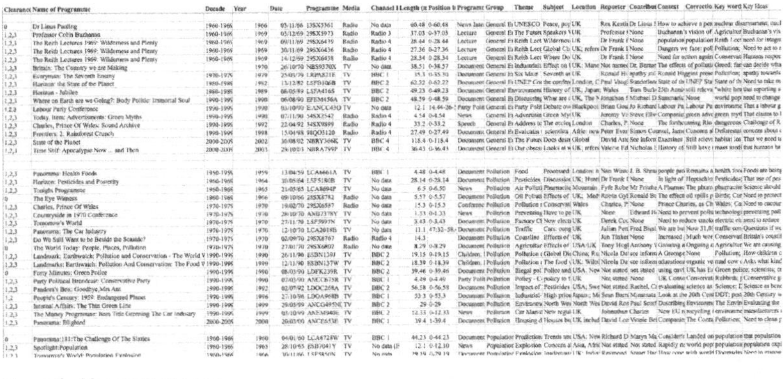

Compiled by project team

Figure 10.2: Detailed glimpse of the Earth in Vision database

Subject	Location	Reporter	Contribut	Context	Correctio	Key words	Key Ideas
Peace, pop	UK	Rex Keating	Dr Linus F	How to achieve a pea		nuclear disarmament; nuclear; genetics; peace; pollution; population; science;	
Speakers \	UK	Professor Colin E	None	Buchanan's vision of		Agriculture; bureaucracy; responsibility; Cambridge un	Buchanan's vision of a
Wildernes	UK	Dr Frank Darling	None	population	population	Reith Lectures; Man and Nature; Wilderness and Plenty	need for integration of
Global Chi	UK; refers to global	Dr Frank Darling	None			Dangers we face: poll	Pollution; freshwater lakes; eutrophication; agriculture;	Need to act to avoid pr
Where Do	UK	Dr Frank Darling	None			Need for action again	Conservation; ecology; population; pollution; wildernes	Humans responsible fo
Effect on	UK: Manchester, Sevenoa	Not named	Dr. Bernar	The effects of pollutic		Greed; farming; factory farming; hedgerows; conservati	can decide what kind c
Seventh ar	UK	Ronald Higgins	apathy still	Ronald Higgins prese		Pollution; nuclear; global crisis; population explosion;	apathy towards global
the confer	London, County Hall	Paul Vaughan	Sunderlan	State of the	UNEP Stat	State of the Planet conference; United Nations Environ	Need to take more glo
History of	UK; Japan; Wales		Tom Burk	25th Anniv	still releva	"white heat"; technological revolution; Horizon; milest	that reporting science
What are t	UK, The Netherlands; Swe	Jonathon Porritt	Michael D	Summarisi	None	world population; material demand; declining resource	need to change attitud
Debate ov	Blackpool, UK	Brian Gould	Jo Richard	Labour Pa		Labour Party; environmental crisis; sustainable development; clean up	That a labour governm
Green Myt	UK	Jeremy Vine	Steve Ells	Companies		green adve	green myth; environmentally friendly; ozone layer, glob	That claims to be envi
The ecolog	London	Charles, Prince of	None	The forthcoming Rio		dangerous times; environmental threats; Rio de Janeiro;	Challenge of Rio is fo
scientists	Afric: new Guinea; UK; S	Peter Evans	Simon Counsel, Jame	Concern al		Deforestation; tropical rain forests; hardwoods; green k	concern about deforest
Does destr	Global	David Attenborot	See inforr	Examines	Still releva	habitat loss; introduced species; pollution; over-harvesti	That we need to take s
Looks at w	UK; refers to global	Valerie Edmond	Nicholas E	History of	Still have r	mass media; science; Armageddon; Jehovah's Witnesse	that humans have a lor
Processed	London: health food shop;	Nan Winton	J. B. Shear	people pro	Remains a	health foods; wholefoods; adulterated foods; unnatural	Foods are being adulte
Discussion	UK; Huntington ;	Dr Frank Darling	None	In light of	Heptachlo	Pesticides; insects; spray; toxic chemicals; battle; natur	That use of pesticides
Phurnacite	Mountain Ash, Aberdare,	Fyfe Robertson	Mr Pritcha	A Phurnac	The phurn	phurnacite; smoke; Clean Air committee; Mountain Ash	Science should be able
Effects of	UK; Medway estuary; Ke	Robin Gyle-Thon	Ronald Bu	The effect	oil spills p	Birds; Curlews; Kent; Medway Estuary; Medway River	Need to protect birds f

Compiled by project team

way of both emphasising the practical, rather than charismatic, qualities of broadcast media and of providing the means for more historically and geographically informed ways into the material.

For example, to contextualise the 1957 broadcast for *Zoo Quest for a Dragon* (and other Attenborough programmes in our sample), we interviewed its presenter Sir David Attenborough, and found associated written archive documents such as Attenborough's 'shopping list' for the dragon trip as well as hand-corrected scripts showing his attention to detail and investment in story development. The extensive interview fed into our research, was made available online and has been embedded in extracts within our e-books. At the same time the careful work in viewing all the content, including the generation of detailed metadata, showed how collaboration between researchers and broadcasters could support meaning-making by users, whether academics, media professionals, teachers, learners or curious publics.

As we added layers of data and context, we were starting to formulate the kind of DBA we would want, and certainly were better able to draw on our sample archive content to write the e-books and develop workshops. As we have written elsewhere (Revill et al, 2018) collaging and reordering media clips into new narratives highlights the importance of archive metadata as a key to opening up and enabling processes of curation. Though we describe the BBC's repository of digitised programming as an 'archive', it is arguable that it only gains this status with the addition of a layer of usable metadata. In other words, indexing or cataloguing conducted with a degree of expertise is a prerequisite for this content to become widely accessible.

Box 10.1: What to wear on a dragon trip

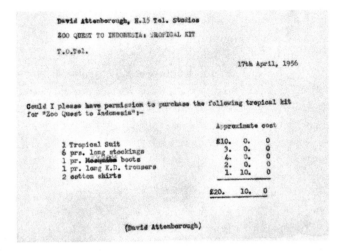

David Attenborough, H.15 Tel. Studios

ZOO QUEST TO INDONESIA: TROPICAL KIT

T.O.Tel.

17th April, 1956

Could I please have permission to purchase the following tropical kit for "Zoo Quest to Indonesia":-

	Approximate cost		
1 Tropical Suit	£10.	0.	0
6 prs. long stockings	3.	0.	0
1 pr. Mosquito boots	4.	0.	0
1 pr. long K.D. trousers	2.	0.	0
2 cotton shirts	1.	10.	0
	£20.	10.	0

(David Attenborough)

'Well, when I started in 1952, I made programmes with one other person, with one cameraman, I did the recording, he did the pictures, it was a clockwork camera and we went off to West Africa and we made programmes and there was only he and I involved. The last 3D programme I made just recently I think I had something like 25 people on location and tons of equipment, tons.' (Earth in Vision interview with Sir David Attenborough, March 2015)[3]

From the BBC written archives, 1956

Engaging digital citizens

Our main methods of engagement have been interviews (with film-makers and media professionals) and workshops, plus a case study school project and research café. All of our workshops have been tailored to the audience/participants. The following section offers a flavour of an extensive body of public participation that has included 14 workshops, which have worked with some 300 people in a mix of schools, clubs and public events.

Environmentally themed storytelling

We are interested in the extent to which archive and web developments could combine to allow for more imaginative but also purposeful future cultural, societal and policy responses to issues of environmental change. Thus, among the potentialities opened up by the release of DBAs is that for new forms of storytelling and an expanded body of storytellers. Our contention is that this can result in new civic mediations, including novel histories, and can generate a new field of opportunities for learning and teaching.

To explore this potential, we devised storytelling exercises, where participants were guided through small carefully selected archive clips in order to write and tell new stories of their own. Examples include voiceover exercises used in our workshop Change the World, during which participants wrote and performed a story to accompany a one-minute climate change-themed archive footage clip. We recorded these, and have an excellent range of stories from teachers, students and diverse publics that illustrate the creative potential of directed use of archives. Secondary school teachers were immediately excited about the classroom possibilities, with one expressing surprise at how quickly their pupils were engaged by the tasks.

Other examples of our workshops include activities designed for secondary school children. They worked with a selection of 25 minutes of cleared BBC archive footage around four environment-themed programmes to produce their own mash-up videos. In another piece of work Oxford Brookes University undergraduate film and media studies students worked with the footage cleared for the e-books to make mash-ups/stories. At our Belfast Science Festival workshop, My Life with Attenborough, participants of all ages (including under 11s) were invited to follow David Attenborough's example and become broadcasters themselves. Using iPads and iMovie they made mini-programmes about wolves, monkeys, bees and hawks. The films made in the workshops, and classroom are presented on the Earth in Vision website, along with the same cleared archive footage, and some guidance, to enable visitors to download and make their own mash-up films (which they can upload if they choose to).

We recognise there is a need, however, to be self-critical in reviewing our own body of activities that have been developed and delivered with our sample of digital citizens. We acknowledge that any creative act of curatorship is always and equally an act of silencing and forgetting. Though this is certainly not solely or even mainly a problem of digital media, by making collage between and across media so simple and easy there is the ever-present danger of investing in a plunder aesthetic. This can easily confine digitised media to an isotropic terrain of contextless data packets. Hence, we recognise that any opening up of such archives has to engage with a politics of curatorship that, among other things, explicitly enables devaluing in order to facilitate processes of revaluation.

Tools and uses

In addition to exploring the storytelling potential of our BBC archive content, in the workshops and interviews we asked people to think about how they might want to use archives, and then collected data about what tools they would want for these purposes.

The answers reflect the broad range of participants, from school children to media professionals. At our secondary school research café, students suggested some innovative tools, for example to categorise programmes or sections of programmes by 'levels of learning (e.g. 1 = general interest/beginner to 5 is highest level of detail for those at expert level' and to enable user generated data, such as being able to 'add comments at particular places in a broadcast (similar to Sound Cloud) to make it easy to find specific things'. Other tools they wanted included being able to link to social media and availability of downloadable transcripts of programmes to use, say, for homework. The students in this case suggested this could be financed by micro-payments, which they insisted they would be willing to pay.

All users, including the school students, pointed to the challenges of navigating archive content. Digital humanities scholars have long wrestled with the problem of how to deal with what has been called 'the infinite archive' (Cohen, 2008: 455). Reflecting on our own experiences, each group of participants we consulted has stressed the need to find ways into and through such vast bodies of material. Hence:

Film makers asked for:

- Well-catalogued archives (detailed data re film makers, context, dates etc.),
- A keyword index
- Clarity of classifications e.g. 'environment'
- An effective tagging system
- Paradigms
- Spatial and temporal locations
- Findability
- Good descriptions
- Good metadata
- An understanding of metadata/architecture

Journalists asked for:

- Ability to search accurately and quickly
- Good search engine

Geography teachers asked for:

- Location
- Date
- Location-linked clips

Users of DBAs need to be able to find particular programmes from the total archive and to choose by genre, subject matter, programme-makers, participants, channel, date and time among other criteria, and they need an index system that enables users to find particular segments of text or audio. Without this, they are condemned to watch through hours of content to find the few seconds or minutes of materials for their needs. While such immersion in the material can be useful for some curators/storytellers, metadata is key to opening up the archives and empowering a wider variety of users, from school students and other publics through to film-makers. It is only by being able to search both within (for example, via time coded transcripts) and between media assets and to log/save those searches, that users can find what they want and begin the process of creating their own stories, presentations, films and audio.

In addition to an extensive body of 'wish lists' for functionality and other tools, we collected 'messages to the BBC' and recorded other interesting responses to the archive content we worked with in workshops. For example, international journalists from the Global South discussed how BBC archive content would help to contextualise historical debates, including the tense final years of colonial rule and the first years of independence. They noted, however, that this could generate as well as resolve tension. Chinese media professionals responded strongly to a 1960s clip on UK smog and the Clean Air Act; they suggested that insights into the UK's industrial and urban past could help to understand their current situation. They went on to suggest that they considered the BBC archives to be world heritage, which they felt they had a right to. The messages to the BBC included a strong and persistent theme that called for an 'opening up' of the archives.

Rights access and creativity

A founding goal of the Earth in Vision project has been to explore ways of making digital broadcast archives available and usable by a diversity of individuals and groups. Differential access is shaped by geographical and socioeconomic disparities and related inequalities in both network coverage and access to technological devices. These kind of disparities and uneven distributions have long been considered (see, for example, Kitchen and Dodge, 2011). However, among the biggest barriers we identified in this work on DBAs is the issue of copyright and the related, although sometimes distinct, issue of intellectual capital. We explored the issues of rights with those who make and, to varying degrees, own broadcast and film content: the film-makers. As the pair of remarks below indicates, for many there is a desire to use archive footage in their own films and, to some degree, to share content, though all acknowledge the thorny issue of rights and responsibility that come with repurposing archive content:

> 'The idea of getting our audience, getting the public to crowdsource metadata into our crown jewels, our archive, is a fascinating idea. It's finding someone to fund it that I think is the real challenge.' (BBC executive producer)

> 'YouTube is a great place because you see all these wonderful and whacky ideas that people are doing ... And there's lots of examples in television where filmmakers have taken real inspiration from YouTube channels...' (BBC programme-maker)

Initiatives such as the Prelinger Archive, Google Books and Project Gutenberg, as well as the obvious candidates such as YouTube and Flickr, all show how much value can be created by working through the challenges involved in making archives publicly available digitally. Yet the issue of copyright and clearance remains an obstacle. Our participants wanted clear rights information (what and how assets can be used), and material cannot be made public until the issue of rights are resolved. This itself provides interesting pointers towards the already composite and collaged nature of broadcast media, which is often so shot through with third-party rights to embedded film clips, images and music that it becomes impossible to thoroughly clear it for use. The rights implications of individual, partial, private and corporate ownership of what are suggestively called media assets is very difficult to square with open access (Barbrook and Cameron, 1996).

Conclusions

Our work with varied publics, teachers and learners has revealed the civic and educational potential of DBAs and the need for media institutions to appreciate their role in developing tools that make such archives both accessible and inviting. The open and experimental formats of our workshops permitted public engagement with the shaping of the specification of the kinds of tools that can underpin civically oriented DBAs. But we view the Earth in Vision project as a valuable but early and partial contribution to dialogues between digital citizens and media bodies. The interactive nature of archive consumption, production and sharing by citizens and learners means that the open and experimental mode needs to be sustained long after any DBA is designed and released: the design of the archive is an ongoing task.

While there are many unresolved questions about who gets access to and permission to use DBAs, their continued release opens up potentialities for new forms of storytelling and an expanded body of storytellers. This might result in new amateur histories and inspiring opportunities for learning and teaching. These opportunities are complemented by the ongoing creation and development of both tools and metadata that permit richer use of media online and that facilitate the reusing and reversioning of DBAs, creating the opportunity for both 'professional' and 'amateur' makers and users to add ever more layers of meaning and value. The challenges presented by rights regimes and financial pressures across the media are formidable. However, our work with public users of our samples of BBC environment archive content offers both impetus and direction to the idea that media archive content should be released from incarceration in broadcaster vaults.

Notes

[1] The three Earth in Vision e-books can be downloaded free of charge from the iTunes iBook library. The three titles are as follows:
Smith, J. (2018) *Earth in Vision: 60 Years of Environmental Change at the BBC*
Revill, G. (2018) *Lives in a Landscape: Imagining British Landscape at the BBC*
Hammond, K. (2018) *David Attenborough: Making Natural History*

[2] Usage statistics from Wikipedia (https://en.wikipedia.org/wiki/YouTube) (last visited 2019) and from https://www.brandwatch.com/blog/youtube-stats/ (last visited 2019).

[3] *Earth in Vision* interview with Sir David Attenborough, March 2015 – can be seen in full at the Open University Open Learn website, Earth in Vision Collection, https://www.open.edu/openlearn/nature-environment/the-environment/creative-climate/earth-vision/sir-david-attenborough-earth-vision?in_menu=463887 (last visited September 2019).

References

BBC (1956) 'Zoo Quest to Indonesia', Memo, David Attenborough, 17 April, Written Archive Centre Folder T6/439/1.

Barbrook, R. and Cameron, A. (1996) 'The Californian ideology', *Science as Culture*, 6(1): 44–72.

Burgess, J. and Green, J. (2009) *YouTube: Online Video and Participatory Culture*, Cambridge: Polity Press.

Cohen, D.J. (2008) 'Interchange: the promise of digital history', *Journal of American History*, 95(2): 442–91.

Kitchen, R. and Dodge, M. (2011) *Code/Space: Software and Everyday Life*, Cambridge, MA: MIT Press.

Hartley, J. (2012) *Digital Futures for Cultural and Media Studies*, Oxford: Wiley-Blackwell.

Revill, G., Hammond, K. and Smith, J. (2018) 'Digital archives and the spaces of environmental story telling', *Area*, 12 March. Available at https://doi.org/10.1111/area.12413

Smith, J., Revill, G., and Hammond, K. (2018) 'Voicing climate change? Television, public engagement and the politics of voice', *Transactions of the Institute of British Geographers*, 43(4): 601–14.

11

Institutional collaboration in the creation of digital linguistic resources: the case of the British Telecom correspondence corpus

Ralph Morton and Hilary Nesi

Introduction

In this chapter we discuss the creation of the British Telecom Correspondence Corpus (BTCC), a searchable database of letters taken from the public archives of British Telecom (BT) that were written by nearly 400 authors on a wide variety of topics between 1853 and 1982.

In the first part of the chapter we discuss our experiences working on the New Connections project, funded by Jisc (formerly the Joint Information Systems Committee) and a collaboration between Coventry University, BT Heritage and The National Archives, focusing particularly on the methodological issues we encountered. The corpus was created to address a gap in existing corpus resources, and so that researchers (primarily linguists) could access and, crucially, engage with the language of the letters.

Since the completion of the BTCC we have put together a funding bid to expand the corpus to include correspondence written to and from the Post Office, an institution with many historical links to BT. This chapter addresses issues surrounding institutional collaboration in both phases of this ongoing research.

Part one: New connections

The BT Archives

BT is the world's oldest communications company, tracing its history back to the formation of the Electric Telegraph Company in 1846.

The Post Office held a monopoly over telecommunications in the United Kingdom from 1912 through much of the twentieth century. In 1969 Post Office Telecommunications became a separate government department and, following the British Telecommunications Act of 1981, British Telecommunications became a public corporation. BT was ultimately privatised in 1984. The BT Archives were established in 1986 to store and preserve the company's historical documents and records.

BT's historical status as a British government department and public corporation means that the pre-privatisation material in the archive is public record and BT is obliged to promote access to it. BT Heritage fulfil this responsibility by maintaining a physical archive of documents in Holborn, London. While this archive is open to the public, access to the offices is limited to six hours on two days a week.

The New Connections project was set up in 2011 to address the limited accessibility of the archives, by cataloguing, digitising and developing a searchable online archive of almost half a million photographs, images, documents and correspondence assembled by BT over 165 years. The project was a Jisc-funded collaboration between Coventry University, The National Archives and BT Heritage. Broadly speaking the roles of the partner institutions were that BT provided the material, The National Archives digitised the material and Coventry University undertook research projects using the digitised material.

Archive aims: the BT Digital Archives

BT's plan for the digital archive was that it should serve as an introduction to the wider collections held in their physical archive. It was important that the records selected demonstrated the cultural importance of the collections and enticed users to explore them further. The material also needed to be of academic interest, as the archive was primarily intended as a research resource for the higher education sector (Hay, 2014: 12). BT worked with an external advisory group of academics and people within the heritage and media sectors to develop approaches to material selection that might balance archival and academic priorities.

The advisory group chose to focus on three areas of archive material. The first area, Category A, consisted of photographic images taken from an engineering series and a publicity series within BT's collections. These series were picked to constitute a visual document of the various developments in communications technology that took place in this period. The photographic material also helped form the mosaics depicting BT-related scenes on the initial BT Digital Archives web interface; these were intended as an access route for the casual user, and could be expanded until individual documents became visible and could be selected for close viewing. Category B consisted of research reports taken from the years 1878–1981, selected to enable detailed research into technological developments in communications technologies. Category C was made up of policy papers and correspondence covering every aspect of the business, from technological innovations to employment and service issues.

While the records in Categories A and B were selected with specific research areas in mind, Category C was intended to be relatively broad and enable a wide range of research. There was, however, some concern that archivists' knowledge of these collections might lead them to cherry-pick 'important' individual documents. To limit this possibility, the advisory group decided that whole folders of material should be scanned. Folders were selected according to a range of topic areas that represented something of the breadth of the material contained in the archive: technology milestones; national events; international reach; government policy; industrial relations; diversity; iconic products and services (Hay, 2014: 8). While these areas reflect as least in part the BT archivists' knowledge of the collection's 'existing and potential research value' (Hay, 2014: 8), they also demonstrate some of the range of topics that the archive covers.

The role of The National Archives: digitising and cataloguing

BT identified 1006 boxes of material for digitisation by The National Archives. Digitisation involved an initial quality check of the material (and, where appropriate, repairs) followed by the production of high-resolution image scans using an ICAM Guardian digital camera workstation manned by two archivists – one to capture each page of material and the other to crop and enhance it.

In addition to the scanning, The National Archives produced metadata for records that had not previously been catalogued by BT, scanning handwritten catalogues of the photographic series and generating basic title–author–date information for the research reports (Hay, 2014: 10). The National Archives worked with BT to fit this new material into the catalogue structure at the subfolder and item level. This involved the generation of extended finding numbers so that each document was contained within the file architecture.

Researcher aims: The British Telecom correspondence corpus

Our role in the New Connections project was to create and analyse a language corpus. By 'corpus' we mean 'a collection of pieces of language text in electronic form, selected according to external criteria to represent, as far as possible, a language or language variety as a source of data for linguistic research' (Sinclair, 2005: 19). We were therefore concerned to capture the language typical of BT correspondence across the time-period covered by the archives.

The period covered by the BT Archives made it a potentially fascinating source of information concerning recent historical developments in business correspondence. The mid-19th century saw a huge increase in letter writing generally, facilitated by the introduction of the Penny Post in 1840 (Dossena and Tieken-Boon van Ostade, 2008: 7–8). An increase in business correspondence was also brought about by the new commercial climate following the Industrial Revolution (Beal, 2004: 116, Del Lungo Camiciotti, 2006: 153). As Del Lungo Camiciotti notes, 'business discourse did of course exist earlier than the nineteenth century. However it is in this period that commercial transactions between England and other countries intensified creating the need for the skill of writing effective letters in English for business purposes' (Del Lungo Camiciotti, 2006: 154).

As the pre-privatisation material in the BT Archives covers the period up to 1984, it has the potential to enable research into the development of business correspondence from this 19th-century boom right through to the advent of electronic forms of correspondence. Very little has been written about the development of business correspondence in this period, perhaps because of the scarcity of publicly available business correspondence hitherto.

For this project, we had sufficient resources to identify and transcribe around 500 letters. Although we were not sure of the exact nature of the material we would be provided with we hoped our corpus could contain (in order of priority):

- a roughly equal number of letters from each decade;
- as wide a variety of authors as possible;
- a variety of topics;
- different letter formats (typed and handwritten).

With a corpus composition of this kind we expected to be able to identify some general trends and historical changes in the language of business correspondence.

Challenges of institutional collaboration

The work that our project partners did in selecting and digitising material was hugely beneficial to us. There were, however, some practical challenges to collaboration, owing to both the circumstances of the project and fundamental methodological differences.

Delivery of the archive material

The research project at Coventry University started in March 2012, the same time that the digitisation process began. This immediately posed the practical problem that there was little or no material when we started work. Our initial literature review had to be kept suitably broad so that we would be prepared to address a range of research areas depending on the nature of the material we received.

The recommendations of BT's advisory team that entire folders should be digitised also greatly increased the time it took for BT to select Category C material (policy papers and correspondence). This meant that we only started receiving Category C material from The National Archives (around 13,000 image scans on an external hard drive) in early June 2012. However, while this represented a significant delay in terms of the digitisation goals of the wider project, BT thought it likely that these files would include at least 500 letters, sufficient for our corpus.

Organisation of the archive material

When we received the scans, there was no metadata attached so the exact nature of the material was unknown. The scans were named and organised according to their 'finding numbers', the main means of searching both the BT and Post Office online catalogues. These describe how records fit into the collections at institutional level (that is, the organisation or part of the organisation from which they originated) in groupings called 'Fonds', within which there are 'Series' of records which originate together or relate to the same activity. Series are made up of 'Files', which are individual folders of files, containing 'items', that is, individual documents.

For example, the finding number POST_30_511B locates a folder within the POST Collection Fond, which contains 'all records created and used by the British Post Office'. The Series POST 30 contains 'Registered files, Minuted Papers (England and Wales, 1792–1952)'. And within that Series, the Folder 511B relates to 'Telegraph: Jubilee

Celebrations (1887)', more specifically a dinner that was arranged to celebrate the 50-year anniversary of the introduction of telegraphy in England.

At Fond and Series levels, the descriptions are too general to assist in the location of any specific material. Folder names more often contain a general topic area and sometimes a date but still not consistent item-level metadata. In our case, as entire files and folders had been scanned, some contained title and contents pages that gave an indication as to what was in the folder, but some had much vaguer descriptions such as 'miscellaneous papers', while others had no descriptions at all.

As it was generally impossible to tell whether a file contained letters or not, the only feasible way to extract the documents we wanted was to manually examine all 13,000 scanned pages. This manual examination identified 992 letters, from which it was possible to select a suitable variety of the material. However, the lack of item-level metadata means that we cannot know exactly what the wider archive contains, and so we also cannot know how representative our sample is of the correspondence in the BT Archives as a whole.

Archives versus language resources: approaches to metadata

The approach to cataloguing taken by BT and similar large public archives reveals a fundamental difference between the mindsets of archivists and corpus linguists. Whereas BT archivists group documents by topic with the history of BT in mind, we, as corpus linguists, are interested in the genre of the documents with the history of the language in mind.

In the early stages of New Connections, BT and The National Archives worked together to catalogue and produce metadata for some of the uncatalogued material in Categories A, B and C. However, this largely involved fitting documents into the catalogue architecture (that is, generating finding numbers) rather than creating item-level descriptions of records. David Hay, the Head of Heritage and Archives at BT, advised us that archiving now tends towards top-level description of a greater amount of material, rather than more detailed description at the item-level. He noted, 'in recent years there has been generally a trend to much lighter cataloguing at a higher level to ensure that more of an overall collection has some kind of catalogue description and finding number' (David Hay, personal correspondence, March 2015).

Given the work involved in operating a massive public archive such as BT's, this approach makes sense. It ensures that as large a proportion of the archive material as possible is described in some form in the wider archive. On the other hand, the approach greatly restricts the possibility of targeted searches.

From our perspective one of the advantages of working with letters is that they contain a lot of metadata. For the majority of letters in the BTCC we were able to collect information regarding author and recipient name, date, location, gender, occupation, company and department, and, for around a quarter of the letters, author and/or recipient age(s). We also ran a series of workshops at Coventry University at which researchers and teaching staff from the English and Languages department were provided with a list of pragmatic functions (which is to say the overall purpose of the letter, for example, 'request') and were asked to assign one or more function to each letter in a sample taken from the BTCC. These classifications were then discussed and the list of potential functions refined. Ultimately each letter was then classified as having one (or more) of the following functions: Application, Commissive, Complaint, Declination, Informative, Notification, Offer, Query, Request, Thanking. This metadata was vital in carrying out our analyses and contextualising findings. It allowed us to compare the key linguistic characteristics of different letter types, as well as enabling more detailed qualitative analyses of individual letter types (for instance, looking at how request strategies developed over time).

The transcriptions and metadata have all been made available to the archivists at BT, although they have not yet been integrated into their digital archive. This is in part because the digital archive was developed in the first year of the New Connections project and launched in July 2013, long before our work on the letters was complete. Furthermore, unlike some other online archives such as The National Library of Australia's Trove, the BT Digital Archive was not designed to facilitate the later addition of transcriptions or item-level metadata by users. As a resource, it makes existing descriptions of the physical archive available online, but does not utilise the interactive potential of digital archive environments to generate new descriptions of collections.

Part two: Working with the Post Office

Expanding the BTCC

The initial analysis on the letters in the BTCC provided many preliminary insights into the development of business correspondence from the mid-eighteenth century to late twentieth century (see

Morton, 2017). However, the corpus has some limitations that reduce the generalisability of the findings. At just over 130,000 words, it is relatively small, and only contains material relating to telecommunications. Moreover, despite our best efforts, there are imbalances in the dataset. Some decades are underrepresented in terms of the overall number of letters, while some individual authors are overrepresented. To try and remedy this, once the initial research on the BTCC was complete, we started looking for ways to expand the corpus.

One of the things we learned while working with archivists on the New Connections project was that the material in the BT Archives used to be part of a wider Post Office archive (hence residual finding numbers in the BT Archives such as POST_30). This means that some of the material in the Post Office archive relates to the shared history of these institutions. Given the close historical and business ties between these two archives, and their public availability, we are bidding for funding to include additional material from the Post Office Museum and Archive in the corpus.

Challenges of working with the Post Office archive material

Integration of item-level and text-level information

Working on New Connections, we learned that even when research produces item-level metadata, it is not always possible for this to be integrated within the architecture of the digital archive. Initial discussions with Vicky Parkinson, the Head of Archives and Records Management at the Postal Heritage Museum, revealed similar issues were we to digitise letters from their collections. In terms of cataloguing, the priority for the archive is to produce a complete top-down description of their collections. By transcribing some of the correspondence contained in their collections, we would be providing an incomplete bottom-up description. As these transcriptions would not provide a complete record of all the items in the originating folder, the Postal Heritage Museum archivists felt that their presence in the digital archive might be misleading to users. While there is a case to be made for including this material with a note flagging to users that they are incomplete records, this would require a significant shift in cataloguing practice, going against the complete top-down description approach employed in the rest of the archive.

Metadata

As in the BT Archives, the material in the Post Office archives is primarily arranged by Fonds and Series, which relate to events in the history of the organisation. One factor that makes the Post Office Archive relatively easier to navigate, however, as of 2014, around 84 per cent of the archive has been catalogued and is available to search online (Gavin McGuffie, Archive Catalogue and Project Manager, personal communication, 5 August 2014). Searches still have to be made primarily via folder descriptions, but because more of the Post Office archive has been catalogued, even before our first visit to the physical archive it was possible to identify folders in which there might be correspondence.

In addition to this, Vicky Parkinson advised us that the Post Office hold a series called 'Treasury Letters' (POST 1) that covers the years 1686–1977. As the Post Office was a government department until 1969, the Treasury supervised all financial aspects of the Post Office's business including correspondence relating to authorisation of expenditure, development of services and applications for pensions. This series contains a large amount of data that relates to a consistent set of topics across time, making it ideal for diachronic study. There is an institutional issue in that, as time went on, the Post Office was less and less under the control of the Treasury, particularly after it became a public corporation in 1969. The result of this is that there is much less Treasury correspondence for later years, which could make it difficult to acquire equal amounts of data across decades. However, the Treasury Letters remain a promising source of data for our proposed language resource, particularly for filling the gaps in 19th-century data that currently exist in the corpus.

Digitisation

For the proposed expansion, we would no longer be able to draw on the resources of The National Archives, and so part of our initial discussions related to the feasibility of digitisation methods. Flatbed scanners are available to use in the Post Office Archive reading rooms, although, given the proposed volume of digitisation, it was felt that quicker methods of image capture using tablet devices might be more appropriate for the majority of material.

Much of the Treasury Letters series is preserved on microfilm and so would be relatively easy to digitise using the scanners and software that are set up in the archive. As in the wider archive, some of the documents preserved on microfilm have been damaged over time and/or ink has bled into the page to the point where the documents are no longer legible. It also appears that quite a large proportion of the type-written documents that survive do so in carbon copy format. We learned working on New Connections that carbon copies are not suitable for OCR scanning owing to the amount of ink bleed; therefore, using these documents would necessitate a large amount of manual transcription.

The relocation

When we first contacted the Post Office to propose this collaboration, they were planning a massive relocation and refurbishment of their archive. There was a provisional timetable for the move, but this was dependent on progress with the construction of the new archive building, which would need to provide the right environmental conditions for the storage of historical documents. Once the relocation was under way it was expected to take two months, but the start date for the move was delayed a number of times. This presented problems in terms of planning our project as it was not entirely clear whether the archive would be open in the months set aside for data collection. Ultimately, we had to propose a very flexible timeline to accommodate a variety of scenarios.

In terms of the timeliness of our proposed project, the relocation presented both challenges and opportunities. In some ways, the relocation and relaunch of the archive made our proposal particularly timely because our digital contribution could be taken by the Post Office as a means of reinvigorating and showcasing their archival holdings. However, the relocation of an archive the size of the Post Office's is a lengthy business, and we entered into discussions with the Post Office relatively late in the course of their relocation plans. As a result, normal impact pathways, such as public talks and exhibitions, were somewhat limited as the Post Office had already developed a two-year programme of launch events. Nevertheless, we have written a public lecture to be recorded as part of the Post Office Archive's podcast series. We have also drawn up plans for a travelling exhibition, scheduled to visit venues in Coventry and London, and we are in talks with additional museums that focus on aspects of the history of communications.

BTPO letter collection

The digital resource that we are proposing will present letters from both archives with links through to the original material. In this way, it will be a standalone letter collection as well as an introduction to both important historical archives. We plan to make the item–level and text–level information available so that it does not need to be integrated into the existing digital archives. Instead, our digital resource and the digital archives of BT and the Post Office will supplement and promote each other. We also intend to make the letters available for linguist and non-linguist audiences alike, presenting them in a simple transcription and manuscript display as well as in the form of a fully annotated corpus. This will enable linguists to engage with the language of historical business, while offering an exploratory space to anyone else with even a passing interest in the history of letters, business, and telecommunications.

Conclusion

Public archives such as those held by BT and The Post Office are invaluable sources of research material. The material provided to us by the New Connections project has enabled us to gain new insights into some of the ways in which business correspondence has changed since the mid–19th century. It has also taught us a lot about the ways in which archives work and has prompted a lot of valuable discussion around questions of how best to digitise material to maximise its research potential. These discussions have not necessarily led to a change in approach either from us or the archivists with whom we have worked. Perhaps this was because the fundamental differences in our approaches are not indicative of a 'right' way and a 'wrong' way of working with historical data; rather, they reflect our different priorities and areas of interest. We are interested primarily in the text and how contextual information can help us make sense of it, whereas documents in archives are traditionally arranged in terms of how they fit thematically into the wider series of events represented by that archive.

It is worth considering, however, that digital archives can provide an opportunity to present material in new ways and that the simple recreation of physical archives online holds inherent dangers. Physical archives are staffed by archivists, on hand to help users make sense of the organisation of records and finding numbers, which can be impenetrable to the untrained. While every archivist we have worked with has been very generous in offering advice, ideally a digital archive should be user-friendly enough to be able to operate without their assistance at any time and anywhere in the world.

Item-level metadata and full text transcriptions have the potential to make collections much easier to navigate and interrogate. The generation of such data may be beyond the purview of archivists, but it is achievable through research collaboration and functions such as crowd-sourced file tagging and optical character recognition correction, which are relatively simple to embed in digital archives. Of course, even when item-level and text-level information has been generated, archivists may be unwilling to include it for only a small fraction of their catalogued material. In such cases it might be worth considering supplementary digital resources that provide new ways of engaging with specific types of document, while also promoting the wider archival collection.

References

Beal, J. (2004) *English In Modern Times*, London: Arnold.

Del Lungo Camiciotti, G. (2006) 'Conduct Yourself Towards All Persons On Every Occasion With Civility and in a Wise and Prudent Manner; This Will Render You Esteemed: Stance Features In Nineteenth Century Business Letters', in Dossena, M. and Fitzmaurice, S. (eds) *Business And Official Correspondence: Historical Investigations*, Bern, Peter Lang, pp 153–74.

Dossena, M. and Tieken-Boon van Ostade, I. (eds.) (2008) *Studies in Late Modern English Correspondence: Methodology And Data*, Bern, Peter Lang

Hay, D. (2014) 'New Connections: The BT Digital Archives Project', Paper presented at the Archives and Cultural Industries Conference, *Girona*, 11–15 October.

Hay, D. (2015) Email to Ralph Morton, 22 March.

McGuffie, G. (2014) Email to Ralph Morton, 5 August.

Morton, R. (2017) 'Public archives as a source of historical linguistic data: The construction and analysis of the British Telecom Correspondence Corpus', paper presented at the Corpus Linguistics 2017 Conference, University of Birmingham, 25–28 July, available at https://www.birmingham.ac.uk/Documents/college-artslaw/corpus/conference-archives/2017/general/paper275.pdf

Sinclair, J. (2005) 'Corpus And Text: Basic Principles', in Wynne, Martin (ed.) *Developing Linguistic Corpora: A Guide To Good Practice*, Oxford: Oxbow Books, pp 1–20.

PART III

Disruptive and counter voices: the community turn

12

Mainstream institutional collecting of anti-institutional archives: opportunities and challenges

Anna Sexton

This chapter uses the Wellcome Library's archive collecting around the treatment and experience of 'mad people' as a case study for exploring the opportunities and challenges that arise from mainstream attempts to introduce counter-narratives into the archive.[1] The argument laid out in this chapter is based on observations at the Wellcome Library undertaken as part of my PhD (Sexton, 2016), where I was embedded within the Wellcome Library and used an auto-ethnographic approach, combined with in-depth interviews with Special Collections staff, to seek to understand perceptions and practice around collection development.

The ethos of collecting at the Wellcome Library can be traced back to the life and outlook of its founder, Sir Henry Wellcome (1853–1936). Henry Wellcome co-founded a successful multinational pharmaceutical company from which he accumulated his personal wealth. He used this increasing wealth during his own lifetime to fund medical research and to fulfil his growing passion as a collector of books and historical objects. His collecting interest lay in his fascination with wanting to understand the art and science of healing across history and cultures. At the time of his death, his personal collection was larger than that of many of Europe's most famous museums (Gould and Faulks, 2007). Although the museum objects collected by Wellcome were transferred to the Science Museum in the 1970s and early 1980s, his book collections were the founding part of the Wellcome Library. Over the years, the Library has been housed in a variety of physical spaces with a sequence of name changes. However, its history during the later decades of the 20th century was one of continuing growth and development, with an ongoing acquisitions programme and a focus on expanding use. In 2007, it became part of the newly conceived Wellcome Collection, which acts as a free destination that 'seeks to explore the connections between medicine, life and art in the past, present and future; at its heart lies the curiosity that drove Henry Wellcome to amass his diverse collection' (Wellcome Library, 2013a).

In the course of the Wellcome Library's history, expanding the archives and manuscripts collections has been, and continues to be, a central concern. The establishment of a Contemporary Medical Archives Centre in 1979 to collect records of important 20th-century medical organisations and individuals is testament to the Library's commitment to specifically grow the archive collections. Another significant addition during the 1980s was the purchase of the manuscripts (and about 10,000 printed books) from the Medical Society of London Library (Wellcome Library, 2013a). The archives and manuscripts collection includes nearly 9,000 manuscripts and over 800 archive collections from the United Kingdom and Europe, and the Library sees itself as holding 'the most important collection of manuscripts and archives on the history of medicine in Britain' (Wellcome Library, 2013b). Archives in the collection are concentrated on English-language material from the 20th century, and the collecting policy focuses primarily on material created in Britain and its former colonies. Broadly speaking, the archives include:

- personal and family papers, correspondence, notebooks and diaries of scientists, GPs and others;
- records of charities, campaigning organisations, and pressure groups;
- records of professional bodies, businesses and research institutions;
- the Royal Army Medical Corps Muniment Collection;
- the Wellcome Archives, including Henry Wellcome's personal papers, the Wellcome Foundation archives, and records of the Wellcome Historical Medical Museum. (Wellcome Library, 2013b)

In seeking to understand the representation of the treatment and experience of 'mad people' within the archives and manuscripts collections held by the Wellcome Library, I focused on madness from the 19th century to the present. In my exploration of the Library's existing archive collections, I found that the most dominant and prevailing archival collection strength across this time period is focused on personal papers of eminent 'psy' experts (psychiatric specialists, psychoanalysts, psychologists and related therapists).[2] The Library holds a number of prominent archive collections in this area, including the personal papers of Melanie Klein (PP/KLE), William Walters Sargant (PP/WWS), Robina Addis (PP/ADD), Ronald Arthur Sandison (PP/SAN) and the art therapist Edward Adamson (PP/ADA). There is also a strong nucleus of collections around professional 'psy' societies and groups, including the Group Analytic Society (SA/GAS), the Jungian Umbrella Group (SA/JUG) and the British Psychological Society (PSY/BPS).[3] The Library also holds the institutional records of a range of private asylums and mental hospitals, including Ticehurst Hospital (1787–1975) and Camberwell House Asylum (1847–53), representing another collection strength. Public and voluntary asylums are also represented across the collections mainly from within the personal papers of prominent 'psy' professionals. For example, an extensive body of material relating to Maudsley Hospital can be unearthed across the personal papers of Carlos Paton Blacker (PP/CPB), William Walters Sargant (PP/WWS), Siegmund Heinrich Foulkes (PP/SHF), Rosen Ismond (PP/ROS) and Henry McIlwaine (PP/MCI). This cross-fertilisation between representation of the individual and the institution testifies to the networks underpinning the evolution of the 'psy' disciplines. There is also a smaller range of material clustered around the personal papers of campaigners, pressure group members and charity workers active in the mental health field, such as Dorothy Silberston (PP/DSI), who was a pivotal member of the National Schizophrenia Fellowship (now Rethink). Here too, the interrelationships between individuals, groups and institutions can be traced. For example, in collections such as the Robina Addis Papers (PP/ADD) there is material relating to her career as a psychiatric social worker, but also material relating to her role as a pivotal member of the National Institute for Mental Health (later MIND), the World Federation for Mental Health, and other bodies. The third sector within the mental health field is represented not just in individual personal papers, but also through a variety of organisational archives, including the archive of the Mental After Care Association (SA/MAC) and the recently acquired archive of the mental health charity MIND (SA/MIN). The library also holds a growing nucleus of material relating to charities concerned with advocating more generally for patient rights, the largest of which is the Patients Association Archive (SA/PAT), where there is a significant body of material concerning mental health patients.

Recognised by the Special Collections staff as areas of notable weakness are archives that represent and document relatively recent sociohistoric shifts in the mental health field. In particular, archive collections relating to the psychiatric consumer/survivor movements that begun to emerge in the 1970s (see Spandler, 2006: 52–67), as well as personal archives of psychiatric consumer/survivors and other individuals with lived experience of mental health. In relation to the latter, two recent acquisitions are indicative of an attempt to shift the sociohistorical weight of the collections away from the 'psy' expert and the mental institution, towards archives in which survivors/consumers are representing themselves more autonomously. The first, donated in 2011 directly from the creator, are the diaries of Pam Maudsley (PP/PMY), which represent a personal documentation of Maudsley's journey through the mental health system and her close relationship with her therapist. The second, donated between 2014 and 2015 by the family of the now deceased creator, is the Audrey Amiss Archive (PP/AMI). However, both of these collections currently remain closed to the public awaiting cataloguing.

The importance of representation within mainstream institutional archives, and the responsibility that falls on archivists to be aware of and address potential marginalisations created through their collecting practices, relates to power. Foucault's body of writing addresses the power/knowledge nexus and its relationship to truth. Across his accounts of the history of madness (1989), the medical gaze (2003) and the creation of expert knowledge categories from human experience (1972), it is possible to trace how the establishment of a discourse that acts as a regime of truth is dependent on the creation of bodies of knowledge. Following Foucault, it is possible to argue that the 'archive' acts as a body of knowledge, as a means of determining what can be said and what can be known, and of what is considered true. Therefore, representation in the archive matters. In Foucauldian terms they can be understood as 'formal systemizations' that give 'functionalist coherence' (Foucault, 1980: 31) to particular perspectives. The processes of capturing, fixing and organising that are inextricably bound into traditional professional understandings of the 'archive' can be understood as mechanisms through which it is possible to objectify those gazed upon, reducing them to categories, data and statistics that can be ordered and controlled. It matters then that individuals with lived experience of madness appear predominately as objects in the archive collections held by the Wellcome Library. It matters that such individuals exist mainly in the case notes of medical professionals, and in the columns of asylum admission registers. It matters that this historical pattern of objectification is still an ongoing reality in most of the material that archives such as the Wellcome Library accession within the present. It matters because the 'archive' has the power to subjugate:

> By subjugated knowledges I mean two things: on the one hand, I am referring to historical contents that have been buried and disguised in a functionalist coherence or

formalized systemization … On the other hand, I believe that by subjugated knowledges one should understand something else, something which in a sense is altogether different, namely a whole set of knowledges that have been disqualified as inadequate to the task or insufficiently elaborated: naive knowledges, located low down on the hierarchy, beneath the required level of cognition or scientificity. (Foucault, 1980: 81–2)

Actively seeking to shift the balance to give the subjugated space to speak becomes an imperative because, as Foucault makes clear, it is the re-emergence of the subjugated that enables critique of the status quo:

I also believe that it is through the re-emergence of these low ranking knowledges (such as the psychiatric patient…), and which involve what I would call a popular knowledge (le savoir des gens) though it is far from being a general common sense knowledge, but is on the contrary a particular, local, regional knowledge, a differential knowledge incapable of unanimity, and which owes its force only to the harshness with which it is opposed by everything surrounding it – that it is through the reappearance of this knowledge, of these local popular knowledges, these disqualified knowledges, that criticism performs its work. (Foucault, 1980: 93)

Yet bringing in archives to counterbalance the predominant 'psy' narrative *into* an institution such as the Wellcome Library, which has been so long aligned with the dominant medical model of mental illness and treatment, is fraught with complexity. Does bringing counternarratives into the walls of the institutional archive release that knowledge from subjugation by clothing it with legitimacy? Or does it in fact further subjugate that knowledge under the weight of the dominant narrative?

The first challenge within mainstream settings such as the Wellcome Library, which I explored with the Special Collections staff, is that unconscious bias towards the institution and the professional remains difficult to break down. Interviewees spoke of the 'seal of institutional approval' that can be attributed to organisations such as MIND and MENCAP. This makes the acquisition of archives of mainstream organisations an unquestionable given, with archives from grassroots settings and from individuals with lived experience coming up against a higher level of scrutiny of their significance and archival value. This echoes with Bourdieu's notion of 'symbolic capital', which is unquestionably carried by institutions and established categories of professionals who have built up a 'heritage of commitments and debts of honour, a capital of rights and duties built up in the course of successive generations' (Bourdieu, 1977: 178) that serve to legitimate their social standing and their merit. This symbolic capital precedes the perception that their archive material is valuable and metaphorically sacred and underscores the assumption that their archives are to be preferred to archive material generated outside their institutional circles. The weight of the symbolic capital ascribed to institutions and professionals renders the archives of those without such credentials into a marginal position. The value of the archive material is more readily questionable, more easily discounted as quasi-profane.

My interviews with staff also revealed how archive professionals at the Wellcome are caught up in a perpetuating cycle that favours the already dominant as they frame and label people and things within the mental health field using the discourse of 'patient' and 'mental illness'. The dominance of the medical framing of madness is carried into the processing and description of collections, where the use of Medical Subject Headings (MESH) as indexing entry points, and the organisation of medically orientated subject guides into the collections, cements the Wellcome Library's overarching alignment with a medical model of mental health. Despite being interested in collecting alternative views and subversive histories, the centralisation of a medical narrative and frame means that archives representing counter-cultures actually become subjugated on entry; defined by what they are counter to; immersed under the dominant frame and its accompanying discourse. Reinforced subjugation is therefore a real danger that is inherent in aligning an oppositional archive under an institutional framework that upholds the norms that the oppositional archive seeks to speak against.

It is useful to think of controlled vocabularies, such as MESH, as a 'symbolic system' (Bourdieu, 1977: 4–68). Bourdieu sees symbolic systems as 'structuring structures' that enable us to understand and order the world, but they are also 'structured structures' with an internal logic related to codes 'that are deep structural meanings shared by all members of a culture' (Swartz, 1997: 83). Symbolic systems, such as MESH, simultaneously function as instruments of communication and as instruments of knowledge (Bourdieu, 1971: 295 in Swartz, 1997: 83). As an instrument of both knowledge and communication, MESH also operates as an instrument of domination and 'dominant symbolic systems provide integration for dominant groups, distinctions and hierarchies for ranking groups, and legitimation of social ranking by encouraging both dominated and dominating to accept the existing hierarchies of social distinction' (Bourdieu, 1971: 114–15 in Swartz, 1997: 83). Therefore, symbolic systems, such as MESH, fulfil a political function. However, there is no straightforward course of action available for disrupting the dominance of the symbolic structures used within the Wellcome Library. There are significant constraints imposed by the infrastructures sitting around the cataloguing system that both locks the team into the use of MESH index terms and enforces a singular top-down hierarchical description of the material, which is difficult to break away from.

During my time with staff at the Wellcome Library, I observed an in-depth collective confrontation of the difficult questions that sit around archival representation in a mental health context, and the Wellcome Library's institutional control of that representation. This confrontation occurred in the context of the Library's handling of the Audrey Amiss collection, which was offered to the institution by Audrey's nephew in 2014. It was accepted as a donation and accessioned in three batches between April 2014 and February 2015. The Wellcome Library's catalogue entry on Audrey states that:

> Audrey Amiss was born in 1933 and died in July 2013 just short of 80 years old. She grew up in Sunderland, was spotted as a talented artist as a child and won a scholarship to the Royal Academy School of Art in London. At the age of eighteen Audrey experienced her first episode of mental health problems. It followed soon after the death of her father, to whom she was very close, and this may have been a contributing factor in triggering her illness. She was diagnosed as a paranoid schizophrenic. Throughout her life, she was in and out of mental institutions, many in south London. (Wellcome Library, 2013c)

I was at the team meeting where the acquisition of the collection was initially considered. At this meeting several team members strongly argued for the value of the collection as a means to bring 'patient voice' into the archive, advocating that the value of the collection was as a first-hand window into a schizophrenic mind. A pivotal shift in the discussion came when the Head of Special Collections began to trouble that notion by introducing more complex underlying ethical concerns into the dialogue. This included raising the issue that as

Audrey is no longer alive to give us her opinion, there is a need to think seriously about the ethical implications of placing her archive into the context of a library of health and medicine in relation to the potential this carries to subsume her artwork beneath a narrative that foregrounds her as mentally ill. After the meeting, during a one-to-one interview, another member of the team reflected:

> I found the meeting you sat in last week really interesting. I was really stimulated by the whole meeting. Thinking about the sketch books – until [name] brought up the ethical issues – the institutionalizing of it – I hadn't considered that [pause] I began to feel more uncomfortable with it – the idea that by taking in that collection we are institutionalizing *her* – I still don't really know where I sit about it to be honest. Should we take it? We want to represent patient views [pause] the agreement was we should pursue it further and consider how we would make it accessible to researchers. How we describe her then becomes an ethical question – that was really interesting actually.

In the surfacing of these complexities at the accessioning meeting and in the team's reflections on that meeting, I sensed a tangible shift away from a simplistic mantra that 'we have a duty to collect patient voice to balance our collections' towards a deeper reflective engagement with the ethics of archival representation. It was the raising of these ethical tensions, the forcing of them out into the open by the Head of Special Collections, that was pivotal in demanding a different response from the team in terms of how they would then act in relation to this collection. The team's commitment to act differently was taken forward through their involvement in a public engagement initiative that took place on 30 April 2015 in the Wellcome Library reading rooms, which sought to engage with some of the questions around representing Audrey Amiss's archive ethically. Towards the end of the discussion at that engagement event there was general consensus on a vision of the catalogue entry for the Audrey Amiss collection. The vision was that it should not resemble a formal, standard, single definitive description. Instead, the catalogue entry should be premised around the series of ethical questions that can be posed around the curation and interpretation of the collection and its presence at the Wellcome Library.

This highlights that where mainstream archive institutions seek out collections from communities and individuals in order to rebalance or diversify their collections, or to create a counternarrative to the dominant discourses threading through their collections, there is a need to pay careful attention to the ethics of representation and the ways in which management practices, including description, indexing and presentation, can further subjugate.

The ethics of representation, and the tendency for the dominant discourse to subjugate, is part of the reason why for many community archives distance and separation from the mainstream is desirable. The work of the grassroots Survivor History Group (SHG) is an example of an existing space in which mental health survivors have voice and ownership over their story and their archive. Their ethos is summarized in their manifesto as seeking to:

> Highlight the diversity and creativity of the service user/ survivor contribution through personal accounts, writings, poetry, art, music, drama, photography, campaigning, speaking influencing … [We intend to] collect, collate and preserve service user/survivor history, make service user/survivor history accessible to all who are interested in or studying mental health, use our history to inform and improve the future, [and] operate as an independent group. The independence of any archive we set up is necessary to prevent limited access to such a resource and to expose the deliberate loss of history – in particular the lived experience of psychiatric system survivors … Our basic founding principle is that service users own their own history. (SHG, 1996)

The SHG can be described as a community archive in the sense that it is a space that has been created, maintained and controlled by community members, by survivors, for survivors 'on their own terms' (Stevens et al, 2010: 60). In this way, the work of the SHG is political and subversive (Flinn et al, 2009) and acts as a direct challenge to the dominant voices presiding over representations of their story. Running through the group's online presentation of their own history and activities is a strong sense of the ways in which their history has suffered when written in the hands of others. The group sees their history as an opposition to narratives written by non-survivors (mainly academics). It is a vehicle that simultaneously points to, and redresses, the lack of acknowledgement by the academic community of the existence of survivor-led historical research.

Furthermore, insight into survivor perspectives on the importance of survivor control over survivor history can be traced through the

SHG's documentation of the 750th anniversary of Bethlem Royal Hospital. This anniversary took place in 1997 and was marked by the creation of an institutionally curated exhibition on the hospital's history, exhibited at the Museum of London. Peter Beresford offers an insightful critique of the exhibition, first published in OpenMind in May/June 1998, reproduced by the SHG in their online archive. His critique is woven into a powerful rhetoric around the necessity of survivors controlling their own history:

> Perhaps most disturbing of all has been its associated exhibition. This is presented in classic modernist terms of centuries of progress, culminating in modern psychiatry and the Maudsley Hospital. It is made all the worse because it is given the respectability of being housed in the Museum of London, which generally shows a sensitivity to issues of difference and discrimination. The current psychiatric orthodoxy that 'genes contribute to most mental illness' is presented as fact. The experience of thousands of inmates is reduced to a handful of indecipherable photographs posed in hospital wards and grounds, and select biographies of the famous and curious few … If mental health service users/survivors are to take charge of our future, then we must regain control of our past. That past, at both individual and collective levels, has largely been appropriated, denied, controlled and reinterpreted by other powerful interests, notably medical professionals, the state, politicians, charitable organizations and the media. This has been destructive to all our futures. In recent years, the survivors' movement has begun to challenge this rewriting of our history. (Beresford, 1998, reproduced in SHG, 1998)

There is a strength of feeling within the SHG around the unique difference that independently created survivor history offers in comparison to other versions of the story, and the necessity of creating this 'different' history. This is coupled with the belief that such a history created by survivors can also be best cared for, most nurtured and made most widely available through independence. Such sentiments resonate strongly with the motivations, positions, values and beliefs found in many other grass-roots community archive contexts (Flinn et al, 2009). Creating, collecting and curating embodies 'the symbolic power to order knowledge, to rank, classify and arrange, and to give meaning to objects and things, through the imposition of interpretative schemas, scholarship and the authority of connoisseurship' (Hall, 2005: 24). Therefore, in order to hold symbolic power, survivor groups need to be in control of the archival process.

In conclusion, institutional archives such as the Wellcome Library that look to enrich their collections with counternarratives that can disrupt or rebalance dominant discourses running through their holdings must carefully engage with the ethics of representation and consider the danger of reinscribing the dominant narrative through process of subjugation in how that material is processed, described, interpreted and made available to the public. Institutions with the resources to do so should consider approaches to support and facilitate the archiving process in grassroots and community settings without seeking to bring those archives into the walls of the institution. Where archives that represent counternarratives do come into the walls of the mainstream, the most ethical approaches to the management, processing and curation of those collections involve a sharing authority and a process of co-production. If sharing authority runs counter to the ethos of the institution, then attempts to collect counternarratives are likely to fall foul of becoming a damaging appropriation of the history and culture represented within the collection rather than a diversification and rebalancing of the narratives that the Institution holds.

Notes

[1] Mad people is used throughout this chapter in keeping with the ethos of the mad pride movement and the related field of mad studies, which seek to reclaim the term 'mad' from negative connotations and redefine its meaning. The inverted commas are used to indicate the contested nature of the term.

[2] As part of my PhD research I conducted a categorisations exercise of the Wellcome Library's archival representation of the treatment and experience of 'mad people' from the 19th century to the present day. Via their online catalogue and accessions database I located 128 relevant archive collections representing this theme within this time period, and I found that 91 of those (71 per cent) could be categorised as being the personal papers of 'psy' experts.

[3] The collections referred to throughout this chapter by their unique identifying code are not cited in the end references. These collections can be searched for on the Wellcome Library website using the unique identifying code given in the text: http://catalogue.wellcomelibrary.org/.

References

Bourdieu, P. (1977) *Outline of a Theory of Practice*, Cambridge: Cambridge University Press.

Flinn, A., Stevens, M. and Shepherd, E. (2009) 'Whose memories, whose archives? Independent community archives, autonomy and the mainstream', *Archival Science*, 9(1–2): 71–86.

Foucault, M. (1972) *The Archaeology of Knowledge and the Discourse on Language*, translated by Sheridan, A.M., New York: Pantheon.

Foucault, M. (1980) *Power/Knowledge: Selected Interviews and Other Writings*, edited and translated by Gordon, C., Brighton: Harvester Wheatsheaf.

Foucault, M. (1989) *Madness and Civilization: A History of Insanity in the Age of Reason*, translated by Howard, R., London: Routledge.

Gould, T. and Faulks. S. (eds) (2007) *Cures and Curiosities: Inside the Wellcome Library*, London: Profile Books.

Hall, S. (2005). 'Whose Heritage? Un-settling 'The Heritage', Re-imagining the Post-Nation', in Littler, J. and Naidoo, R. (eds) *The Politics of Heritage, The Legacies of Race*, London: Routledge, pp 23–35.

Sexton, A. (2016) 'Archival activism and mental health: Being participatory, sharing control and building legitimacy, PhD thesis, University College London.

Spandler, H. (2006) *Asylum to Action: Paddington Day Hospital, Therapeutic Communities and Beyond*, London: Jessica Kingsley.

Stevens, M., A. Flinn, A. and Shepherd, E. (2010) 'New Frameworks for community engagement in the archive sector: from handing over to handing on', *International Journal of Heritage Studies*, 16(1 and 2): 59–76.

SHG (Survivor History Group) (1996) 'Survivor History Group: Long manifesto' [online], Available from: http://studymore.org.uk/mpu.htm#ManifestoLong2006 [Accessed 14 February 2013].

Survivor History Group (SHG) (1998) 'Survivor History Group: past tense, Peter Beresford on the need for a survivor controlled museum of madness', originally published in *OpenMind* (May/June 1998) [online], Available from: http://studymore.org.uk/mpuhist.htm#1 [Accessed 14 February 2013].

Swartz, D. (1997) *Culture & Power: The Sociology of Pierre Bourdieu*, Chicago and London: University of Chicago Press.

Wellcome Library (2013a) 'Wellcome Library: a brief history of the Library' [online], Available from: http://www.webarchive.org.uk/wayback/archive/20130219055014/https://library.wellcome.ac.uk/about-us/history-of-wellcome-library/ [Accessed 19 February 2013].

Wellcome Library (2013b) 'Wellcome Library: Archives and manuscripts' [online], Available from: http://www.webarchive.org.uk/wayback/archive/20130219055004/https://library.wellcome.ac.uk/about-us/about-the-collections/archives-and-manuscripts/ [Accessed 19 February 2013].

Wellcome Library (2013c) 'Audrey Amiss Catalogue Description' [online], Available from: http://archives.wellcomelibrary.org/DServe/dserve.exe?dsqIni=Dserve.ini&dsqApp=Archive&dsqCmd=Show.tcl&dsqDb=Catalog&dsqPos=0&dsqSearch=%28%28%28text%29%3D%27audrey%27%29AND%28%28text%29%3D%27amiss%27%29%29 [Accessed 9 February 2013].

13

Silver hair, silver tongues, silver screen: recollection, reflection and representation through digital storytelling with older people

Tricia Jenkins and Pip Hardy

Introduction

Narrative approaches to research have gained prominence in academia, particularly in the fields of social science and health. Digital Storytelling (DS) is rapidly becoming recognised as a way for people – especially those whose voices are marginalised – to shape, voice and share their stories.

In this chapter, we discuss the use of DS with older people. We look at the benefits of participation in the DS process before considering how these self-representations – organised, selected and told by individuals and shared on their terms – can break down traditional bureaucratic power structures represented by the notion of 'archive'.

We present two case studies: one from Patient Voices,[1] which curates and archives digital stories made under its auspices with the intention of transforming health and social care by conveying the voices of those not usually heard to a worldwide audience; and another from DigiTales's work with older people through the transnational action research project Silver Stories,[2] which generated an archive of over 160 stories by older people and those who care for them, from five European countries. 'Digital storytelling creates new possibilities for participatory and collaborative approaches to discovering and developing new knowledge, re-positioning participants as co-producers of knowledge and, potentially, as co-researchers' (Hardy and Sumner, 2018: 11).

Digital storytelling – practice, product, research and archive

Digital stories are short (two to three minutes), first person, multimedia presentations consisting of images, a voiceover, sometimes video and occasionally music or other sound effects. Stories are often created in DS workshops during which storytellers are carefully facilitated to find their stories (participating in a Story Circle), draft scripts, record voiceovers, select suitable images and edit their own short videos. The restrictions imposed by the form require storytellers to focus on what really matters to them; the commitment to empowerment and collaboration required of facilitators ensures that storytellers are helped to tell the story only they can tell and offers them complete control over what goes in and what stays out. Users and viewers of the stories value their brevity; as one of the authors of this chapter found while conducting MSc research: 'Their brevity was felt to be more than adequately compensated for by their intensity, and the two/three minute format was a decided benefit, with the combination of visual images, voice and music providing a richly textured opportunity to understand another's world' (Hardy, 2007: 29).

The process is creative and reflective, encouraging participants to make meaning of the experiences of their lives; the resulting stories have an immediacy and authenticity that allow viewers to see the world through another person's eyes. Indeed, our own views were echoed following a viewing of a collection of stories created by parents of children who had been severely brain-damaged as a result of contracting malaria in early childhood. A medical director at Tanzania's National Institute of Medical Research commented that, 'These stories allow us to walk in someone else's shoes for a few minutes.'

Combining the ancient art of storytelling with new technologies, DS enables participants to create and share personal stories and use them as powerful forces for change. As each story is digitally preserved, it can be shared online as well as 'in any lecture theatre, Board Room or conference venue anywhere in the world' (Hardy, 2007: vii). Each story can be added to the growing archive of data that is being generated by DS initiatives throughout the world, comprising the evidence of experience presented from the individual perspectives of thousands of storytellers. In the case of Patient Voices, for example, once a story is released by the storyteller, the story joins hundreds of others on the Patient Voices website (www.patientvoices.org.uk), where all the stories are freely viewable under a Creative Commons non-commercial, no-derivatives, attribution licence. The decision not to put the stories on

YouTube was made in order to preserve the integrity of the stories and ensure that they do not ever appear in a mash-up or derivative film of, for example, 'The Ten Worst Things That Patients Say'.

DS is now a global movement of committed practitioners working with stories in community, educational, health and therapeutic environments, gathering momentum as practitioners join from around the world. Meanwhile DS, along with other narrative approaches, is gaining traction as an audio-visual means of expression, and as an innovative way of carrying out research, as evidenced by the growing number of PhDs undertaken in the field (Thumim, 2007; Alexandra, 2015; Hardy, 2016) and the proliferation of books about the use of digital stories and digital storytelling (examples being (Lundby, 2008; Hartley and McWilliam, 2009; Jamissen et al, 2017; Dunford and Jenkins, 2017; Hardy and Sumner, 2018).

Narrative has shifted from being a marginal approach to gathering data to a key concept in social science research, especially in relation to personal histories, biography, framing identity and coping with illness (Cobley, 2014: 212). Riessman (1993: 4) foregrounds the importance of 'meaning-making structures' that contribute to the richness of data that can be captured through narrative research and acknowledges that the 'subjects' or 'informants' of the research will create an order and use a voice or voices to articulate their stories. She states that, in narrative analysis:

> the methodological approach examines the informant's story and analyses how it is put together, the linguistic and cultural resources it draws on and how it persuades a listener of authenticity. Analysis in narrative studies opens up the forms of telling about experience, not simply the content to which language refers. We ask, why was the story told that way? (Riessman, 1993: 2)

In relation to DS, we can explore the pre-narratives that emerge through the Story Circle process, consider the choices that participants make about how to tell their stories and analyse the additional layers of meaning produced by the selection, construction and ordering of images, the 'scripting' of voice, the choice of tone, the performance and participants' interpretation of what makes a *story*, rather than an account of a whole life or life event, or responding to interviewers' questions. The form trades linearity and length for brevity and depth, as the case studies later in this chapter will demonstrate. A collection of family albums may provide a photographic record of many decades.

However, through the DS process a selection of photos most illustrative of a significant moment can give them new life through their narrative sequencing, opening up new readings and prompting new insights: 'A past which seemed disconnected from the present is inserted into the present through the personal narratives that were created to accompany them, as digital storytelling powerfully combines the promiscuous meaning of photography with the power of the spoken narrative' (Dunford and Rooke, 2014: 213).

Digital storytelling with older people

Indisputably, we are ageing from the moment we are born. However, there is a point at which 'one is labelled as *aged* or *older* (older than whom?) and life beyond that point is labelled as 'ageing' (Baars, 2010: 108). Most definitions of ageing are derived from clinical measures (degenerative symptoms associated with ageing) or social measures (such as the age of retirement) based on the chronological measurement of age. Such measurements displace ways of articulating what it *feels like* or 'what it *means* to grow old?' (Cole et al, 2010: 1). Humanistic gerontology is an interdisciplinary approach to the study of ageing that prioritises qualitative research methods, particularly narrative approaches, and pays attention to such philosophical questions. To quote Baars again, 'micro-narratives remain important for empirical studies of ageing as they articulate human experiences' (2012: 1). Digital Stories are micro-narratives and the processes of creating them, including the discussions and chats that occur within the Story Circle, are potentially rich sources of data that can shed light on how people from diverse backgrounds and different ages within the 'older people' category experience the ageing process.

Most important, though, is the potential for DS not only to provide a space in which older people can voice their experiences and tell their life-stories, but also distribute them and make them accessible. Participants often move beyond reminiscence (the focus of so many creative projects with older people) to find ways in which their stories, photographs and memories, when combined with digital technology, provide them with 'an opportunity to think about the ways in which they may wish to narrate their experiences into the future *and* the means of doing so' (Rooke and Slater, 2012: 21).

Within the context of archive, we applaud the philosophy behind the Museu da Pessoa (Museum of the Person), a virtual museum based in Sao Paulo, Brazil, founded in 1991. The Museum has established a virtual archive that values the cultural diversity and history of each and every person by capturing and presenting their stories. They are, individually and collectively, important and valid contributions to Brazil's national history and identity and 'an opportunity to create and include alternative and additional narratives to a country's history by building a critical mass of stories as a source of knowledge, understanding and connection between all people and peoples'.[3] DS enables personal stories to contribute to nation stories and to institutional stories, providing alternative perspectives, micro-narratives that can illuminate macro-stories. As illustrated in the case studies 'Who is Bertha' and 'The Story of the Teething Ring', these stories offer us the potential to understand many perspectives into the minutiae of everyday life, as well as the experiences of their tellers, of living through major historic events – in this case the First and Second World Wars. These are perspectives that may otherwise be absent from more conventional accounts that find their way into traditional models of archive, enabling us to question and challenge dominant narratives, and gain perspective into aspects that might otherwise be considered not important enough to include.

Case study: Patient Voices – The Society of the Holy Child Jesus

The Patient Voices Programme was established in 2003 to provide an alternative form of data to that usually used in healthcare design and delivery, that is, quantitative data elicited from randomised control trials, surveys and statistics. Digital stories created by patients, carers and staff are intended to prompt reflection and promote greater humanity and compassion. The archive has grown to more than 1000 stories; they are used in healthcare education and improvement initiatives around the world.

Although the majority of Patient Voices' work takes place in healthcare, this case study focuses on a project with an elderly community of nuns, serving as a reminder that health and well-being do not rely only on the absence of disease. The Society of the Holy Child Jesus (SHCJ) is an international religious community dedicated primarily to education, health and social care. In common with many religious orders, numbers have fallen, and the community was concerned to recruit new members, eager to reveal the members of the community as 'ordinary' human beings, with flaws and foibles, just like the rest of us. The decision to create digital stories coincided with the redesign of the Order's website to exude a more modern appeal in the hope of attracting younger women to join the community.

After a successful reconnaissance visit from two senior sisters, four more sisters participated in a Patient Voices DS workshop, including 82 year-old Sister Eva Heymann who has since returned to make a total of four stories, documenting her early life and later diagnosis of dementia (Heymann, 2009, 2010). The creation of these stories, and the possibility of archiving them on the Society's website, highlighted the growing importance of gathering and preserving the stories of the community. In 2008, Patient Voices was invited to work with some of the oldest sisters to help them create digital stories that would go into the Society's archives.

The first day of the workshop arrived. A circle of nuns awaited us, some in wheelchairs, some on mobility vehicles, some slumped, unknowing, others bent over with age. More arrived, some wheeled in by nurses or other sisters – 'We don't want anyone to feel left out'; the circle grew, along with our consternation. How would we manage such a large story circle? Bolstered by the presence of two additional facilitators, there was nothing for it but to begin. We offered the microphone to the first volunteer, rather like a talking stick. She told a touching story not so much of vocation but of choices made by parents and teachers from another era.

The microphone was passed to the next sister, who told of the solace she found in solitude on a Welsh mountainside surrounded only by sheep. The microphone passed hands again, and Sister Gemma described her first calling – to marry her sweetheart Tom – rapidly succeeded by her father's decision to send her to a convent. Then 104-year-old Sister Marie Cecile spoke of her memories of the first Armistice Day in her small village in France and of her subsequent decision to join the Order. At some point, one of the sisters commented to another, 'I've known you for 50 years and I never knew that about you!' Whether this new insight could be attributed to the microphone or to what we regard as the almost sacred opportunity to listen to one another's stories is not certain, but the new, stronger connection between the sisters was obvious.

At last the microphone arrived at Sister Josephine, slumped in her wheelchair and hitherto unresponsive (see Figure 13.1). The sister who had just finished telling her story reached across Sister Josephine to pass the microphone to the next sister, commenting, 'Oh, Sister Josephine won't tell a story – she hasn't spoken for years. We just don't want her to feel excluded.' To the amazement of everyone in the circle, Sister Josephine sat up, grabbed the microphone and, clearly and succinctly, told a perfectly formed short story about her first memory of her father, a soldier returned from the First World War when she

Figure 13.1: Sister Josephine slumped in her wheelchair and Sister Mary telling her story

Photo by Pip Hardy

was three years old. At the conclusion of the story, Sister Josephine slumped over once again, and the microphone dropped into her lap.

By some magical combination of skill, experience and a winning way with nuns, my colleague, Tony Sumner, managed to persuade Sister Josephine to retell her story so that he could record it. Unlike most of the other sisters she had no photos, so some picture research was necessary in order to complete her digital story. An old photo of a small girl and another of a First World War soldier were used to enhance the audio recording, reinforce the humanity of her story and highlight both the uniqueness and the universality of her experience. Furthermore, her story, which might otherwise never have been heard, is preserved for posterity in the archive (Turnbull, 2009).

In total 11 digital stories were created. This was accomplished in a variety of ways, depending on the preferences of the individual sisters, and with four facilitators to support the work. Dementia, arthritis and Parkinson's compounded lack of confidence with technology. Facilitators worked closely with storytellers, helping with selection of images, creation of storyboards and editing the videos under the direction of the storytellers. Such careful attention to individual needs and abilities reinforces the DS ethos that 'every story matters' and has enabled these extraordinary stories of service and vocation to be preserved in both the Patient Voices and SHCJ archives.[4]

It is our custom to screen all stories on the last day of the workshop. It was decided that a proper celebration was in order, complete with cake and prosecco. All the sisters in the community were invited to join the storytellers and we duly gathered in the sunny conservatory to rejoice in the accomplishments and the stories of these remarkable women. Most of the sisters who participated in that workshop have now died, so it is even more important that their stories are preserved in the community's archive, where they continue to illuminate the challenges and the joys of vocation, the uniqueness of individual sisters, and the loving and supportive community that cherishes the stories of all its members.

Case study: DigiTales – Silver Stories

Silver Stories was an action research partnership spanning nine organisations across six countries between 2013 and 2015.[5] It was funded by the European Commission's Lifelong Learning: Leonardo da Vinci Transfer of Innovation sub-programme and built upon the results of an earlier, award-winning project, Extending Creative Practice,[6] which ran from 2010 to 2012. The partnership included higher education establishments and smaller practice-based companies that were to 'transfer' DS skills into the higher education environment. The main purpose of the project was to test the use of digital storytelling with older people by training students and professionals who were working with older people in community or residential care settings to use digital storytelling in their work. The stories were also to generate a growing archive that could be used in the training of future students working in, for instance, social work, occupational therapy or nursing and care settings.

In the United Kingdom, DigiTales worked with residents in a sheltered housing scheme near Maldon in Essex. We departed from the 'classic' three-day intensive workshop model and instead ran a programme for eight residents over six months, for half a day per week. One of the most frequently voiced anxieties about participating in a workshop is 'I don't have a story to tell'. To combat this concern, we ran a range of Story Circle games to help participants to 'find' their stories and help them to think about how to use image, text, voice and other music or sound effects to maximise the impact of their storytelling. The supportive atmosphere of the Story Circle enabled the most shy and reticent members of the group to participate.

JM, who had been reluctant to speak, was encouraged by other members of the group to develop a story she started to tell upon passing round the silver teething ring that she had been given by her grandmother and that had survived a bomb blast during the Second World War. Figure 13.2 shows the moment when another participant, DM, encouraged her to develop her story and, despite her shyness and lack of confidence, JM was the first to record her voice-over of 'The Story of the Teething Ring'. The story describes awaiting the return of her father on leave from the Navy, her mother washing her hair at her grandmother's in anticipation, the dropping of a bomb nearby, the discovery that their own flat had been razed to the ground, the finding of a naval hat and the assumption that her father had perished, to the revelation that he had never boarded the train.[7] The story shines a light on the personal 'near-miss' experience of a family that adds another dimension to the idea of what is archived to document 'big' stories such as the impact of the Blitz on London and Londoners. It goes beyond a simple account of what happened, providing context in its descriptions of the family relationships; developing empathy through the detail of washing hair, and Grandmother saying to Mother 'don't go home with your hair all wet'; building an element of suspense when the neighbour knocks on the door to relay the news of the bomb and the finding of the hat; a sense of relief on discovering that the father had not fallen

Figure 13.2: Extract from transcript of Story Circle, 20 March 2015

```
200
201   DM:   Can I just poke in and say I think JM
202         ought to tell her little story again
203         because I thought that was really
204         lovely.... the little ornament,
205         because M hadn't heard that. I
206         thought it was really lovely J.
207
208   JM    [shows her teething ring and a
209         photo]. That is my Mum and Dad.
210         Dad was in the navy and this is a
211         little story. We were bombed out,
212         me and my Mum in London.
213         We...eee, we lost everything (voice
214         cracks). Er... my Mum lost
215         everything. But when ... ... it was
216         just a crater – everything went. My
217         Mum said the bed was still made
218         (others join in – still made, yeah)
219         at the bottom of it. But they
220         managed to get that out for me it's
221         mine [shows the silver figurine] and
222         it's a little – can I give it to you
223         (passes to MW) – it was a key ... not
224         a keyring, a teething ring that my
225         other Nan got me for my first
226         Easter.
227
228   RC:   They got that out?
229
230   MF:   (looking at the teething ring) That's
231         wonderful.
```

victim to the bombing; and a final conclusion showing the teething ring as a talisman that had been with JM all her life. Figure 13.3 shows key images from the story, combining photographs from the family album, archive images and a current image created for the story. The sequencing of family album with 'stock' imagery, anchored by the content of the story and its narration in the storyteller's own voice, at her own pace, using her own words, brings added layers of meaning to the archive imagery of the bombed-out East End of London. It provides an insight into families and family relationships at that time; of neighbours and communities (coming to 'break the news', searching the bombed out site); it enables us not simply to see the shattering of a community in terms of its physical destruction, but also to feel the anxiety, the constant fear of losing one's life or the life of a loved one. The audible crack in the storyteller's voice as she nears the end of the story, as she attempts to control the tears, tells us something about how such experiences can affect a person for the whole of their life. The digital story can, in two or three minutes, take us far beyond the gathering of information from archive material.

Eve's story, 'Who is Bertha?',[8] is the story about the absence of a story. Eve's father was a prisoner of war during the First World War. Her story begins by describing her father, how he met her mother, and how he was a 'carman' before and between the two world wars.[9] Eve had hoped to enlist our help in finding out what had happened to her father while he was a prisoner of war, but in fact, because he was 'only' a private soldier, very little information is recorded. 'The records were not kept very well … all he said was that he worked on a farm and the girl who looked after him was called Bertha – he seemed to like her quite a lot!' (Story Circle, 20 March 2015).[10] Eve's story is a record about the lack of records, a prime example of the prioritisation of some stories over others in archival collections. Listing the few facts that were known by the family, she states, while showing an image of an entry about her father in the war records (Figure 13.4):

> But I always wondered what had happened to him during World War I. We know he was at Ypres – Wipers he used to call it. We know he was hurt in his right arm – he used to like to show me his war wound … we know his regiment – here's the evidence from the war records. But this is all we have, and that is where it stops. However hard you try, when you're looking for the history of ordinary soldiers, and their experiences as prisoners of war, they just don't seem to exist. These documents tell us everything and nothing.

Figure 13.3: Key images from the 'The Story of the Teething Ring'

(a) J's father, thought missing

(b) The teething ring that survived the blast

(c) The teething ring as a lucky talisman

Figure 13.4: War record

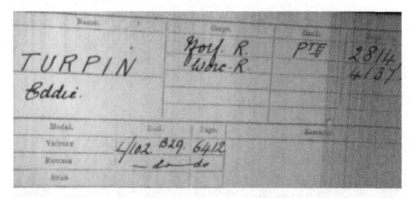

Digital Stories – 'authentic' contributions to archive?

Archival documents or artefacts are usually thought of as 'primary sources', created at the time of the events they describe by people who were there. Many definitions also state that they have been selected (by whom? – our question) as evidence of 'historically significant events'.[11] Archive material is often kept in secure environments, is not freely available (that is, it needs to be requested) and is interpreted by researchers or writers for particular audiences. What archive material, then, is privileged, how is it shared and whose interpretation of its significance is at the fore?

Within DS, the primary source materials may be a storyteller's own personal images – photos from the family album or images specifically created for the digital story. However, they may also use archive or stock images, chosen for their relevance or impact on the telling of the story. They may choose to add music from a completely different context, to guide or influence the viewer's reading of that story. They may embellish the way the story is told, lace it with humour or pathos, anger or bathos. Does the constructed nature of a digital story and its creation, not necessarily at the actual time of the event, make it less authentic? But what could be more authentic than a storyteller's own unique voice, recounting experience in a way which has meaning for *that person*?

Our case studies demonstrate the potential of stories to strengthen communities, by anchoring meaning in place and experience, valuing personal stories and creating valuable artefacts for the archive. Those who participate in DS workshops generally want to share their stories (although some are wary of the potential for their distribution online to be out of their control and limit their distribution to screenings with people that they trust).

DS offers opportunities to preserve the experiences of ordinary people in a way that is under the control of the storyteller, shifting power from interviewer and archivist to individual storyteller in terms of decisions about what is important, and challenging the conventional concept of archive as a repository of data controlled by those whose power has been traditionally unchallenged.

Notes

1 https://www.patientvoices.org.uk/.
2 http://arts.brighton.ac.uk/projects/silver-stories.
3 From Museu da Pessoa website www.museudapessoa.net.
4 The digital stories from this project can be seen at www.patientvoices.org.uk/shcj.htm and www.shcj.org.
5 http://arts.brighton.ac.uk/projects/silver-stories.
6 www.extendingcreativepractice.eu.
7 JM did not wish her story to be uploaded to the internet, but the screen shots show some of the key images used.
8 Who is Bertha? is available on the Silver Stories website at: https://vimeo.com/142780687.
9 A 'carman' was a driver of horse-drawn vehicles for transporting goods, often employed by railway companies.
10 From the transcript of the Story Circle, 20 March 2015, at Hazelwood Court.
11 http://www.kings.cam.ac.uk/archive-centre/introduction-archives/definition/libraries.html.

References

Alexandra, D. (2015) 'The politics of voice and listening; audio–visual anthropology; digital storytelling and co-creative documentary; asylum and contemporary migration in Ireland', PhD thesis, Centre for Transcultural Research and Media Practice, Dublin Institute of Technology, Dublin, Ireland.

Baars, J. (2010) 'Philosophy of Aging, Time and Finitude', in Cole, T.R., Ray, R.E. and Kastenbaum, R. (eds) *A Guide to Humanistic Studies in Aging*, 3rd ed., Baltimore, MD: The Johns Hopkins University Press, pp 105–20.

Baars, J. (2012) 'Critical turns of ageing, narrative and time', *International Journal of Ageing and Later Life*, 7(2): 143–65.

Cobley, P. (2014) *Narrative*, 2nd ed., Abingdon: Routledge.

Cole, T.R., Ray, R.E. and Kastenbaum, R. (2010) *A Guide to Humanistic Studies in Aging*, Baltimore, MD: The Johns Hopkins University Press.

Dunford, M. and Jenkins, T. (2017) *Digital Storytelling Form and Content*, London: Palgrave Macmillan.

Dunford, M. and Rooke, A. (2014) 'Extending Creative Practice', in Gregori-Signes, C. and Brígido-Corachán, *Appraising Digital Storytelling across Educational Contexts*, Valencia: University of Valencia, pp 205–21.

Hartley, J. and McWilliam, K. (2009) *Story Circle: Digital Storytelling around the World*, New York: John Wiley.

Hardy, P. and Sumner, T. (2018) 'The Journey Begins', in Hardy, P. and Sumner, T. (eds) *Cultivating Compassion: How Digital Storytelling is Transforming Healthcare*, 2nd ed., London: Palgrave Macmillan.

Hardy, P. (2007) 'An investigation into the application of the Patient Voices digital stories in healthcare education: quality of learning, policy impact and practice-based value', MSc dissertation, University of Ulster, Belfast.

Hardy, P. (2016) 'Telling tales: The development and impact of digital stories and digital storytelling in healthcare', PhD thesis, Manchester Metropolitan University.

Heymann, E. (2009) 'From darkness into light: New worlds', Pilgrim Projects [online], Available from: www.patientvoices.org.uk/flv/0345pv384.htm [Accessed 26 September 2019].

Heymann, E. (2010) 'The sun also rises', Pilgrim Projects [online], Available from: www.patientvoices.org.uk/flv/0517pv384.htm [Accessed 26 September 2019].

Jamissen, G., Hardy, P., Nordkvelle, Y. and Pleasants, H. (2017) *Digital Storytelling in Higher Education – International Perspectives*, London: Palgrave Macmillan.

Lundby, K. (2008) *Digital Storytelling, Mediatized Stories: Self-Representations in New Media*, Oxford: Peter Lang.

Riessman, C. (1993) *Narrative Analysis*, New York: Sage.

Rooke, A. and Slater, I. (2012) *Extending Creative Practice*, London: Centre for Urban and Community Research, Goldsmiths, University of London [online], Available from: www.extendingcreativepractice.eu [Accessed 26 September 2019].

Thumim, N. (2007) 'Mediating self representations: tensions surrounding "ordinary" participation in public sector projects', PhD thesis, London School of Economics.

Turnbull, J. (2009) 'The feet on the sofa', Pilgrim Projects [online], Available from: www.patientvoices.org.uk/flv/0286pv384.htm [Accessed 26 September 2019].

14

'Wibbly-wobbly timey-wimey' LGBT histories: community archives as boundary objects

Niamh Moore

> People assume that time is a strict progression of cause to effect, but actually from a non-linear non-subjective viewpoint, it's more a bag of wibbly-wobbly timey-wimey stuff.
>
> Steven Moffat, 'Blink',
> episode of *Dr Who*, 9 June 2007

This chapter offers a 'wibbly-wobbly' account of a Lesbian, Gay, Bisexual and Transsexual (LGBT) community history and archiving project, How We Got Here (see also Moore, 2015). The project was initiated by The Proud Trust (TPT), 'home of LGBT+ youth', a regional network of LGBT youth groups across Manchester and North West England, who partnered with a number of organisations, including Schools OUT UK.[1] The project traced three interrelated threads of LGBT activism that were particularly focused on Manchester and the north-west of England, but both the project and the original activism also paid attention to how the city and region are inevitably enmeshed in national and global politics. The three strands of activism centred on:

1. the establishment of the first purpose-built gay centre in Europe, in Manchester in 1988; this is now managed by TPT;
2. work in schools, supporting teachers and pupils, including the setting up and campaigning of Schools OUT UK (formerly called the Gay Teachers' Group);
3. histories of LGBT youth work in Manchester.

Thus, the project also centred on histories of LGBT activism that rarely receive attention – including the campaigning of teachers and youth workers in schools and youth clubs and beyond. Such sites of intergenerational exchange are useful for thinking about change, how change is understood and how what counts as change itself changes over time in the context of LGBT activism. The youth work practised by TPT has a strong emphasis on participation and informal learning. This ethos was reflected in the project, which was conceptualised as participatory community history involving young people from a number of LGBT youth groups across Manchester.

This participatory project, focusing on the creation of queer histories, forms the basis for the current chapter which draws on Susan Leigh Star's (2010) concept of 'boundary objects' to explore the often invisible work of collaboration. In particular, I explore the making of queer transgenerational histories and archives, and highlight differences and tensions across the project, around matters of whose histories are included and whose are excluded.

How we got here

This participatory oral history project was led by TPT but many organisations and individuals were involved and actively participated. Young people belonging to youth groups were trained in oral history skills and were involved in facilitated discussions about LGBT history. They then carried out oral history interviews with older LGBT activists, teachers, youth workers and people who had used LGBT services. The interviews formed part of organised 'memory days' at the LGBT Centre, as well as following the Schools Out Conference. Ultimately all the materials created were deposited in Manchester Central Library's Archives +, a facility for community archives. They were also used to make a number of outputs including YouTube videos, an exhibition and a collaborative book (LGBTYNW, 2015).[2]

The project was funded by the Heritage Lottery Fund in the United Kingdom (UK), which has a strong history of supporting community history projects, including LGBT history projects. The funding supported a project manager, youth workers to carry out some of the work, equipment for recording, transcription costs, artists and a videographer, book design and printing, as well as travel, refreshments and materials on the way. I was fortunate to be a part of the project team and provided input on design and methodology. I also provided training in oral history interviewing skills, worked alongside youth workers and young people on the project outputs, as well as contributing to these. I came to this project as part of ongoing involvement in projects with TPT, sometimes through funding gained by them, sometimes as a volunteer and sometimes through funding gained through academic grants (including a series of Connected Communities projects) – the differences in funding are not irrelevant, as funding changed the governance and everyday practices of projects as well as the nature of outputs planned.

Wibbly-wobbly timey-wimey histories

The use of the term 'wibbly-wobbly timey-wimey' by one of the young people in our first oral history training session was hardly a coincidence. We were working in a building that has often been referred to as a TARDIS (Time And Relative Dimension In Space), the time travel machine from the BBC science fiction series *Dr Who*. This evocation captured an apparent capacity of the building to able to house a multitude of people and stories over time, and to transport people to different realms, parallel universes and to other pasts and presents, and to hold onto the messiness of lives and time. This early recognition of the complexities of time and history was easy for project participants to work with and to do so in ways that also echo recent accounts of 'queer time' – Halberstam's 'queer failure' and Stockton's 'growing sideways' (Stockton, 2009; Halbertsam, 2011).

Like many other LGBT projects, this one emerged out of complex urges to document ephemeral histories, to try and insist on, and mark, a series of changes, while at the same time also recognising that there is much work yet to be done and an ongoing pressing need for LGBT Centres, and for organisations like Schools Out UK. Part of the ambition of the project was to point to the crucial role of youth workers, teachers and young people in LGBT activism. Another ambition was to dislocate London as *the* site of gay activism in the UK. Manchester-based LGBT activists have always been particularly determined, with a long history of displacing London-centrism or national narratives, and with a commitment to developing practices such as LGBT youth work. Such practises do not necessarily flourish to the same extent elsewhere – after all, TPT does not have any other regional counterparts in England or Wales. Shared LGBT stories in Manchester have a wider significance. For example, the anti-Section 28 March in Manchester was much larger than the one in London. 'God's cop', James Anderton, Chief Constable of Greater Manchester (1976–91), made national press for his verbal attacks on gay men, as well as his increased policing of the gay community. The Centre has hosted international solidarity events, including some hugely significant visitors, such as Ugandan gay rights activist, David Kato (later murdered in Uganda in 2011).[3]

The knots of history

One of our early activities – aimed at teasing out some of the complexities of LGBT histories – involved us unfurling four long ribbons across our large meeting room, each ribbon to be put to work to enact the different strands of LGBT lives. We picked up the ribbons and played purposefully with them – we made knots in ribbons to mark specific historic moments, and crossed and tangled the ribbons together to signal moments of connection or tension between the different histories. It was a game with serious intent that was evocative and sometimes painful, as well as being playful and fun. That the trans youth worker was literally bound up in knots with the ribbons was both a demonstration of the complexity of trans lives now, as well as a moment of playful excitement; the exhilaration for some of the sheer significance of having a trans youth worker in the room, centrally involved in the project. That the ribbon for bisexual histories was the one that turned out to be the most lacking in any knotty detail was a potent way of making visible missing histories. This activity was in part inspired by Donna Haraway's work on string games and her use of the game cat's cradle as a way of materialising the work of creating patterns and passing on stories, making new patterns, new knots, with care (Haraway, 1994; Moore, 2017).

Our early ambitions for complexity and care in telling histories remained present throughout the project – but these queer ambitions were sometimes undermined by the exigencies of practice, the tangle of people, professions, passions involved and the relentless march of project time. One enduring memory of the project comes from the first 'Memory Day' held in the Joyce Layland LGBT Centre. The first participants had arrived, they had been paired up with a young person and interviews were taking place in smaller rooms off the main room. New participants were arriving, being offered cups of tea and were looking at some of the materials related to the history of the Centre on the walls, or were sitting around chatting with other arrivals or with those of us tasked with the logistics (looking after the digital recorders, consent forms, batteries and laptops for uploading interviews once they were done). I looked around at one stage and saw that an impromptu focus group had formed in the central communal space. Four people who, it turned out, had been centrally involved in the early years of the Centre had arrived, not all together. They had somehow identified Amelia Lee, youth worker and Strategic Director of TPT, as a key figure and gathered around her, capturing her attention and filling her in on stories about the history of the Centre and their roles in starting

LGBT youth groups and in making the Centre happen. These white, middle-aged professional-looking gay men stayed and talked non-stop for several hours. It was a compelling sight and also a profound moment of recognition of the capacity of projects such as this to draw people (back) in, of the very different histories of involvement in the Centre and of the power of particular stories – of how some stories get told and others remain marginal, and how it can require significant work to bring these other stories to the centre of attention.

As part of this work, not long afterwards and no doubt influenced by that particular event, we decided to organise a separate day for women activists. Although many women have been involved in the Centre over many years and, indeed, the two current strategic and organisational directors of the organisation are women, when it came to getting stories of activists we were faced with the uncomfortable fact that women were less likely to volunteer themselves. Despite organising a separate day for women's stories, not many women attended. This provides an interesting contrast with Feminist Webs – a previous feminist youth work histories project that provided a model for the current project.

Building on Feminist Webs: community archiving as boundary object

Feminist Webs was led by the Young Women's Project, a group affiliated with TPT and involving some of the same people. It is a loose collective of feminist youth workers, young women, academics, artists, archivists and allies who have been collaborating with a focus on reinvigorating feminist practices of youth work and work with girls, in a way that unsettles any sharp separation of academia, activism, archiving and semi-professional domains such as youth work. Central to Feminist Webs has been the process of creating an archive of feminist youth work (oral histories as well as materials from girls' work groups around North West England over the past 40–50 years), and (re)using this archive in a number of ways. It has also involved a participatory oral history project, the creation of an online and physical archive, exhibitions, bringing the archive on tour and a book (Feminist Webs, 2012). While 'how we got here' was a more defined, year-long project, Feminist Webs is an open-ended project about histories and futures of feminist youth work and girls' work in Manchester and the North West. As much as 'how we got here' built on Feminist Webs, this chapter also develops previous work (Moore, 2017), using Susan Leigh Star's conceptualisation of 'boundary objects' as a way of understanding the collaborative working practices of the project involving youth workers, academics, artists, archivists and young people in youth groups, and, in particular, the process of creating an archive.

While the term 'boundary object' can seem a little awkward, it is perhaps an appropriate phrase to describe something that does not quite fit – the awkwardness seems especially appropriate for a queer history project. Star used boundary object as a way of conceptualising collaborative working; for her, the boundary was not intended to point to edges or limits, but rather to point to a collectively generated 'shared space where the sense of here and there are confounded' (Star, 2010: 602–3). The concept of boundary object avoids an account of the work of creating a community archive that would reduce it to a contest between professional and amateur practices, or official institutions and grassroots organisations. Describing Feminist Webs as a boundary object allows us to confront the orthodox sense of the nature of the archive as a formal institution and practice, a ready-made structure into which messy community materials might not fit or that would need to be tidied up and restructured into order to fit into the given orders of the archive. Archive as boundary object draws our attention to the evolving archive and to the ad hoc infrastructures emergent from different but intersecting and overlapping approaches to the archive. So the archive remains in a dynamic relationship with its necessary infrastructures. We can then think of the archive, any archive, as a flexible capacious changing space, rather than a contest between different places and spaces or archival practices. And that it is this flexibility, this wibbly–wobblyness of the sharedness of the meaning, that holds people together who have different understandings of the archive.

In using the idea of boundary object here, I am developing and extending work on community archiving. This particularly includes work initiated by Andrew Flinn and colleagues on community archives, as well as those writing on feminist archival practices (Flinn, 2007; Flinn et al, 2009; Eichhorn, 2010, 2013; Stevens et al, 2010) and work on post-custodialism, including Terry Cook's account of four archival paradigms, which situates community archiving as a key challenge and opportunity for the archival profession (Cook, 2013).

I was particularly drawn by Star's own account of the origins of the model – she noticed that some projects first worked on building consensus and then cooperation could begin; but in other groups there was no consensus 'but cooperation continued, often unproblematically' (Star, 2010: 604). And this is what I noticed in Feminist Webs from the beginning. There were lots of different people involved, and we were all working together and managing to collaborate to produce this unwieldy project, Feminist Webs, that drew us in and spoke to our different commitments. It also felt as if no one person fully owned the project, but at the same time we all felt responsible, if in different ways. Feminist Webs was compelling and tangible enough that we were all drawn in and felt we had something to contribute, and at the same time it was vague enough that we all felt that it had some significance and value for each of us individually, in different sectors, and had something that we could take away that would resonate in our own 'locals', as Star would say (Burman, 2004: 370; Star, 2010). Arguably it was the success of Feminist Webs that led to the idea of a further project that would build on the same model. While many of the practices from Feminist Webs carried over to How We Got Here, there were also adaptations. How We Got Here was planned as a time-bound project, over the one year of funding, not as an ongoing project.

Key to the concept of 'boundary object' is the notion of 'interpretative flexibility', which can be seen in how Feminist Webs flourishes as an entity that is a youth work resource, a grassroots community archive and a site of feminist activism, all at the same time. Star (2010: 602) also pointed to how boundary objects often involve the creation of ad hoc 'boundary infrastructures' to support the non-standard working practices that emerge in these kinds of collaborations. At the same time, existing domains and infrastructures do not disappear, so she recognised the process of 'tacking back and forth' between well-structured local and particular versions of boundary objects, and vaguer more general shared versions. This is suggestive of the challenges both to professional archival standards and to academic research that are posed by community archiving projects. While Feminist Webs tacks back and forth across the domains of youth work, academia, community and activism, as well as across amateur and professional archival and research practices, other feminist and community archives have taken different approaches (see, for example, Nestle, 1998 on the Lesbian Herstory Archives in New York).

Interpretive in/flexibility and ad hoc boundary infrastructures: boundary object as diagnostic

I suggested previously that 'tracing the extent to which community archives are more or less successful in creating boundary objects might help to explain why some projects flourish more than others' (Moore, 2017: 134; see also Fox, 2011). Turning to examine the flexible infrastructures of the collaborative process as a key site for thinking through success and failure may be productive. There are times when the interpretive flexibility, the ad hoc boundary infrastructures and the tacking back and forth between different 'locals' does not always work and tensions emerge. Star's model does not necessarily provide an account of if and when these tensions should be ameliorated or accommodated.

There was one, almost fleeting, incident late in the project, close to the deadline to get our book, *Prejudice and Pride*, which drew on the oral history interviews, to the printer, when we ceased to hold onto the complexity of wibbly wobbly LGBT histories. One participant, a gay man who had been interviewed as part of the project, learned that Peter Tatchell, a well-known gay activist in the UK, and an often controversial figure, was also interviewed and involved in the project.[4] After some equivocation, he reluctantly withdrew his interview from the project, because he did not want to be associated with, and implicated in, a project and a publication that also involved Tatchell. He was concerned with how Tatchell dominated in UK gay politics, how he knew so many people and had so many contacts, that his reach was extensive – as indeed was demonstrated by his showing up in this Manchester-based project. He was also concerned about Tatchell's politics, about his treatment of other queer activists and academics, and in particular that his work contributes to rather than contests discourses of racism and Islamophobia. Tatchell has long been controversial, from public outing of closeted public figures, especially those who in their public roles, as MPs, teachers and so on, were actually involved in implementing homophobic legislation, policies or practices. More recently, Tatchell has again been at the centre of controversy over the silencing of work that criticises him. An edited collection, *Out of Place: Interrogating Silences in Queerness/ Raciality* (Kunstman and Miyake, 2008), which carried a chapter by two queer junior academics, briefly critiqued Tatchell's work, as part of a wider argument about gay imperialism, about how gay rights is increasing taken up as a marker of western 'progress' against the supposed 'backwardness' of certain forms of racialisation. In this way gay rights is drawn into justifications for certain political interventions, including the War on Terror. The chapter was described by Tatchell as 'false and libelous' (Ahmed, 2011: 120). The book publisher, a small independent, feminist press, Raw Nerve Books in York, issued an apology, or perhaps was forced to issue an apology, and ultimately closed down (Ahmed, 2011). One consequence is that the collection is now no longer in print. While Tatchell subsequently argued that he did not actually threaten the authors with litigation, Sara Ahmed suggested in her article on the controversy that it does not matter whether he did or not; the use of the language of 'libel' was sufficient (Ahmed, 2011: footnote 2). Tatchell's actions, his threats, whether literal or figurative, have been widely understood as enacting the kind of silencing and censorship that he himself was objecting to, as closing down debate about queerness and raciality, and as resulting in one of the first collections on queer raciality in the UK being silenced.

Because Tatchell was drawn into our project, one participant withdrew their interview from our archive and from our book; their story would have provided a rather different account of solidarities with gay activists, including an account of David Kato's visit to the Centre. This was a moment in the project when some stories prevailed over others, when some histories were told and not others. In the end, there are not many quotes from Peter Tatchell in the final book. This was not by design, but rather echoed how independently different authors worked on different chapters and made their own decisions about what quotes to include. Even though his testimony is not dominant, Tatchell is in the book, and his influence prevails. And other gay activists are not; other gay politics are not.

With the deadline for the printer looming in days, those of us writing and editing chapters, myself included, were frantically writing, rewriting, editing drafts. We were all exhausted. I tried, arguably half-heartedly, to intervene, to suggest a need to stop and think about an interview withdrawn, about whether Tatchell should be in 'our' book, about the stories that were being told and the stories that were being silenced. My feeble intervention might have been seen as a certain kind of academic obsession about detail, and an unworkable and impracticable intervention at this late stage; my half-heartedness might have been anticipating these responses, rightly or wrongly. It was not 'my' book alone; I did not feel as if I could take a stand or veto, insist on the standards that prevailed in my 'local'. The book went to the printer. Interpretive flexibilities congealed and the ad hoc boundary infrastructures that had sustained the movement back and forth between different locals solidified in one particular configuration. The ambition to undermine 'London-centric' histories and the metropolitan centre was weakened.

Queer failures

This chapter has used a collaborative archival project to describe ways in which communities are remaking archives and providing new models of collaborative working in a post-custodial landscape.

Star's model of the boundary object provides insight into the often invisible processes of collaborative working, beyond oppositional models of communities against archivists (or vice versa). Conceiving of community archives as boundary objects allows a focus on the dynamic nature of an emergent archive – and for attention to ad hoc and flexible infrastructures being built around archival materials and their communities. This is a generative alternative to imposing formal structures on community archives or conceiving of community archives as lacking professionalism and standards. There might yet be a shift from talking about 'official archives' and 'community archives', to talking about archives and their infrastructures, without the need for modifiers that suggest a hierarchy of value, or expertise or professionalism.

While Fox's work (2011) has drawn attention to using the boundary object as a mode of diagnosis and analysis, allowing us to see which projects might succeed, and which fail, Star's conceptualisation of the 'interpretative flexibility' and ad hoc 'boundary infrastructures' necessary for boundary objects provides further tools for tracing the work of collaboration, for recognising and diagnosing success and failure, for describing and analysing what happened and why. We created and documented some histories and failed to tell others. There was a moment when different queer histories – and futures – were possible, before some domains were overdetermined and the boundary infrastructures collapsed into their local specificities, and communication across boundaries failed. Halberstam (2011) has given 'queer failure' a recuperative gloss, for understandable reasons, and when writing in the context of the failure of queer lives to always measure up to heteronormative lives, this account has some purchase. The recuperative potential of queer failure can feel different when we don't live up to our queer intentions to do the best we can by and with other queers.

Acknowledgements

Thanks to Amelia Lee for the invitation to be involved in the project, and to all Feminist Webbers for the ongoing feminist fun. Thanks also to Kim Beasley for discussions on post-custodialism and community archiving; and to Ali Hanbury and Joan Haran for comments on an earlier draft.

Notes

[1] See https://www.theproudtrust.org/. The Proud Trust were previously named Lesbian, Gay, Bisexual, Trans Youth North West (LGBTYNW), and changed their name in 2016.

[2] The videos are available on The Proud Trust YouTube channel https:// www.youtube.com/user/LGBTYouthNorthWest. The films from this project are not specifically identified as such, but can be identified as they are the interviews with a rainbow flag as a backdrop.

[3] See also http://queerbeyondlondon.com/ for another exploration of gay life in other cities in the UK.

[4] Tatchell was drawn into the project through Schools Out; some key figures in Schools Out knew him and at some point someone had asked him to get on board, arguably largely because as a public figure he could bring some further media attention to the 40th anniversary conference of Schools Out, as well as to the project more broadly.

References

Ahmed, S. (2011) 'Problematic proximities: Or why critiques of gay imperialism matter', *Feminist Legal Studies*, 19(2): 119–32.

Burman, E. (2004) 'Boundary objects and group analysis: Between psychoanalysis and social theory', *Group Analysis*, 37(3), 361–79.

Cook, T. (2013) 'Evidence, memory, identity, and community: Four shifting archival paradigms', *Archival Science*, 13(2): 95–120.

Eichhorn, K. (2010) 'D.I.Y. collectors, archiving scholars, and activist librarians: legitimizing feminist knowledge and cultural production since 1990', *Women's Studies*, 39(6): 622–46.

Eichhorn, K. (2013). *The Archival Turn in Feminism: Outrage in Order*, Philadelphia, PA: Temple University Press.

Feminist Webs (2012) *The Exciting Life of Being a Woman: A Handbook for Women and Girls*, Bristol, HammerOn Press.

Flinn, A. (2007) 'Community histories, community archives: Some opportunities and challenges 1', *Journal of the Society of Archivists*, 28(2): 151–76.

Flinn, A., Stevens, M. and Shepherd, E. (2009) 'Whose memories, whose archives? Independent community archives, autonomy and the mainstream', *Archival Science*, 9(1): 71–86.

Fox, N. (2011) 'Boundary objects, social meanings and the success of new technologies', *Sociology*, 45(1): 70–85.

Halberstam, J. (2011) *The Queer Art of Failure*, Durham, NC: Duke University Press.

Haraway, D. J. (1994) 'A game of cat's cradle: Science studies, feminist theory, cultural studies', *Configurations: A Journal of Literature, Science, and Technology*, 2(1): 59–71.

Kuntsman, A. and Miyake, E. (2008) *Out of Place: Interrogating Silences in Queerness/Raciality*, York: Raw Nerve Books.

LGBTYNW (ed.) (2015) *Prejudice and Pride: LGBT Activist Stories from Manchester and Beyond*, Bristol, HammerOn Press.

Moffat, S. (2007) 'Blink', *Doctor Who*, BBC, 9 June.

Moore, N. (2015) 'Wibbly Wobbly Timey Wimey LGBT Histories', in LGBT YNW (ed.) *Prejudice and Pride: LGBT Activist Stories from Manchester and Beyond*, Bristol, HammerOn Press, pp 13–31.

Moore, N. (2017) 'Weaving an Archival Imaginary: Researching Community Archives', in Moore, N., Salter, A., Stanley, L. and Tamboukou, M., *The Archive Project: Archival Research in the Social Sciences*, London: Routledge, pp 129–52.

Nestle, J. (1998) 'The will to remember: the Lesbian Herstory Archives of New York', *Journal of Homosexuality*, 34(3–4): 225–35.

Star, S.L. (2010) 'This is not a boundary object: Reflections on the origin of a concept', *Science, Technology, & Human Values*, 35(5): 601–17.

Stevens, M., Flinn, A. and Shepherd, E. (2010) 'New frameworks for community engagement in the archive sector: from handing over to handing on', *International Journal of Heritage Studies*, 16(1–2): 59–76.

Stockton, K. (2009) *The Queer Child, or Growing Sideways in the Twentieth Century*, Durham, NC: Duke University Press.

15

Locating the Black archive

*Hannah Ishmael, Ego Ahaiwe Sowinski, Kelly Foster,
Etienne Joseph and Nathan E. Richards*

There is a definite desire and determination to have history,
well documented, widely known at least within race circles,
and administered as a stimulating and inspiring tradition for
the coming generations.

Schomburg, 1925: 215

I hoped that my relatively insignificant memories would
provide a starting point for developing a collective memory
and cultural archive to which other people who knew
Olive [Morris] could contribute. I felt that those of us who
had known Olive needed to make sure that we passed the
memories on.

Obi, 2010: 7

We have it if we look for [our history]. It's in the oral
history testimonies, it's in the oral tradition, it's in sculpture,
it's in music. It's always been there in culture, but it's also
in the record offices, it's in the cemeteries, it's in the hard
documented evidence. So we want to combine those
kinds of tangible and intangible heritage and start to tell
fascinating stories through this archive.

Paul Reid, Director of Black Cultural Archives[1]

Introduction

Reflecting on Stuart Hall's *Constituting an Archive* (2001), we embrace
the concept of the 'living archive' that he describes as 'present, ongoing, continuing, unfinished, open-ended' (Hall, 2001: 89). This
affords us the space to practically and theoretically comprehend 'how
heterogeneous a practice collecting and archiving is' (Hall, 2001: 91)
and to interrogate the concept of archives and archival practice, outside
traditional frameworks. Perhaps more importantly, we are cautioned

against accepting the burden of a tradition whose tenets construct the archive as a 'prison-house of the past' (Hall, 2001: 89) and to broaden our view on what 'constitutes' archival practice in the African Diaspora.

Taking this concept of 'living heritage' as a starting point, we will show the ways in which focusng on tangibility and intangibility, the formal and the informal, can be used to stretch the concepts of archival practice. We understand archival practice in its broadest sense to include not only traditional documentary practice, but also song, dance and the digital. Throughout this work we highlight the intellectual framework(s) within which we are working; the intellectual forebears who have guided our thinking as well as those whose work we have written about. These have included Arthur Schomburg, Toyin Falola and V.Y. Mudimbe among others. We place value on the cultural and intellectual traditions, tangible and intangible, found within the Caribbean, Africa and across the Diaspora. Accordingly, we acknowledge that the institutions, organisations, concepts and practices we discuss here have a 'pre-history' both internationally and here in the United Kingdom (UK); a prehistory inseparable from the development of the intellectual and cultural history of African and Caribbean communities in the Diaspora. Despite this, we are yet to develop an archival science capable of dealing with these complexities. The issue is further vexed when we consider the implications of these traces in the digital realm. The Western habit of prioritising the physical, over time, could conceivably result in an historical amnesia, particularly for African heritage, induced by archival theories and practices that are simply not fit for purpose (Marable, 2006: 22).

Our contribution to this volume gives us the opportunity to consider the ways in which Black-led archival practices in the UK have historically sought to both disrupt and define heritage practices. Unlike Jenkinson (1922) and the myth of archival neutrality, we make a claim for the active, political and cultural incursions, disruptions and interventions in the heritage sector by Black-led archives and heritage practitioners. We are mindful that this subjectivity should not end with the act of recording. Hall reminds us that a collection, whether tangible or intangible, is simply a beginning. We are therefore interested in the ways in which history and heritage are recorded, remixed, reused and repurposed for our contemporary uses. We want to suggest that Black Cultural Archives' Director Paul Reid's ambition to 'tell fascinating stories' (Ellis-Petersen, 2017) through the combination of tangible and intangible heritage is representative of a re-emerging current of conscious thought and action in the UK's

Black heritage practice. This chapter is intended to serve as a catalyst in the ongoing reintegration of these tangible and intangible aspects in African and Diasporan heritage working.

Of readers

In the 1920s, Arthur Schomburg, founder of the Schomburg Center for Research in Black Culture in New York, saw an obligation to harness heritage materials to 'remake his past in order to make his future' (Schomburg, 1925: 231). His work heralded a (re)construction of African and African Diaspora archives that has continued until the present day. The collection and publication of materials corroborating the existence and achievements of people of African heritage has enabled successive generations to engage in the practice of Sankofa – to 'go back and fetch it' for use in the present (Temple, 2010: 137). 'Living' heritage as embodied through Sankofa, and the blueprint laid down by Schomburg, is the 'constituting' moment for three archives in London, the Black Cultural Archives (BCA), the George Padmore Institute (GPI) and the Huntley Collection deposited at the London Metropolitan Archives (HCLMA), which is administered by the Friends of the Huntley Archives. There is not scope to detail their individual histories, but in the space in which they overlap it is clear that their focus on collection is an active and functional practice of Sankofa. Their collection of material seeks to anchor the contemporary experiences of the Black communities in Britain to the history of political activity of the Caribbean and the African Diaspora. This political activity includes the ending of the Atlantic Slave Trade and spans the decline of Empire and decolonisation. These institutions can be considered as touchstones and memorials to this history of activity, as well as holding both the tangible and intangible manifestations of this history.

These three archives were borne out of the fights of the Black, specifically African Caribbean, communities in the UK within the sphere of educational activism. Their founders wanted to ensure that Black children, newly migrated or born in the UK, were provided with resources that positively reflected their African heritage. The founders of BCA wanted to provide educational resources to be used within the education system to provide positive reference points and role models for Black children (Walker, 1993), while the founders of GPI and HCLMA were actively involved with the creation of the Black Supplementary School movement (Andrews, 2013). They provided independent and autonomous schools, often operating on

Saturday mornings. These institutions offered full alternative curricula focusing on African history and heritage, while providing support with reading, writing and mathematics (Warmington, 2014). Many of these educational resources drew on the histories of resistance for the Caribbean community, highlighting key individuals and groups within the Pan-African movement who fought and overcame racism and colonialism within the Caribbean, Africa and the UK. Returning to Hall and his 'living archive' (Hall, 2001), such initiatives invoked the ancestral and foregrounded the functional – standing, as Hall expresses it, 'in an active, dialogic relation to the questions which the present puts to the past' (Hall, 2001: 92): being functional implies being *practical*, being *useful*, being *active*. At their core, all these organisations attempt to actively capture the experiences of the Black communities in the UK to ensure that a fuller and more balanced record of the history of the 20th century can be told. For the founders, one of the key purposes of the collection of tangible archival material was to counteract the negative stereotypes of Black communities; focusing instead on positive material that evidenced the contributions of Black people to the historical development of the UK and Europe. Equally important was the provision of resources that showed how Black communities have been active agents in social change.

Of rituals

Sankofa as archival practice need not be confined to the searchroom, classroom, exhibition hall or lecture theatre. Professor Toyin Falola's positioning of 'ritual archives' (Falola, 2016), for example, transfigures the archive as we have been taught it into forms accommodating of active, physical and metaphysical cultural expressions. Falola challenges the 'conventions of Western archives. Namely, what is deemed worthy of preservation and organization as data… [and the restriction of] archives inside the location of the library or university or museum' (Falola, 2016). He simultaneously applies 'the techniques and resources of academic archives' to the traditions and practices of his people whenever it is beneficial to do so. It is this spirit that our reconfiguration channels: a cohabitation of Western and non-Western archival principles calibrated in favour of cultural understandings and philosophies that are familiar to Black people. Toyin Falola's schema for ritual archives includes: 'images … performances … languages … literatures … philosophies … the visible and invisible world … the non-world … sounds … orality … musical compositions … dancing…' (Falola, 2016)

Transposing Falola's ideas from their Yoruba-infused epistemological foundations to the UK's cultural landscape is an exercise that bears much fruit. Applying the mindset of the ritual archive to Notting Hill Carnival in the UK, for example, allows what might have been thought of as an ephemeral and largely intangible event to be considered in archival terms. Cast in this light, the Carnival is an active repository for the continuing traditions of the Caribbean on the streets of the UK. Theorists have pointed to the role of carnival as a vehicle for transmitting and sharing Caribbean history and culture (Bastian, 2009). This transmission operates through the lyrics of the traditional music of calypso as social critique and historical record, in addition to the use of masquerade to teach aspects of Caribbean history (Owusu and Ross, 1988). The development of Notting Hill Carnival also highlights key themes in the history of the Black communities in the UK, particularly the melding of different traditions from across the Caribbean, and later from across the African Diaspora more broadly. The origins of Notting Hill Carnival are hotly contested. But, whatever its origins, London's Carnival has its roots not only within the Trinidadian carnival tradition but with cross-cultural elements such as the inclusion of Jamaican reggae sound systems during the 1970s (Owusu and Ross, 1988). This bringing together of cultures from across the Caribbean has created a uniquely British event.

As well as the Carnival itself being representative of historical tradition, a physical enactment of Caribbean culture and artistic creativity, it was also a site of political and cultural agitation during the late 1970s and 1980s (Race Today Collective, 1977). Notting Hill Carnival became a visible legacy of the Caribbean community in the UK and to this day remains under threat with ongoing calls for closure (Mcleod, 2016). At the same time, it is celebrated and is a major draw for visitors to London during the August Bank Holiday when it is held (Time Out London, 2017). It is a vehicle for transmitting and validating historical social and cultural traditions, and also ensures that these traditions and experiences contribute to the development of new ones. The ephemeral and intangible nature of the Carnival makes it difficult to capture, but perhaps there is the need to rethink the very idea of 'capturing' an event if we are to truly understand the active nature of Black heritage. For many, the participation in Notting Hill Carnival and the fight for it to take place on the streets represent aspects of the struggle to ensure that it continues to live on and inspire new generations. It is in this act of living and regeneration that its true preservation occurs.

Capture, reification and privileged access have been at the heart of the Western archival endeavour since its very inception (Jenkinson,

1922; Schellenberg, 1956). It is therefore no exaggeration to label the application of living principles to the Black archive as a decolonial act. The Decolonising the Archive organisation, of which one of the authors is a co-founder, focuses on independent heritage practice by people of Africän descent (Decolonising The Archive, 2017). Its recent (2017) Forward Ever project deploys material archives mostly created and housed outside Western institutions, with no demand for external funding. The project revisited the Grenadian Revolution (1979–83), using film, music, movement, physical archives and orality. Project sessions presented archives relating to the activities of the People's Revolutionary Government of Grenada within a therapeutic context,[2] that of an 'Emotional Emancipation Circle',[3] followed by an informal post-workshop 'grounding' allowing space for feedback on the main workshop, socialising and a little dancing. The core intentions of the workshop were to explore the psychological impact of the revolution in Grenada (and other allied movements) on the wider African Diaspora. This exploration was used as a foundation for developing strategies for material and psychological resilience among the participants and their wider networks.

The workshop intervention cannot be understood as a religious ritual of the kind of which Falola speaks. Still, the use of images (ambient projections in the space and as part of more traditional presentation of archival material), performance (both as music, and workshop facilitation), languages/orality (communication in patois, pidgins and creoles), dance (as a social element performing shared cultural understandings) and philosophies (the invocation of the human circle as a metaphor for the African philosophies of collective interdependence and continuity articulated by Mbiti (Mbiti, 1969) allow bold connecting lines to be drawn to his theory and practice of 'ritual archives'. Important to the understanding they seek to furnish is the fact that each 'living' element is in itself archival, 'intangible heritage' referencing the centuries of nature and nurture that participants bring to the space. Walidah Imarisha puts it thus: 'the past is never really past. What those who came before survived, what they protected, what they grew in hostile soil -- that is as present as the air we are all breathing. All moments of time live as one' (Imarisha 2017).

Let us not be naïve, however – the archive as we know it can never truly be decolonised. It is scarcely possible in 2018 to apprehend, theorise, constitute or deploy an archive divorced from the 'archontic' principles encouraging authority to be drawn from those who possess, classify and interpret the material archive (Derrida, 1998: 3).

However, the common function of 'the archive' across cultures – as a repository of memory – invites the cutting, splicing, dubbing and remixing of Western and non-Western ontologies, methodologies and epistemologies; giving rise to forms that are at once brand new and second-hand.

Of remixing

Outside the formal realm of participatory practice, Black public heritage engagement online has taken on more dynamic, social and creative forms. In her essay 'Techno-Vernacular Creativity and Innovation Across the African Diaspora and Global South', Dr Nettrice Gaskins provides a framework that affords us insight into the ways Black communities engage, employ, exploit and create technologies that inform, and are informed by, their cultural realities and existing technological practices. Gaskins calls this culturally specific engagement the 'techno-vernacular' (Gaskins, forthcoming). While Gaskins's work is principally concerned with understanding how Black and Latin American communities enter so-called STEM subjects (science, technology, engineering and mathematics) via their embodied and existing creative modalities, her framework provides us with a point of entry to begin to think about the ways Black communities have traditionally interrogated, preserved and performed the past; as well as the tools and institutions they have developed to facilitate that process – their 'techno-vernacular' of the past.

Institutions such as masquerade, ancestral veneration and carnival, and technologies such as drumming, sculpture, dance and oral traditions are well-established modalities of the past developed by Black communities. These creative technologies and institutions are grounded in participatory and performative practices and retain a dynamic and often ephemeral quality. We are beginning to see new iterations of these technologies and institutions of the past as they merge, define and are redefined by contemporary digital technologies.

Reappropriation, improvisation and conceptual remixing are all central tenets of Gaskins' framework, and we see these activities emerging among African descended heritage enthusiasts online, though primarily outside the formal heritage realm. Institutional digital, and digitised archives are being mined, unhoused (as Steven Blevins writes) from their colonial epistemologies, to be performed and engaged online as part of a performative and participatory practice: 'If the archive houses, such performances of public history unhouse, materializing the past in and as present, and making the past relevant for – and indispensable to – public discussion and debate' (Blevins, 2016: 11).

In addition to the mining and remixing of formalised collections, Black communities are increasingly contributing and preserving their own material, as well as carrying out their own interpretative processes to ensure the past retains relevance to the present.

Black in the Day (BITD) (blackintheday.co.uk, 2017) is a recent heritage project that regards itself as a digital archive; it collects images of what the project co-ordinators see as an oft-neglected theme in formal archival institutions – everyday Black life. The project scans a range of photographs that depict Black African and Caribbean communities in Britain over the last five decades: house parties, coach trips, work and school friends, lovers on cold rocky beaches, smiling children with birthday presents in hand, grandparents in their Sunday best.

Beyond the everydayness of the images BITD collects (the filling in of life beyond protest, conflict and racism), what sets this project apart from more formal archives, and is arguably its strength, is its collection methods and access model. Images can be submitted by anyone online after agreeing to rights and usage terms, with no prohibition on themes or period, and contributors are free to add the metadata and tags they deem fitting. Two thirds of the project's acquisitions are gained at what the coordinators call 'scanning socials'. These events have been hosted at various institutions across London, including the Victoria and Albert Museum and SPACE. While Lovers Rock music plays raucously in the background, contributors mingle, discussing the photographs and memories they have chosen to have scanned, attributed and uploaded to the project's cloud-server – with the computational process projected onto the wall for all to see.

The images lack a level of metadata attribution for the co-ordinators' long-term goals – to become a resource for teaching and scholarship. However, as a brainchild of individuals who have grown up sharpening their social, cultural, and even historical, knowledge via a range of transnational participatory digital platforms, BITD's activities fit into the emerging techno-vernacular of African Diaspora communities. They are a heritage Instagram for millennials, both creative and performative, and above all else are a shareable experience. BITD's aims for the images to be freely available online, under a Creative Commons licence with remix and reuse an accepted, and expected, part of the collection's function.

There is an increasing number of projects that illustrate the merger of traditional memory vernacular and contemporary digital technologies.

For example, the sharing of video footage of Igbo masquerade ceremonies with Diaspora populations via YouTube and other participatory networks; the collection and digitisation performance, art and symbolism and their use in immersive technologies. These practices ground archival material in more context-rich environments (Richards, forthcoming)

Engagement with Black heritage online is visceral, creative, dynamic, and like yesterday's news content it exists for a moment on newsfeeds before fading. Black digital heritage, and the emerging techno-vernacular, is facilitating the production of content akin to mnemonic devices; it encourages participation in collective remembering, while folding the past into the present moment to forge new, subjective, meaning around it. Online, unburdened by the lore and power dynamics of traditional practices, we are beginning to see an engagement with African and African Diaspora heritage that reflects the memory traditions of African communities. As discussed by V.Y. Mudimbe, empowered by the visual, sonic and dynamic potential of the digital:

> Africans tell, sing, produce (through dance, recitation, marionette puppets), sculpt, and paint their history. Just like other peoples, they have always sought to master their past, have had their historic discourses which render and interpret the facts of the past, placing them in an explicative and aesthetic frame producing the sense of their past. This sense of the past creates a line between the past, the present, and the future of Africa. This sense allows the production, in the domain of a historic science now enlarged to fit the dimensions of the world, of a discourse which is useful, true, and believable in itself as well as in its relationship with the facts that it interprets. (Mudimbe and Jewsiewicki, 1993: 3)

Conclusion

The time is ripe to (re)locate, revisit and renew theories and practices of 'Black archives'. The decolonial project set forth by Chinweizu, Wa Thiong'o, Diop (Chinweizu, 1987; Wa Thiong'o, 1986; Diop, 1996) and others has breached the walls of the archival institution. African and African-descended heritage practitioners are attempting to decolonise concepts of the archive formed *about us* rather than *for us*; reaching beyond an intellectual remaking of an African past towards a living, breathing and *healing* forging of African and Diasporan futures.

While we are conscious that this complexity is not unique to Black communities, we are hopeful that taking these active approaches to locating and working with our heritage might serve as inspiration for others grappling with the re-visioning of the archive to accommodate their own. The loud grating of our cultural understandings against the accepted body of archival science galvanises our determination to pick up the baton held out by those who have come before. We leverage our cognisance of Western and non-Western approaches to heritage working in order to develop new ways of working and to define our own practices. In committing aspects of our developing theories, methodologies and ideas to print. We increase the probability of building a critical mass, a tipping point of theory and practice, creating, as Hall, Falola, Imarisha and others have done for us, a space from which to 'reopen the closed structures into which they have ossified' (Hall, 2001: 89).

About us

Transmission is a group of five individuals who share thoughts and ideas on the current heritage landscape. We are developing a framework for interrogating what it means to be a Black archive, advocate and/ or archivist in the 21st century with a view to share skills and build capacity within the sector.

Notes

[1]　Comments made by Paul Reid following the unveiling of the Black Cultural Archives in 2014. For more context and information, please access the following link: https://www.theguardian.com/culture/2014/jul/29/black-cultural-archives-new-centre-brixton.

[2]　Delivered by the Caribbean Labour Solidarity organisation.

[3]　Hosted by African-centred psychologists Rameri Moukam and Davy Hay.

References

Andrews, M. (2013) *Doing Nothing is Not an Option*, London: Krik Krak.

Bastian, J. (2009) '"Play mas": Carnival in the archives and the archives in carnival: records and community identity in the US Virgin Islands', *Archival Science*, 9: 113–25.

BlackintheDay.co.uk (2017) *Black in the Day* [online], Available from: http://blackintheday.co.uk [Accessed 13 August 2017].

Blevins, S. (2016) *Living Cargo: How Black Britain Performs its Past*, Twin Cities: University of Minnesota Press.

Chinweizu (1987) *Decolonising the African Mind*, Lagos: Pero Press.

Decolonising The Archive (2017) 'Forward ever' [online], Available from: http://decolonisingthearchive.com/forward-ever/ [Accessed 29 July 2017].

Derrida, J. (1998) *Archive Fever: A Freudian Impression*, Chicago: University of Chicago Press.

Diop, C.A. (1996) *Towards the African Renaissance*, London: Karnak House.

Ellis-Petersen, H. (2017) 'Black Cultural Archives unveils new centre in Brixton' [online], Available from: https://www.theguardian.com/culture/2014/jul/29/black-cultural-archives-new-centre-brixton [Accessed 23 August 2017].

Falola, T. (2016) 'Ritual archives' [online], Available from: https://www.loc.gov/today/cyberlc/feature_wdesc.php?rec=7711 [Accessed 23 August 2017].

Gaskins, N. (forthcoming) 'Techno-Vernacular Creativity and Innovation Across the African Diaspora and Global South', in Benjamin, R. (ed.) *Captivating Technology: Race, Technoscience and the Carceral Imagination*, Durham, NC: Duke University Press.

Hall, S. (2001) 'Constituting an archive', *Third Text*, 15(54): 89–92.

Imarisha, W. (2017) 'Sankofa, survival and science fiction: a graduation speech' [online], Available from: http://www.walidah.com/blog/2016/6/12/sankofa-survival-and-science-fiction-a-graduation-speech [Accessed 23 August 2017].

Jenkinson, H. (1922) *A Manual of Archive Administration*, Oxford: The Clarendon Press.

Marable, M. (2006) *Living Black History: How Re-imagining the African American Past can Remake America's Racial Future*, New York: Basic Civitas.

Mbiti, J.S. (1969) *African Religions and Philosophy*, London: Heinemann.

Mcleod, M., 2016. *Why is Notting Hill carnival's success always measured by its crime levels?* Available at: https://www.theguardian.com/commentisfree/2016/sep/01/notting-hill-carnival-success-crime-rate-glastonbury-london-culture. [Accessed 4 April 2018].

Mudimbe, V.Y. and Jewsiewicki, B, 1993. Africans' Memories and Contemporary History of Africa. *History and Theory* 32(4): 1-11.

Obi, L. (2010) 'Remembering Olive: Time to Pass the Memories On', in Colin, A., Lopez De La Torre, A. and Springer, K. (eds) *Do You Remember Olive Morris?*, London: Remembering Olive Collective (ROC), Gasworks.

Owusu, K. and Ross, J. (1988) *Behind the Masquerade*, Edgware: Arts Media Group.

Race Today Collective (1977) *The Road Make to Walk on Carnival Day*, London: Race Today Collective.

Richards, N.E (forthcoming) 'The Black British past: History memory and the digital', PhD thesis, University of Sussex.

Schellenberg, T.R. (1956) *Modern Archives: Principles and Techniques*, Chicago: Society of American Archivists (1996 reprint).

Schomburg, A. (1925) 'The Negro Digs Up His Past', in Locke, A. (ed.) *The New Negro*, New York: Simon and Schuster (1997 reprint).

Temple, C.N. (2010) The Emergence of Sankofa Practice in the United States: A Modern History. *Journal of Black Studies* 41(1): 127-150.

Time Out London (2017) 'Notting Hill Carnival' [online], Available from: https://www.timeout.com/london/things-to-do/notting-hill-carnival [Accessed 23 August 2017].

Walker, S. (1993) 'Directors Report', BCA/1/1/1. [Document], Black Cultural Archives.

Warmington, P. (2014) *Black British Intellectuals and Education: Multiculturalism's Hidden History*, London: Routledge.

Wa Thiong'o, N. (1986) *Decolonising the Mind*, London: Heinemann.

16

The public and the relational: the collaborative practices of the Inclusive Archive of Learning Disability History

*Helen Graham, Victoria Green, Kassie Headon,
Nigel Ingham, Sue Ledger, Andy Minnion,
Row Richards and Liz Tilley*

Q: Why is it important that people with learning disabilities tell their stories?
A: I think it's to let other people know what's happened to them and make it aware of people so that it doesn't happen. People doesn't go around hurting other people, it's not fair. So I think if they write their story it makes people aware, because years ago it wasn't aware of people with learning disability because they were put away. So now it's time for people with learning disability to write their story and to let other people know. (Cooper, 2008)
Mabel Cooper, former resident St Lawrence's Hospital, self-advocate, broadcaster and founder member of the Open University's Social History of Learning Disability Group.[1]

This book's title – *Communities, Archives and New Collaborative Practices* – raises the question of who or what is collaborating. The reading of the title most immediately available might be that the collaboration is between communities and those that work in archives. Yet we want to focus on another type of collaboration here, one that is equally crucial in developing new collaborative practices for archives. In a recent action research project to develop an Inclusive Archive of Learning Disability History,[2] it became clear that in seeking to produce an archive we needed to conceive of collaboration not only in terms of people but also in terms of a collaboration between different political theories. In developing the Inclusive Archive, we recognised that we needed to seek a collaborative relationship between the political ideas derived from public political logics – public service, public sphere, 'on behalf of the public' and for posterity – and those that derive from relational and personal-centred politics. While there was constant debate in the team with some of us favouring one set of political logic and some the other, we realised that for an archive to be an archive, and for it to be an inclusive one, we needed to develop an approach to archival practice that held both the public and the relational political traditions in dialogue. Both political traditions have a history of being very effectively expressed in the learning disability self-advocacy movement as speaking up and being heard, and of arguing for services to start with the individual by being more 'person-centered' (Brownlee-Chapman et al. 2017). The task of our archive was to explore fruitful combinations and collaborations between the two political traditions.

Archival politics and the politics of the social history of learning disability

The Inclusive Archive project emerged from an inclusive research group based at the Open University, set up almost 25 years ago, called the Social History of Learning Disability Group (Social History of Learning Disability online). The Social History of Learning Disability Group is made up of researchers with and without learning disabilities, and over the years the group has produced many co-authored and co-edited books, alongside running an annual conference. A central issue for the group from its outset was the viewpoint of 'learning disability' offered in the majority of archives.

Archives, as we know, are never neutral; they exist for specific purposes. What becomes an 'archive' is always produced from specific knowledge systems (Schwartz and Cook, 2002; Cook, 2013; Gilliland and McKemmish, 2014). The archives of what we now call learning disability, but was then termed 'mental deficiency' or being 'feeble-minded', often derive from the institutions of the late 19th and early 20th century and were bound up with eugenic science (Thomson, 1996).[3] The main way in which people with learning disabilities have been represented in archives is as patients, as people to be regulated, picked up from the streets, separated from their families and given medical treatment.

A crucial Social History of Learning Disability Group collaboration – and one that was fundamental to the inception of the Inclusive Archive project – was between Dorothy Atkinson, an academic at the Open University who taught health and social care, and Mabel Cooper, who lived in learning disability institutions, including St Lawrence's long-stay hospital in Caterham, from a young child until she was in her 30s (Atkinson 2001). Mabel was part of the self-advocacy activist movement where people with learning disabilities speak for themselves about their needs and hopes, a crucial aim when so many people had been deprived of any agency over their own lives. Mabel and Dorothy together wrote Mabel's life story. One aspect of their work together included going to the archives and reading the only formally archived records of Mabel's life. Mabel reflected on this experience (Cooper, 2001) in the following way:

> These are some of the things the records said about me when I first went to St Lawrence's:
>
> • I was an 'imbecile'. This really hurts.
> • I was 'educationally very backward'.
> • I was 'ignorant of the four rules of numbers'.
> • I was 'dull and slow in response' and that I did not seem to have any general knowledge at all.
> • I was 'not able to learn to tell the time'.
>
> You see, for me, it did upset me for them to say I wasn't teachable. I think if someone goes around and says something like that are you going to learn? You are not! And then they turn round and say 'Oh, you're not teachable'. And for them to say, you know, that I need to be looked after, trained for life. I don't know who made that decision, or who makes those assumptions. Who were they to make these assumptions?

The Inclusive Archive project – like the Social History of Learning Disability Group before it – came about through a strong desire to challenge the archives to ensure that what is left of people's histories is not only these objectifying records produced through the state and medical management of people's lives but their own stories in, as with Mabel's, their own words. This was never seen by the Social History of Learning Disability Group only as an academic endeavour but – as with many alternative history movements – as one that was actively political (Atkinson et al, 2000; Mitchell et al, 2006).

What happens to the politics of archives when the archive becomes person-centred?

Many of the people who influenced, or were collaborators in designing, the Inclusive Archive are self-advocates. There is a strong tradition of telling stories in self-advocacy; it is often called 'speaking up' or 'speaking out'. From the work of the Social History of Learning Disability Group and self-advocacy inspired organisations such as our project partners Carlisle People First Research Team Ltd, it is clear that people with learning disabilities wish to add their perspectives to archives as a way of challenging public perceptions and creating a world where people with learning disabilities can live lives they choose.[4] The desire to speak out in public works very much with the grain of traditional archives and museums as public institutions that seek to inform public debate with collections kept for posterity and future generations. Yet, there is another well-developed tradition in self-advocacy known as being person-centred. Person-centred approaches – in contrast to older professional interactions with people with learning disabilities – aim to start with that person and the world from their perspective and to avoid imposing external values about what is important or desirable.[5] This tradition indicates an approach to archives that also makes no assumptions about what taking part might include. Both political traditions – both very much consistent with self-advocacy activism – needed to be deployed in our Inclusive Archive design.

When we were briefing for the design of the archive, we developed a diagram (Figure 16.1) to illustrate the 'different ways of thinking about archives' and to ensure that our design would enable people to choose their own pathway. Where the left-hand side was about engaging archival politics on its own terms, adding new stories into a public sphere, the right-hand side was driven by the person-centred and the relational.

The idea of the significance of 'relationships' has become a crucial way of conceiving contemporary life, whether in art practice as 'relational aesthetics', in psychology and medical contexts as 'relational ethics' or, as we will develop here, as 'relational politics'. Taking a cue from a feminist emphasis that the personal and everyday life is political and politics does not operate in a separate domain, a number of theorists have drawn out the implications of relational political theorising. As Kenneth J. Gergen has put it, 'Politics in the relational mode may be subtle, fluid and unceasing – not the work of specific groups on specific sites identified as "political", but the work of us

Figure 16.1: Different ways of thinking about archives that navigate the different logics of the public and the relational

From the Inclusive Archive Project

all, in all relationships' (2001: 180). This chimes in tone with a series of significant works in a learning disability context looking at the everyday production of disability and ability in social care practices (Rapley, 2009; Williams, 2011; Antaki and Kent, 2012). This work – often drawing on very close readings of conversation – shows how people's lives can be closed down or radically enabled through seemingly very small everyday actions. If the negative denial of people's ability and choices are produced and reproduced through many small everyday interactions, a relational form of learning disability politics is one where the means are the ends and making space for dialogue with people on their own terms for its own sake is a way of creating positive change.

As suggested in Figure 16.1, in designing the digital archive, we sought to make the archive flexible and varied in the kinds of contributions produced:

Share with everyone/Share with people you know
The first shift here was to enable people to have choice over who they shared their contribution with. They might share it publicly, only with people they knew or not share at all. To design this aspect of the digital archive we drew on established social media conventions that enable selective sharing of media with identified 'friends' or 'groups' or across public networks. Many we worked with were familiar with such conventions through Facebook, and such choices are made more explicit and simple to understand in the accessible learning disability social media sites that we drew from as we developed the inclusive archive Multi Me (www.multime.com) and the RIX Wiki (www. rixresearchandmedia.org/rix/home-media).

What is important to others/What is important to you
One concern many people articulated was that their life could not possibly be interesting to others. We needed a way to break down that barrier, and so we wanted to emphasise that people could share whatever they wanted and *they* were able to say what was 'important' (or 'significant' in heritage terms).

Share forever/Share for a while
The idea of posterity was an issue for many people. For some it was important that experiences, especially of institutionalisation and long stay hospitals, must not be forgotten. But for others 'forever' seems like a long time. And having to consent for something to be shared publicly forever became a big barrier in enabling consent. We wanted to ensure that people could share for a while and, if then they chose, to change their minds.

Easy to find/Easy to put in
We wanted to ensure that documentation and metadata were accessible as well. One of the researchers on the

project, Nigel Ingham, in collaboration with Carlisle People First Research Team Ltd, developed an accessible survey to produce catalogue entries.

Use disability labels/Choose your own labels
For some people the label of 'having a learning disability' is an important political statement, while for others it is not an important description – or it could even be a label they might reject. We wanted people to be able to label – tag – their contributions in ways that made sense to and for them.

Lives on in buildings/Lives on in people
From the outset, we were interested – as many have been in archive and heritage contexts – in conceptualising the archive as living. This draws on the biological definition of living: that it grows, changes, adapts and gets energy from feeding. We wanted the energy of the people who care about the archive to be important in sustaining its future, not only institutional structures.

Speaking up in public: issues of capacity to consent

As explored here, the left-hand side of Figure 16.1 reflects more traditional ideas of what the archive might do and how it might be sustained. Many of our collaborators were very clear that the public side of archives must not be forgotten and should remain crucial to the Inclusive Archive. We were reminded by self-advocates, social care providers, and supporters and family members that in social care service contexts the presumption is always against the open and public approach. Risk aversion in staff and lack of clarity over the law and good practice tend to stop people with learning disabilities being supported in speaking out, using social media, being filmed or appearing on TV. This is especially the case for people who might not be able to consent themselves to any of those things. As a result, it was essential that we addressed questions of consent and of the law on capacity to consent.

The crucial piece of legislation for our project was the Mental Capacity Act (MCA) England and Wales 2005. This governs decision-making for people who may lack capacity 'because of an impairment of, or a disturbance in the functioning of, the mind or brain' (MCA, 2005, section 2 (1). Through the diagnostic threshold component of the MCA, people labelled with learning disabilities fall under its jurisdiction and can therefore be subjected to a functional capacity test to ascertain whether or not the individual has capacity to make a specific decision at a specific time. Important principles underpinning the legislation include: a presumption of capacity in the first instance; that a person is not to be treated as unable to make a decision unless all practicable steps to help him/her to do so have been taken without success; the right to make an unwise decision; and that because you cannot consent to one thing does not mean you cannot consent to another. Someone might be able to consent to what to have for dinner or to moving house but not to spending money on a holiday. Under the Act, capacity relates to being able to understand, retain and weigh up information that pertains to the decision, and to be able to communicate that decision. When designing our digital archive, we wanted to ensure that we built in processes that supported people to do – and demonstrate – these things. When we asked our wider research community what would support inclusion,[6] participants highlighted the need for greater understanding of how to support communication and a legally compliant decision-making pathway that is easy to follow and yet keeps the person right at the centre.

To build people's capacity to make an informed decision to consent to sharing in archives, we drew on the definition of decision-making that was articulated by our Research Associate, Vicky Green. Vicky describes herself as a researcher who has mild learning disabilities. Drawing upon her lived experience, including attending school alongside individuals with more complex learning disabilities, she reflected:

> To make a good decision you must:
> 1. Know about it.
> 2. If you do not know about it, you have to try it.
> 3. Then you decide. (Brownlee-Chapman et al, 2017: x)

Under the Mental Capacity Act, if a person is judged not to have the capacity to consent to a decision, then a substitute decision is made by those that know the person in what must be their 'best interests'.[7] This presented another potential barrier for our archive, as families and service providers who support people with very complex disabilities (including those who communicate in non-formal ways such as facial expressions and gesturing) were anxious about whether they could make a best interest decision about depositing in archives. This boiled down to one key question: what counted as 'best interests' in this matter? A wider idea of public benefit is included in the MCA in relationship to research but could this count for archives? Could best interests be read broadly to include the wider public sphere arguments Mabel made?[8] In discussions with a QC, we were reassured to understand that the case law has developed to include 'altruistic sentiments and concern for others',[9] including a concern for other people in the future (Lee, 2017). In addition, case law is increasingly emphasising the importance of maximising capacity (*CH v A Metropolitan Council* [2017] EWCOP 12), involving the person in every stage of the decision-making process, with a particular focus on ascertaining the individual's 'will and preferences' (Lee 2017). With this in mind, the project undertook a piece of work – led by one of us, Sue Ledger – to explore with people the practicalities of legally supporting someone with complex needs to deposit to an archive. As Sue has put it elsewhere:

> This involved working with an individual (Cherry) and her closest supporters, alongside an outreach and learning officer at The Keep Archive, Brighton, Isilda Almeida-Harvey, to explore:
> 1. What material Cherry may wish to deposit
> 2. How Cherry could be best supported to make an informed decision about whether or not to deposit her items in an archive by exploring ways to maximize her understanding of what an archive is – for example by using photos, making films, identifying and learning from an individual's past and present experiences of sharing with the public, visiting.
> 3. If Cherry was unable to make the decision for herself, to work through a robust best interest decision making process.
> 4. Transparent documentation of Cherry's step by step decision-making process – whether or not to deposit in her local archive through the use of photography, film and examples of documentation completed by Cherry and her circle of support. (Brownlee-Chapman et al, 2017: x)

Crucially, through working to build the possibilities for an individual to consent our team had to thoroughly break down what an archive is and what it means. We had to explore creative and experiential ways for people to understand archiving and the ideas of 'the public' and of 'the future'. As Sue has described in terms of the collaboration with the archivist at The Keep and Cherry:

To explore Cherry's own wishes and feelings we undertook a number of visits to the archives where Isilda (the archivist) introduced Cherry to the stories and to archival boxes. We also actively considered whether Cherry enjoyed sharing things about her life with other people – including people she didn't know personally. A key indication used to determine the best interests decision was that Cherry had publically exhibited her art work in the past and had clearly really enjoyed this process. (Brownlee–Chapman et al, 2017: 9)

As is indicated in Sue's description, through this strand of the project we have come to see that the public forms of 'speaking up' and the relational 'person-centred' forms are, in fact, highly productively connected. The route to Cherry being supported to explore public depositing in an archive and, in this case, for a 'best interests' decision to be made, was enabled and structured through detailed relational work, between Sue, The Keep, Cherry and her mum and her wider support circle, and between the idea of the public archive, keeping in view constantly the very person-centred sense of what was important to Cherry.

When we first conceived the 'different ways of thinking about archives' illustration, we called it 'the binaries' as a shorthand. We conceived this as a heuristic to enable design; to guide us there would be differentiated ways of being part of our archive. Yet we always knew that 'binaries' was not quite right as we saw the different choices set out in our diagram as being in dynamic relationship. The work of the project – and especially in the context of people with complex needs and the MCA 2005 – showed that the route to the political logics of the public has also to begin in a person-centred way. But being person-centred also meant that we needed to anticipate in our design that not all engagements with the archive would necessary lead to public sharing.

Public *and* relational: a new collaborative practice?

In designing the inclusive archive we needed a rich variety of archival practices to enable a variety of ways of being, of taking part and of reflecting different theories of how positive change in people with learning disabilities' lives comes to happen. We wanted to ensure that the archive enables both those who want to speak up and claim the space of the public sphere and also for those who want more person-centred, networked and relational ways of being part of an archive. As part of enabling speaking up, as we have just shown, we also needed to draw on emerging MCA 2005 case law to understand 'best interests' not only as very bounded and private but as including more expansive ideas of altruism and claiming a space in the world for the benefit not only of yourself but also for others and future generations too.

Archives, legislation, oral histories and everyday conversations are not passive representations of the stories and dynamics already there; they are productive; they are ways in which we produce the present and the future. Archiving requires varieties of ways of knowing, and of accounting for, the complexity of power, varieties of ways of being and to be designed to make way for a variety of possibilities for political change. The politics of the public sphere, of public service and of posterity remain crucial in speaking up and contesting policy and prejudice, but they also need to be open to different person-centred modes of small and everyday change. What we found was that both these political logics needed to be planned in. We also found – through our work linked to the MCA – that the route to public depositing is also a highly relational one, whose legitimacy comes ultimately from being person-centred. It is likely that 21st-century archival politics and its new collaborative practice will also benefit – inspired by the learning disability self-advocacy movement as well as women's liberation and civil rights movements more generally – from a very active collaboration between these two different political genealogies: the public and the relational.

Notes

[1] A self-advocate is someone who is developing skills in speaking for themselves and making decisions about their own lives. Self-advocacy groups – such as People First – have been crucial in supporting people with learning disabilities to do this.

[2] The Inclusive Archive of Learning Disability History Project ran from 2014 to 2017, funded by the Arts and Humanities Research Council. Its key aim was to increase people with learning disabilities' access to, and participation in, heritage, through the co-production of an online archive of learning disability history and through the co-development of new systems, processes and guidance in public archives.

[3] Over the past 25 years as the large long-stay institutions have closed, considerable efforts have been made to record, reveal and share the histories of those who lived, and worked, in these places. The wide-ranging scope of the work in this area spans both the United Kingdom (UK) (Potts and

Fido, 1991; Ingham, 2003; Keilty and Woodley, 2013) and the rest of the world (Manning, 2008; Johnson and Traustadottir, 2005; Malacrida, 2015).

[4] From its very first event in the 1990s, people with learning disabilities have shared their stories and perspectives at the Social History of Learning Disability Research Group's conferences and seminars (http://www.open. ac.uk/health-and-social-care/research/shld/). Archives have often been seen as an important site of activism in other contexts too (Bastian, 2002; Flinn et al, 2009; Flinn, 2010; Costa et al, 2012; Buchanan and Bastian, 2015).

[5] Valuing People guidelines describe person-centred practice in the following terms: 'A person-centred approach to planning means that planning should start with the individual (not with services), and take account of their wishes and aspirations' (DoH, 2001: 49).

[6] Consultation with our wider archive research community included people with learning disabilities, advocates, families, archivists, heritage sector workers, health and social care staff, academics, technicians, photographers and performers.

[7] In 2009 the UK ratified the United Nations (UN) Convention for the Rights of Disabled People. At the time of writing in 2017 the UK is undergoing formal UN review of its progress towards full compliance. The use of substitute decision-making in accordance with current MCA legislation is the subject of further legal examination following concerns raised by the UN review that this approach contravenes Article 12 (Equal recognition before the law). The committee has recommended replacement by supported decision-making (see Martin, 2017; Ruck Keene, 2017).

[8] The idea of a legitimate Best Interest decision that is based on an idea of benefit to others exists in the MCA explicitly only in terms of research: '5) The research must—(a) have the potential to benefit P without imposing on P a burden that is disproportionate to the potential benefit to P, or (b) be intended to provide knowledge of the causes or treatment of, or of the care of persons affected by, the same or a similar condition' (MCA, Section 5).

[9] *Aintree University Hospitals NHS Foundation Trust v James* [2013] UKSC 67 (paragraph 24).

References

Aintree University Hospitals NHS Foundation Trust v James (2013) UKSC 67 (paragraph 24). Available at: http://ukscblog.com/case-comment-aintree-university-hospitals-nhs-foundation-trust-v-james-2013-uksc-67/ [Accessed 11 October 2019].

Antaki, C. and Kent, A. (2012) 'Telling people what to do (and, sometimes, why): contingency, entitlement and explanation in staff requests to adults with intellectual impairments', *Journal of Pragmatics*, 44: 876–89.

Atkinson, D. (2001) 'Foreword' to "Mabel's Story"', [online], Available from: http://www.open.ac.uk/health-and-social-care/research/ shld/resources-and-publications/life-stories/mabels-story/foreword [Accessed 11 October 2019].

Atkinson, D., McCarthy, M. and Walmsley, J. (eds) (2000) *Good Times, Bad Times: Women with Learning Difficulties Telling their Stories*, Kidderminster: BILD Publications.

Bastian, J.A. (2002) 'Taking custody, giving access: a postcustodial role for a new century', *Archivaria: The Journal of the Association of Canadian Archivists*, Spring. Available at: http://archivaria.ca/index. php/archivaria/article/view/12838 [Accessed 11 October 2019].

Brownlee-Chapman, C., Chapman, R., Eardley, C., Forster, S., Graham, H., Green, V., Harkness, E., Headon, K., Humphreys, P., Ingham, N., Ledger, S., May, V., Minnion, A., Richards, R., Tilley, L., Townson, L. (2017) 'Between speaking out in public and being person-centred: Collaboratively designing an inclusive archive of learning disability history', *International Journal of Heritage Studies* [online], Available from: doi: 10.1080/13527258.2017.1378901 [Accessed 11 October 2019].

Buchanan, A. and Bastian, M. (2015) 'Activating the archive: rethinking the role of traditional archives for local activist projects', *Archival Science*, 15: 429–51.

CH v A Metropolitan Council (2017) EWCOP 12. Available from: https://www.courtofprotectionhub.uk/cases/ch-v-a-metropolitan-council-2017-ewcop-12 [Accessed 11 October 2019].

Cook, T. (2013) 'Evidence, memory, identity, and community: Four shifting archival paradigms', *Archival Science*, 13: 95–120.

Cooper, M. (2008) '"An interview with Mabel Cooper', at the Forgotten Citizens Conference, Learning Disability Week 2008' [online], Available from: https://vimeo.com/1406390 [Accessed 15 August 2017].

Cooper, M. (2001) 'Mabel's story' [online], Available from: http:// www.open.ac.uk/health-and-social-care/research/shld/resources-and-publications/life-stories/mabels-story/part-2-quest [Accessed 11 October 2019].

Costa, L., Voronka, J., Landry, D., Reid, J., McFarlane, B., Reville, D. and Church, K. (2012) 'Recovering our stories: a small act of resistance', *Studies in Social Justice*, 6(1): 85–101.

DoH (Department of Health) (2001) *Valuing People: A New Strategy for Learning Disability for the 21st Century*. Available at: https://www.gov.uk/government/publications/valuing-people-anew-strategy-for-learning-disability-for-the-21st-century [Accessed 11 October 2019].

Flinn, A. (2010) 'Independent community archives and community-generated content: 'writing, saving and sharing our histories', *Convergence: The International Journal of Research into New Media Technologies*, 16(1): 39–51.

Flinn, A., Stevens, M. and Shepherd, E. (2009) 'Whose memories, whose archives? Independent community archives, autonomy and the mainstream', *Archival Science*, 9: 71–86.

Gergen, K.J. (2001) *Social Construction in Context*, London: Sage.

Gilliland, A.J. and McKemmish, S. (2014) 'The role of participatory archives in furthering human rights, recovery and reconciliation', *Atlanti: Review for Modern Archival Theory and Practice*, 24(1): 79–88.

Ingham, N. (2003) *Gogarburn Lives*, Edinburgh: LMA.

Johnson, K. and Traustadottir, R. (eds) (2005) *Deinstitutionalization and People with Intellectual Disabilities: In and Out of Institutions*, London: Jessica Kingsley Publishers.

Keilty, T. and Woodley, K. (2013) *No Going Back: Forgotten Voices from Prudhoe Hospital*, Sheffield: Centre for Welfare Reform.

Lee, A. (2017) 'In the matter of The Open University and a proposal to establish a learning disability archive', legal advice received from 39 Essex Chambers, private correspondence.

Malacrida, C. (2015) *A Special Hell: Institutional Life in Alberta's Eugenic Years*, Toronto: University of Toronto Press.

Manning, C. (2008) *Bye-bye Charlie: Stories from the Vanishing World of Kew Cottages*, Sydney: UNSW Press.

Martin, W. (2017) 'Capacity, incapacity, and human rights: A CRPD perspective, Paper given at Keele University, 15 February [online], Available from: https://autonomy.essex.ac.uk/crpd/ [Accessed 1 October 2017].

Mental Capacity Act (MCA) (2005) London: HMSO [online], Available from: http://www.legislation.gov.uk/ukpga/2005/9/contents [Accessed 15 August 2017].

Mitchell, D., Traustadóttir, R., Chapman, R., Townson, L., Ingham, N. and Ledger, S. (eds) (2006) *Exploring Experiences of Advocacy by People with Learning Disabilities: Testimonies of Resistance*, London: Jessica Kingsley.

Multi Me [online], Available from: www.multime.com [Accessed 11 October 2019].

Potts, M. and Fido, R. (1991) *A Fit Person to be Removed*, Plymouth: Northcote House.

Rapley, M. (2009) *The Social Construction of Learning Disability*, Cambridge: Cambridge University Press.

RIX Wiki [online], Available from: www.rixresearchandmedia.org/rix/wikis [Accessed 11 October 2019].

Ruck Keene, A. (2017) 'Capacity assessments', Presentation given at COMMUNITY CARE LIVE LONDON CONFERENCE, Business Design Centre Islington, London, 25 September.

Social History of Learning Disability Research Group [online], Available from: http://www.open.ac.uk/health-and-social-care/research/shld [Accessed 11 October 2019].

Schwartz, J.M. and Cook, T. (2002) 'Archives, records, and power: The making of modern memory', *Archival Science*, 2: 1–19.

Thomson, M. (1996) 'Family, Community, and State: The Micro-politics of Mental Deficiency', in Wright, David and Digby, Anne (eds) *From Idiocy to Mental Deficiency; Historical Perspectives on People with Learning Disabilities*, London: Routledge, pp 207–30.

Williams, V. (2011) *Disability and Discourse: Analysing Inclusive Conversation with People with Intellectual Disabilities*, Oxford: Blackwell Wiley.

17

Archive utopias: linking collaborative histories to local democracy

Lianne Brigham, Richard Brigham,
Helen Graham and Victoria Hoyle

We want to introduce the work we did together, and we will explore it in this chapter from three starting points:

In the York Guildhall – the historic meeting place of the Guilds and now the full City of York Council Chamber – there is a sign probably put up in 1891 (Figure 17.1). It reads: 'No manifestation of feeling from the public will be allowed during the council meetings'. Lianne Brigham and Richard Brigham photographed and shared this photograph on their York Past and Present Facebook 17,000-strong group to much amusement: 'typical!'.

Lianne, Richard and Helen Graham – as part of a previous research project – had noted a serious problem with 'them' and 'us' culture in local democracy. On one side there is a lot of 'just moaning' as Richard calls it, where the council gets blamed for everything and people are not constructive. On the other side, the council and other public organisations do not find it easy at all to respond to offers to help from local people and find it very difficult to find ways of sharing responsibility (Bashforth et al, 2015).

Victoria Hoyle, City Archivist, spoke at an event ran by Lianne, Richard and Helen called 'What has heritage ever done for us?', where she called for a closer relationship between the archive and creating democratic presents and futures: 'I would like to see it used more as a resource by council officers and also by residents to access information about how the city governs itself … I would like to think that there is a future where "look it up in the archive", "visit the archive", "have you thought about the archive?", is the first step in designing solutions to problems and celebrating our past achievements'. (Hoyle, 2015)

From these three starting points a project was born that explored how York's city archives could be used to open up different kinds of democratic relationships. It focused on archival collections relating to Hungate, an area of York that was designated a 'slum' and demolished by the council during the 1930s. We looked at health inspection records, explored maps and the 1911 census, and read angry letters from people whose lives were being affected by local government decisions. Seeing the breakdown in relationships between local people and local government – and the way in which this is reflected in cynicism towards the council today – led us to develop a conceptual intervention we called the Utopian Council, which sought to imagine and stage a more positive and reciprocal relationship between the council and local people. While sometime utopia is seen almost like an impossible blueprint for a perfect world, in our approach to utopia we drew on Ruth Levitas's definition: 'The core of utopia is the desire for being otherwise, individually and collectively, subjectively and objectively. Its expressions explore and bring to debate the potential contents and contexts of human flourishing. It is thus better understood as a method than a goal…' (Levitas, 2013: 1).

Figure 17.1: The 1891 sign in the City of York Council Chamber next to the sign made to take to the Utopia Fair at Somerset House in 2016

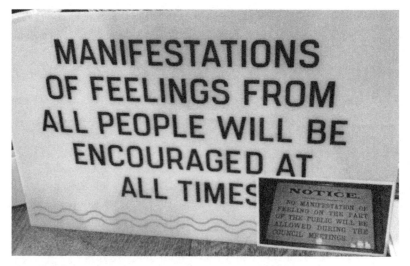

Photo by the project team

Along the way we learnt a lot about how archives can be used 'against the grain', as Victoria puts it, to create a shared space for discussion of urgent issues. In our final section we draw the focus out to reflect on participation in heritage more generally and suggest that a feeling of insurgency tends to be more powerful than a managed form of community collaboration.

Using the archives for local democracy

We started looking at the Hungate archive because housing is a crucial and urgent issue in York. York is the most unaffordable place to live in the north of England, when average wages are compared to housing costs (Lloyds Bank, 2017). As Richard has put it elsewhere:

> If we look at York at the moment, there are two big problems. The first is gentrification. If you look at the underlying values, you know why things are being sold off. It is always for expensive flats or a new hotel. It's good to have nice, beautiful-looking buildings, they are attractive to look at. But they are only for certain very wealthy people. Are these people going to live there every day? Are they going to use the local town and local shops? The worry is that it is just more rich people buying up property as investments or holiday lets. You are near enough kicking us out of our own city. (Brigham et al, 2018)

After it was cleared, Hungate was used for light industry and commerce until 2008, when it was purchased by an executive housing developer. Redevelopment was ongoing during the project and the building of expensive apartments on the site of a former 'slum' seemed indicative of this process of gentrification. During the period of the project, York was also seeking to develop and pass its Local Plan, which would set agreed levels of house building over the next decades (City of York Council, online). Many people in York want greater governmental intervention to ensure low cost and social housing is made available for local people, raising the question of the role of government in people's everyday lives. For these reasons, going back to the politics, hopes and realities of the early 20th-century 'slum clearances' provided a useful focus. In early 2016, Lianne and Richard advertised on the York Past and Present Facebook group, and a core group of eight people visited the archive over a six week period (Graham, 2016a).

In order to collaboratively write this article we decided to record our conversations, which we then transcribed and edited.

Victoria: The project had quite an unusual motivation in that we wanted to think about the future and the present, not just the past. A lot of research that has looked at similar kinds of archives has been focused on thinking about the early 20th century and what the early 20th century was like, whereas this was much more about using the archive to think about today. It made me think of the archive as more than a frozen past. It is also a repository of potential futures. The only future we know about is the one we are living in now but going to the archive you can see what the people at the time *thought* the future was and all the possible trajectories that York could have travelled down.

I remember from the research session Catherine [another member of the project group] finding a document about what they'd planned to do in Hungate after the clearances. There was a swimming pool, a bus station and civic space for the public. And we know what actually happened was that it became a commercial development and a bit unused, a brown field site until it was developed very recently with the Hungate flats. But that struck me at the time as quite a surprise. A 'sliding doors' moment, when things could go off in lots of different directions.[1]

Richard: I loved working with the archives. In clearing Hungate and building a new council housing estate in Tang Hall, the council thought they were giving people a better way of life, 'look what we're giving you', but I wonder how many people would have wanted to stay in Hungate. All that community they'd built in the area, was ripped to pieces. The community around there, the help they gave each other was huge.

Lianne: I found going through the archive quite upsetting because I was going through all the illnesses.

Victoria: The archive speaks a very formal language, like the health data you were looking at Lianne or with the housing inspections which were focused on 'how many windows?' or 'where is the toilet?' There were these very occasional insights into the personal experience of the clearances but it is an imaginative leap from these types of records to what the people involved were thinking at the time: Did they want to be moved? Or were they thinking, this is my home with my friends and family around me. In the archive all you can really see is the will of the council pushing forward the changes.

Helen: This question of what different types of record enable you to know or understand was an issue when we designed the project. Did we need a formal structure to our collaborative research that reflected the type of archival material (e.g. start with the legislative context or the census) or should we just dive in and see what emerged? We went for the latter and it paid off.

Victoria: A lot of archivists would consider the way we went about the archival research to be a bit chaotic and unmanaged. People in the group took a couple of weeks to find something they were interested in and during that time we did a lot of rummaging and we had a lot of discussions and slowly, slowly, slowly we started to settle into a groove. Some people were interested in the maps. Catherine was interested in the detail of the census and the houses [Sotheran, 2016a, 2016b]. From people's interests different ways of valuing the archive started to emerge. The archive wasn't just being valued for evidence or historical information. It was being valued for what it could tell us about today, about people's lives today, and what it could tell us about the future. The thing which struck me was that archivists tend to structure archives by the administrative order of the council. Yet the way we were structuring it during the research was based on the place and being in the place. It wasn't anything about which department created those records. It struck me how not useful the kind of cataloguing we [archivists] do is because it doesn't allow you to ask the kind of questions we were asking.

Helen: I like the idea that by just getting in there and starting to use the records we created different pathways through the archive, based on what different people in the group were interested in. That by experimenting as a group, yet finding our own individual interests, we were collectively forging different lateral connections in the archive that, if you approached it top down or on your own, you wouldn't have found. Crucially I think these different routes created a context for us to think collectively about the role of government in people's lives today, which took us to our question of utopia.

Victoria: Some of the motivations for the clearance could be read as utopian. The idea of creating better living conditions for people was very radical. In the context of the building of the new estate at Tang Hall: the big houses, gardens, cul-de-sacs where everyone was facing each other. We talked a lot about how negative that experience was for those whose lives were affected, but in the motivations there was that element of building a utopian environment for people to live in.

Helen: Yet these utopian intentions reveal a certain lack of democracy. At that time it was the council that wanted to make something better *on behalf of*, rather than *with*, the people concerned.

Lianne: They didn't ask the people who lived there. They didn't know what was going on – all they could do was write letters to the council. Working with the archive has given me an insight into where the problems are with the council today. They've got good intentions and good ideas but it is really about how they work with people.

Victoria: I felt that by us exploring the archive and becoming 'experts' in it, we created a space where anyone can know about the place: anyone can know about Hungate because that knowing is there in the archive. Thinking about the public workshop we did afterwards, everyone that came had something to bring and to contribute that other people might not have known.[2] It gave people the basis for speaking as experts in other ways, whether through personal memories, the perspective generated through family memories or having a view on the legal issues. The archive allowed everyone to get involved in that conversation

Helen: The archive worked to hold a space. Whether that was looking at photos or plans, it offered a tangible point of connection which we used as a way of entering into what might otherwise be more difficult conversations to convene in the present.

Manifestation of feelings: the Utopia Council

Prompted by this problematic relationship between local people and the local council then – that their utopian ideas on behalf of people of Hungate did not extend to collaborating with the people affected – we designed, in collaboration with Reet So, a Leeds-based creative collective, a utopian intervention as part of the Arts and Humanities Research Council Connected Communities Utopia Fair at Somerset House, London, 24–6 June 2016. Our point of inspiration was the sign Lianne and Richard had photographed in the Guildhall Council Chamber: 'No manifestation of feeling from the public will be allowed during the council meetings'. Our first act was to invert the sign: 'Manifestations of feelings from all people will be encouraged at all times'. Our invitation to people visiting our stall read:

> We are the Utopian Council. We are a collaboration of minds and hands. Together we are the ears to your queries, dreams and fears and a catalyst for your actions.
>
> The idea of this 'council' derives from an ancient concept left behind from earlier days, where cities, towns and constituencies were ruled by tiered management structures and elected members. However, the Utopian Council is open to your interpretation. There are no limits to our duties as a council, or yours as 'the people', we are here for you as you are for us. (Graham, 2016b)

We had 51 letters, and the four of us got together to respond to them in the Guildhall itself (Figure 17.2). We reflected together on that experience of sorting and making sense of the letters.

Figure 17.2: Sorting out the letters posted to the Utopian Council

Photo by the project team

Victoria:	The thing I found really powerful about the London event was this idea of being able to bring your emotions into the interactions of the Utopian Council. I'm still very struck by that sign.
Richard:	'No manifestations of feelings'.
Victoria:	What was significant was being able to express the way you feel about change and not only the reasons why a change should or shouldn't happen. It was what was missing from the archive about Hungate. We imagined what people would or would not have experienced, we injected the feelings. But the feelings weren't present in the archive in the way that they were in the idea of the Utopian Council.
Richard:	My favourite thing was answering the letters people wrote.
Lianne:	It made us log into our creativity and our creative mind in how we replied to people's letters. I liked that bit.
Richard:	These days that is few and far between. If you wrote to a council they'd be like, shrug. But as the Utopian Council we were saying, 'you are one in a

million people but you are so important, we're so sorry we missed you'. You had to write as if that person was so important, 'you've written to us, we must deal with it immediately!' It was good fun.

Helen: What I liked was that everyone who wrote – because of the questions we asked – were not just demanding, they were offering something as well. We were – as the Utopian Council – connecting people up to make something happen. As a result, it indicated a different kind of relationship between government and people. People tend to treat the relationship between government and people like demand and supply: I want this, the Council should supply. The Utopian Council allowed us to feel out how local democracy might become more reciprocal.

Lianne: When I was answering the letters I thought of it as a bartering system so they were willing to offer something and then we were willing to offer them something. With one of the letters, I was putting them in touch with someone they could help or with someone who could help them. So we had a whole network of people helping each other.

Victoria: What is at the heart of the bartering system idea is that what you have to offer is as valuable as what the council has to offer. Supply and demand assumes that the supplier has everything of value, but in the Utopian Council both sides have things of value and can contribute to address a problem rather than asking for something and receiving it.

Helen: We did have ourselves a bit of an archival challenge with the 51 letters, in terms of how to organise them!

Richard: People could add which department they were writing to on the letter. But then we had piles and some letters didn't fit because they addressed more than one department or issue.

Helen: Or their ideas was so holistic that it challenged the whole premise of 'departments'. Victoria brought the structure of the City of York Council as it is now just to experiment with how useful that was. But the idea that we could even vaguely use that structure fell apart very quickly.

Victoria: The structure of the council is doubly problematic because it's quite rigid but it also changes all the time. It makes it very difficult to communicate because you have to know who will be responsible for the inquiry. To be responsive to what our letter writers were proposing, we had to develop a more flexible system. Things were being handled – through the way we were working – more individual to individual rather than via this bureaucratic system.

Richard: It would be nice to think it could work in reality.

Lianne: It showed how it would feel if the council was more approachable and if we could pull down some of the barriers. And if the council was more approachable, people wouldn't moan as much.

Victoria: Sometimes there is a communication style that reinforces the expertise that certain people might have. For example, 'health and safety risk' is repeated by the council like a ritual, like a prayer. I think that immediately sends a flag up: 'I know things that you don't know.' It's designed to say: 'there is nothing to debate here because I know that it is dangerous'. When you do get lots of people together, it is difficult to get to a place where people are not using that language of expertise against each other. It's something that happens in archives when we say 'preservation risk'. It's a way of saying 'no' and asserting ownership.

Helen: Our Utopian Council tried to imagine completely other ways in which people, public organisations like archives and local government could work together creating different social capacities for living together. I remember one of the poetic responses we wrote which tried to sum up that difference:

You were not asking for us to take actions on your behalf.
You wanted to work with us to create conditions.
To make spaces where things can happen.
To connect up.
To collectivize infrastructure (waste; electricity).
To spread good ideas.

To reflect back and recognize your successes.
And to be something more multiple than a 'you' and an 'us'.

(Graham, 2016b)

Collaboration or Insurgent movement?

Alongside the questions of archive and local democracy, one of the issues that we have long been researching together is the nature of collaboration between archives and heritage organisations and communities (Bashforth et al, 2015; Bashforth et al, 2017). During the conversations we had to prepare this chapter we also reflected on the wider issues of 'collaborative practice' as framed by this book.

Lianne: Victoria, when we first met you, you came across as quite protective over the archives. Now you've seen people using them and pulling out their own questions would you say you are still as protective over them now?

Victoria: My idea of why archives are valuable has changed. I've really moved away from the idea that my role is to protect the archive from damage and physical danger; the 'health and safety' thinking that is used as a way of shutting down conversations and saying 'no' to things that are not within established patterns. In the balance of things I'd much rather things get used and that the archive was being active in the world rather than sitting safe in a store. And if that means taking some risks, then that is the trade-off.

Richard: That's a key idea for York Past and Present. You can have it behind closed doors, but get it digitised then everyone has access.

Victoria: Richard, you often ask why does it cost an archive thousands to digitise when York Past and Present can do it for free? I think it's because digitisation threatens to take power away from the archival institution, so you say, 'no, because it has to be done in certain ways and so it's very expensive'. That was where I was at five years ago. You've demonstrated other ways through your website and Facebook.

Richard: There are a lot of people who don't require any amount of money, they are willing to give their

245

time and expertise. There are hundreds of people more than happy to help.

Lianne: Just because we do things for free doesn't mean we won't care as much.

Victoria: Speaking as someone who is in the system and has colleagues across the archive and heritage sector, I sense their desperation to be able to reach the big audiences that you have with York Past and Present. They feel like, 'we really tried, we put it online and no one commented. We did events and no one came.' York Past and Present is a mystery to them. 'How does it work?' You must have people asking how you did it all the time.

Helen: But it is to do with the relationships Richard and Lianne have built. If we are co-running an event and we want people to come to things I have to get you to post it because it doesn't work if I post it because I haven't got the relationships in the same way. You organise coffee mornings, you talk to people and you are always posting on the Facebook group. You have an ability to use the York Past and Present network that almost no-one else can, the network is not equally accessible to all those 17,000 people.

Richard: We've tried to do things that previously people have said that you can't, 'no'. And there is no more powerful words in the English language than 'no, you can't'. It tends to get people interested.

Helen: The tours you have been running at the Guildhall have been so successful, with demand far outstripping your ability to supply. Yet I firmly believe that if the tours had been set up professionally no one would have come.

Richard: In fact, someone who works at the Guildhall said they had done a long time ago and it had stopped due to lack of interest.

Victoria: That is also how the council experiences consultation, they experience that no-one wants to engage, but do it differently and they do. They don't have the relationships.

Helen: But I wonder whether one of the reasons it works it because you – York Past and Present – are not exactly collaborating with the archives or the other heritage organisations you've worked with. It is like this idea of 'no' being a powerful motivation. It's a bit like you are breaking down the doors, you are wrestling your way in. You say to the York Past and Present group: 'we had to fight and this is now possible – come and do it with us'! Believe me, if the archives did a call out for a digital photographer to help with digitisation they'd get very few takers. If you said, 'we've made the argument that we can do it just as well as those that get paid – are you up for it?'. If you said that, you'd get 500 volunteers.

Richard: It's a trust thing.

Victoria: It is a trust thing, the feeling you're going to be respected and be with people who understand you and respect you.

Helen: Yes, but I can't help feeling it's also that you make it clear that they are taking part in something hard won, big, important and urgent.

Conclusions: Utopia feelings, ways forward

As you can see from our conversations in the Hungate archives project and the Utopian Council, there was a productive intermeshing of a variety of practices that mutually illuminated each other and have opened up new future directions. The variety of practices include working with the archive in slightly anarchic ways, the creativity of feeling out different relationships between local government and local people through the Utopian Council and, finally, exploring how we might in very practical ways rework the relationship between communities and heritage organisations.

Victoria: As someone who works in archives, I know that it is extremely challenging to think beyond structures and systems. Archives produced by local government replicate local government ways of seeing the world, which are reinforced further by archival processes like cataloguing that are all about hierarchy and order. What we did with the Hungate archive, it was a powerful experience. We took something that was uncatalogued so it didn't have that extra layer of archival structure and tried to use it in a way that was against its grain, in a disruptive way. A lot of the responses people had over time, as we got to the end of the project, were indicative of how some of those barriers – both to using archives and to engaging with local government – could be, if not be taken away, then at least negotiated.

Helen: Part of what we've learnt, it seems to me, is the creative potential for archives, heritage organisations and local government in welcoming disruption and for participation to be openly seen in that way. Seeking to co-opt York Past and Present into a safe collaboration is both impossible and pointless. Yes as part of this project, and others before, we did, and do, collaborate but what makes the dynamic powerful and galvanises so many people is the very real sense that you are fighting very hard to open doors.

Richard: As I've said before, we now have a higher security clearance locally with heritage professionals (Brigham et al, 2018). So when I phone someone for a meeting, it's now 'next week? Yes, no problem'. But one of my friends on York Past and Present has been ignored for three months by the same person I have no trouble getting a response from. But four years ago, before York Past and Present went from 3 to 17,000 people, that was me being ignored. But we're fighting now so that everyone can have the same access.

Lianne: We said when we went to do a talk in Leeds years ago now that we were taking on the whole city.[3] Well, we were right, that's what we've been doing.

Notes

[1]   *Sliding Doors* (dir. Peter Howitt) was a film where there were two realities based on whether the heroine caught, or failed to catch, a train.

[2]   We ran an open public workshop called 'Hungate in the archives: Histories of hopes for York's housing' to share the work we'd done on 21 June 2016, 3–5.30 pm.

[3]   The Leeds conference mentioned was for the Connected Communities Heritage Legacies project (PI Jo Vergunst).

References

Bashforth, M., Benson, M., Boon, T., Brigham, L., Brigham, R., Brookfield, K., Brown, P., Callaghan, D., Calvin. J.P., Courtney, R., Cremin, K., Furness, P., Graham, H., Hale, A., Hodgkiss, P., Lawson, J., Madgin, R., Manners, P., Robinson, D., Stanley, J., Swan, M., Timothy, J., Turner, R. (2015) 'How should heritage decisions be made?: Increasing participation from where you are' [online], Available from: http://heritagedecisions.leeds.ac.uk/ [Accessed 11 October 2019].

Bashforth, M., Benson, M., Boon, T., Brigham, L., Brigham, R., Brookfield, K., Brown, P., Callaghan, D., Calvin. J.P., Courtney, R., Cremin, K., Furness, P., Graham, H., Hale, A., Hodgkiss, P., Lawson, J., Madgin, R., Manners, P., Robinson, D., Stanley, J., Swan, M., Timothy, J., Turner, R. (2017) 'Socialising heritage/socialising legacy', in Facer, K. and Pahl, K. (eds) *Valuing Interdisciplinary Collaborative Research: Beyond Impact*, Bristol: Policy Press, pp 85–106.

Brigham, L., Brigham R. and Graham, H. (2018) 'Curiosity can fuel democracy: People making heritage and much loved places', in Halme, Anna-Maija, Mustonen, Tapani, Taavitsainen, Jussi-Pekka, Thomas, Suzie and Weij, Astrid (eds) *Heritage is Ours: Citizens Participating in Decision Making*, Helsinki: Europa Nostra, pp 20–9.

City of York Council, 'Local plan' [online], Available from: https://www.york.gov.uk/info/20051/planning_policy/710/new_local_plan [Accessed 11 October 2019].

Graham, H. (2016a) 'Hungate Histories: Lots of paperwork … and people's lives glimpsing through' [online], Available from: http://myfutureyork.org/hungate-histories-lots-of-paperwork-and-peoples-lives-glimpsing-through/ [Accessed 11 October 2019].

Graham, H. (2016b) 'An open letter to our Utopian Fair letter writers' [online], Available from: http://myfutureyork.org/an-open-letter-to-our-utopian-fair-letter-writers/ [Accessed 11 October 2019].

Hoyle, V. (2015) in Graham, H. (ed.) 'York: What has heritage ever done for us?' [online], Available from: http://heritagedecisions.leeds.ac.uk/2015/11/04/york-what-has-heritage-ever-done-for-us/ [Accessed 11 October 2019].

Levitas, R. (2013) *Utopia as Method: The Imaginary Reconstitution of Society*, Basingstoke: Palgrave Macmillan.

Lloyds Bank (2017) 'Home affordability in cities at its worst since 2008' [online], Available from: http://www.lloydsbankinggroup.com/media/press-releases/press-releases-2017/lloyds-bank/affordable-cities3/

Sotheran, C. (2016a) 'No. 2 + 4 Garden Place: The saga of 2 owners, some back windows and an unpaid bill' [online], Available from: http://myfutureyork.org/no-2-4-garden-place-the-saga-of-2-owners-some-back-windows-and-an-unpaid-bill/ [Accessed 11 October 2019].

Sotheran, C. (2019b) 'Hungate: An analysis of the 1911 Census' [online], Available from: http://myfutureyork.org/hungate-an-analysis-of-the-1911-census/ [Accessed 11 October 2019].

18

Community archives and the health of the internet

Andrew Prescott

For almost all of the projects discussed in this volume, the facilities afforded by different types of digital technology for mutual cooperation have been vital for the creation of a successful community archive. The different chapters illustrate the extraordinary variety of digital tools and methods used in community archives, ranging from the use of familiar commercial platforms such as Facebook to highly innovative exploitation of digital broadcast archives. Some projects enhance community access to heritage materials by digitising them, while others explore the potential of emerging technologies such as 360-degree image capture to allow communities to record and explore their heritage in novel ways. Techniques such as digital storytelling and oral history record experiences of ordinary people that are often missing from conventional archives. Video allows performances, ritual and ceremonies of black minority groups to be recorded. Projects such as Pararchive and tools such as Yarn encourage users to tell their story and turn the archive into a space of yarning. By using three-dimensional printing, communities are encouraged to experience data in new, more tactile and engaging ways. We sometimes speak of the digital as if it is a single integrated technology, but it is not. The variety and diversity of approaches illustrated in this volume shows how it might be more appropriate to talk of the digital*s*.

The story of the growth of community archives is not only the story of an insurgent community movement seeking to create archives that capture the diversity and plurality of human experience. It is also a story of the way in which digital tools lower those barriers that historically excluded and suppressed the voice of the ordinary, marginal, poor and oppressed. The importance of digital affordances in the development of community archives has been noted by many recent commentators. Elise Chenier (2016) argues that digital methods can reclaim the lesbian archive:

> Because open-access and digital environments encourage and enable collaborative knowledge construction across time and space, the digital humanities provide a democratic platform that supports anti-hierarchical and anti-elitist imperatives. (Chenier, 2016: 171)

Similar claims have been made for archives of indigenous peoples. Since 2012, a major digital repository called Sípnuuk has been created by the Karuk tribe, as a 'Karuk-centered and decolonized space where knowledge can be accessed and shared through a self-representative lens in alignment with Karuk protocols and laws' (Karuk Tribe et al, 2017: 312).

The digital success story of Sípnuuk has been repeated many times by various communities in different ways and contexts. Andrew Flinn (2010: 42–5) noted at an early stage of the development of Web 2.0 the potential of digital technologies for the sharing and development of community archives. Examples cited by Flinn included Eastside Community Heritage in East London (https://www.hidden-histories.org/), which celebrated its 20th anniversary in 2018. During that time, it has worked with over 20,000 beneficiaries, delivered 2000 reminiscence sessions and 3000 school workshops and worked with 1000 community groups. Another long-standing community archive noted by Flinn with a strong digital presence is the Waltham Forest Oral History Group (http://www.wforalhistory.org.uk/), London's oldest oral history group. My Brighton and Hove (http://www.mybrightonandhove.org.uk/) has now grown to over 13,000 pages of content and is being transferred to a new platform.

Despite these success stories, the use of digital technologies by community archives is a complex and conflicted issue. Community groups often find that the technical, financial and logistical demands of maintaining digital resources are considerable. This tempts them to use commercial platforms whose longevity is not assured and which raise issues of privacy and manipulation. As we all increasingly work in a digital environment, the quality of that environment affects our day-to-day life almost as profoundly as our physical environment. The health of the digital ecosystem on which we all depend affects the ability of community archives to achieve their aims of creating shared spaces of self-representation, collaboration and memory. Every day seems to bring further revelations of the manipulation of social media, security breaches, personal abuse and digital disinformation. These anxieties can make it seem that the vision of a digital space promoting community self-representation and collaboration is under threat.

Within the archives profession itself, the relationship with the issues presented by the digital boom is complex and goes beyond exploring new methods of community engagement. Formal archives are run by and for the benefit of government and other corporations, and the issues associated with preserving and making available the enormous quantities of digital records now being produced by these bodies are formidable. The development of big data and the predictive analytics that are now feeding into the growth of artificial intelligence provide new opportunities and challenges for archives that may impact on their engagement with communities. There is a risk that big data and artificial intelligence approaches will promote a 'top down' approach whereby data and the information in archives are used for greater control of communities rather than to empower communities. Can community archives promote the growth of a more decentralised and open digital environment that will enable the internet to become less the plaything of large commercial interests and more of a space for community empowerment?

For many community archives, while digital methods have proved enabling, the issues of funding and accessing suitable technical expertise are problematic. The builders of the Karuk Tribe repository Sípnuuk, while noticing the great success of the repository in preserving and documenting the Karuk Tribe, see funding and sustainability as their major challenges:

> Although actively supported by collaborators providing abundant resources, our greatest challenge remains a lack of sustained funding to ensure fundamental site maintenance, let alone steady staffing and growth. Sípnuuk is dependent on grant-based funding. This not only is unpredictable but also seldom provides needed support to fund personnel and the endless pursuit of further grant funding, creating a situation in which staff are chronically charged with more work than they have the resources to accomplish. Programs such as Sípnuuk are often fuelled as a 'labor of love,' impacting the lives of people dedicated to maintaining the resource. (Karuk Tribe et al, 2017: 311)

Failure to use open standards, lack of access to technical expertise and funding issues have already led to the loss of many community archive activities. Many of the local digital resources created in the first years of this century by the lottery-funded New Opportunities Fund did not have sustainability plans. Some of these projects were never completed and many others are now unavailable (Thomas and Johnson, 2015: 191).

Given these difficulties, it is not surprising that many community groups use commercial platforms to create their archives. Not only does this reduce the funding pressure and the requirement for technical expertise, but also many users of the archive already use these platforms and are very familiar with them. The use of platforms such as Facebook, YouTube, Flickr or Instagram creates the illusion that the community archive is in a place where the community often meets and gathers. As increasingly the experience of many users in using the internet is mediated by packages such as Facebook, they seem an obvious solution to the creation of community archives. Like other Facebook users, I belong to a number of groups which deal with the area of South London in which I was born and the school I attended as well as with my academic interests such as medieval history. The local groups contain many postings about local history and topography. The process of gentrification in London has caused the working-class community in which I was brought up to become widely dispersed and Facebook groups are one means by which the memory of this community is sustained. Social media groups such as these represent the largest and most widespread current community archive activities.

The range and extent of such social media groups is enormous. The popularity of coming out by uploading a video to YouTube means that YouTube has become in recent years an enormous archive of lesbian, gay, bisexual, trans, queer, intersex plus (LGBTQI+) experience (Cover and Prosser 2013; Namaste 2018). In imitation of the Facebook groups documenting memories of cities, a network of Lost Gay Facebook groups has developed that document places associated with LGBTQI+ groups and memories, such as Lost Gay Perth and Lost Gay Adelaide, which urges members to 'Invite your friends, add relevant LGA pics, videos, events, discuss Ye Olde Days' (Cover, 2019: 4). Cover argues that an important characteristic of such groups is the way in which their incoherence challenges the structure of the conventional archive:

> The chaotic, non-linear temporality of the contributions is presented on walls, feeds, albums and document bays on group Facebook pages. These contributions thus reflect a pattern of randomness given the *individual, personalised* and *customised* manner in which members might contribute an image, a death notice, a comment, a memory, a text in their own time and not in a chronological order that

reflects a community history. This framework competes, therefore, with older, traditional classificatory systems that derive from a desire for cataloguing contents in settings related to history and time, and arguably demonstrates the difficulty of transposing a traditional, procedural activity into a crowdsourced social network setting. (Cover, 2019: 5)

Commercial platforms such as Facebook or YouTube are not structured in such a way as to allow the mass of information contained in groups such as these to be readily categorised, catalogued or retrieved. While there can be no doubt that the lively conversations within Facebook groups, whether about south London schools or gay meeting places, are enormously rich historical and cultural resources, the informality of these archives militates against the implementation of structured metadata. Moderators of forums such as Lost Gay Melbourne urge members to remember to provide names, dates and places for uploaded images, and may provide more detailed instructions to ensure the coherence of the archive:

> UPLOAD YOUR MATERIAL INTO AN ALBUM: If you're uploading a whole batch of images etc, create an album first and upload the entire collection of images to that album at once. That way, it will only appear once on the group wall and not flood the entire wall with individual posts … DO NOT POST SONGS OR MUSIC unless they have some direct relationship with the GLBTIQ community of Melbourne. ACCEPTABLE POSTS INCLUDE: Drag shows and special performances etc, videos that relate to Melbourne. (Cover, 2019: 5)

Despite such injunctions, however, finding and retrieving material in such Facebook and other social media archives can be enormously difficult.

The use of platforms such as Facebook by no means assures the sustainability of an archive. The problems caused for the Pebble Mill archive by the use of Facebook have already been noted. In June 2018, the account of a musician who had died six months earlier was deleted by Facebook without reference to his family, who bought a legal action to ask Facebook to reveal who requested the deletion of the account. The musician's partner complained that 'Lots of Mirza's profile included me and our travels, our photos, music he shared, some for me, some for friends, his profile stated that he was in a relationship with me – they could have dropped me an email to check [before deleting it]' (Keating, 2018). The outlook of American corporations may be at odds with the needs of, for example, political activists, leading to the destruction or suppression of archives. A Facebook page in memory of Khaled Said, who had been killed by Egyptian police, which was an important focus of Egyptian opposition to the government, was briefly deactivated by Facebook in 2010 because its owner had used a pseudonym to avoid detection by Egyptian authorities (Poell and van Dijck, 2018). Similarly, YouTube videos showing violence by government authorities in Syria and Egypt posted by opposition journalists were removed for contravening community guidelines (Poell and van Dijck, 2018).

Recent controversies over Facebook and the drop in its share price are reminders that the long-term future of any digital platform is never assured, regardless of its commercial success. It is possible that in ten years' time Facebook will seem as outmoded and forgotten as MySpace. The literature is already full of references to community archive websites that have disappeared. The Manchester Outright archive of coming out stories reported by Cover and Prosser (2013: 87, 93) is already frozen and unavailable, just six years later. But anxieties about the use of commercial social media for community archives are not just restricted to concerns about metadata and sustainability. The revelations about the way in which Facebook uses personal data have led in the past year (2018–19) to government inquiries, a drop in Facebook share value and the deletion of millions of accounts, both by users disillusioned with Facebook and by Facebook itself, anxious to clean up its act.

Communities that create their archives on platforms such as Facebook, YouTube, Flickr or Instagram make the data in those archives available to those corporations for commercial and other forms of exploitation. These corporations will use that information to direct suggestions for further contacts, advertisements, links and other marketing at everyone involved in the archive. The South London memory groups that I subscribe to on Facebook may seem harmless enough, but I can see readily enough in my Facebook feed how they are being used to suggest potential friends (sometimes very unlikely) and are helping to shape the advertisements I see. They also affect the sequence in which Facebook prioritises the posts on my feed. It is intriguing to wonder how my membership of these groups affects the assumptions made by Facebook and other social media about my political opinions. Most of my Facebook contacts seem to fall into the normal urban middle-class liberal European Union-remaining type that might be expected of a British university professor. But the heavy representation of the South London working-class diaspora in my Facebook memory groups mean that pro-Brexit opinions frequently surface there. Are these discounted by Facebook? How are these archives used by it?

The detailed use made by Facebook of the vast quantities of community archive data it owns is of course shrouded in mystery. But the key point is that, once it is mounted on Facebook or a similar platform, the contents of this archive are no longer owned or controlled by the community that created it. This breaches the fundamental rule of community ownership and control of its archive. And it is clear that the algorithmic manipulation by Facebook of group sentiment and connection that has caused such controversy over matters such as the Trump presidency or Brexit is also affecting Facebook group discussions on matters that at first sight might seem less contentious. For example, Amy Hale (2015) has meticulously documented the attempts of the alt-right to infiltrate and subvert digital communities devoted to the discussion of modern Paganism and esotericism. Similar concerns have arisen about White Supremacist infiltration of fan groups for punk and heavy metal music (Ross, 2017). These concerns about White Supremacist cultural appropriation received extensive public coverage at the time of the Charlottesville disturbances in August 2017, when many White Supremacists wore pagan, medieval, punk, heavy metal and martial art insignia. My own Facebook groups saw an explosion of anger about racism in the study of the middle ages, with the young medieval scholar Dorothy Kim receiving intimidatory threats from another medieval scholar and the far-right activist Milo Yiannopoulos (Kim, 2018). Much of this confrontation was played out in Facebook groups of which I was a member, and I was struck by the way in which the Facebook algorithms quickly polarised the participants, so that I was identified as being linked with one camp and received only information likely to confirm my views – the 'echo chamber' in action.

If Facebook can fuel culture wars in medieval studies, then almost any community archive that makes use of Facebook (and other social media) is at risk of being similarly subverted and manipulated. As increasingly our social relations, memory, intellectual explorations and cultural understanding take place on, and are mediated by, the internet, so the health of the digital ecosystem on which we are all dependent is just as important to our collective well-being as the air we breathe, the water we drink and the food we eat. The scandals of the past couple of years have made us all increasingly aware of this, but the extent to which engagement with these issues will be vital for the continued success and development of community archives has not been sufficiently recognised. By exchanging the power hierarchy of the conventional bureaucratic archive for the opportunities offered by the corporations of Silicon Valley, there is a risk that the community archive may have exchanged one form of power relation for another that is much worse. Will the memories and voices enshrined in community archives become part of the data fuel that fires the development of artificial intelligence and predictive analytics by firms such as Google with its Deep Mind machine learning technology?

Among the most important initiatives launched in response to recent security and privacy controversies is the Mozilla Foundation's monitoring of the health of the internet. Mozilla issued a prototype internet health report in November 2017, and followed with the first full open source report a year later (Mozilla Foundation, 2018). The report assesses the health of the internet with reference to the following topics:

- Privacy and security: is the internet safe and can we trust the systems that protect us?
- Openness: how far can everyone participate and innovate on the internet?
- Digital inclusion: It's not just about how many people have access to the Internet, but whether that access is safe and meaningful for all of us.
- Web literacy: how far does everyone have the skills to read, write and participate in the digital world.
- Decentralisation: a few large players dominate the online world, but the internet is healthier when it is controlled by many. (Mozilla Foundation, 2018)

The key elements identified by the Mozilla project as essential for the health of the internet are also vital for the creation and preservation of community archives that offer neglected and marginal communities a chance to record their voice and to preserve their own heritage. It may seem that archivists, historians and researchers should not feel obliged to get involved with the wider advocacy for a healthy internet by organisations such as the Mozilla Foundation. But we are all today so dependent on the internet and what happens on it that we cannot avoid engaging in action to ensure that our digital ecosystem remains healthy.

However, there are signs that developments in such key areas as archives administration, historical research and local government may be hostile to the conditions under which community archives prosper. While the world of community archives is one of small-scale decentralised activity, many historians are engaging in more large-scale big data approaches, using tools such as Google Trends or Google Ngram viewer. Tim Hitchcock has described how, drawing on the world of big data, some historians are trying to create suites of tools that offer a 'macroscope', a visualisation tool that allows broad trends to be easily discerned from large collections of data (Hitchcock, 2014). Hitchcock admits that this form of 'big history', which privileges a certain type of empirical quantification associated with the social sciences, can provide interesting insights, but he emphasises how such big data approaches exclude the telling detail that speaks of the forgotten, the excluded and the oppressed:

> By locating the use of a 'macroscope' at the larger scale, seeking the *Longue durée*, and the ear of policy makers, recent calls for how we choose to deploy the tools of the Digital Humanities appear to deny the most powerful politics of the Humanities. If today we have a public dialogue that gives voice to the traditionally excluded and silenced – women, and minorities of ethnicity, belief and dis/ability – it is in no small part because we now have beautiful histories of small things. In other words, it has been the close and narrow reading of human experience that has done most to give voice to people excluded from 'power' by class, gender and race. (Hitchcock, 2014)

Community archives exist precisely to give voice to the traditionally excluded and silenced, and they potentially provide a substantial counterbalance to the dangers posed by the creation of digital humanities macroscopes.

Big data and big tech may also cause archivists to turn their attention away from community voices towards the formidable problems of dealing with born-digital corporate information. Increasingly, archivists have to develop new ways of curating, preserving and making available the tsunami of digital information being created by government and business. The scale and quantity of data being created poses challenges that can only be met by innovative computer science techniques. According to John Sheridan, Digital Director at the National Archives, archivists are facing an onslaught of an untamed second generation of born-digital content already accumulating within government departments – a 'Digital Wild West' where we can no longer depend on the traditional certainties of robust authenticity or clarity over who created a record, its timescale and consistency of format. It's likely to be extremely difficult to discipline this lawless data within the strictures of a traditional online catalogue. (Sheridan, 2018)

Sheridan (2018) points out how these demands will require a fundamental rethinking of many central tenets of the archive, and by extension a rethinking of much of the methodology of historical research. The nature of the catalogues we use to locate material in the archive will fundamentally change, and they may become unrecognisable from the kind of lists we have been accustomed to. The record will not be a self-contained unit whose authenticity can be readily established – metadata will be essential for understanding the record and the nature of that metadata cannot necessarily be guaranteed. In order to navigate and use these vast quantities of data, techniques which would have be anathema to 19th- and 20th-century historians, such as probabilistic linking of names, will be essential.

The computing pioneer Ted Nelson coined the term 'intertwingling' to describe how different types of information interact with and illuminate each other. Sheridan (2018) argues that the 'intertwingling' of records will become commonplace, and records will contextualise each other. While the National Archives will provide the essential element of trust in this process, it is likely that large-scale commercial operators such as Amazon or Google will have to get involved in dealing with this digital archive, because they are the only corporations with the facilities to deal with such large-scale computing requirements. It is vital that the National Archives achieves the mission outlined in its digital strategy of creating a disruptive digital archive, since it will ensure that the data that governs our lives is available for future interrogation, but this is a high-tech big data world, in which the voices represented in the community archive seem pushed out.

Many governments in the Western world have stressed the value of open data and at first glance this might seem to chime with the agenda of community records, but closer examination suggests once again a clash between such big data approaches and the philosophy of community archives. There is a risk that 'smart city' initiatives can be more about using data to control communities rather than empowering citizens. New York is regarded as being at the vanguard of the 'smart city' movement and is proud of its open data and data analytics work. Recent examples of community use of civic data include mapping of stop, question and frisk incidents by the police, mapping of child well-being indicators and a visualisation of street trees (NYC Open Data, 2019). However, the New York Police Department also uses this data for 'predictive policing' software that is biased against minorities (Rieland, 2018).

New York State is using facial recognition technology, whose reliability in identifying people of colour, women and children is poor, to identify drivers and passengers at toll booths and New York City has expressed interest in using facial recognition technology to develop a free-flow highway environment (MTA Bridges and Tunnels, 2016). Data analytic techniques have also been used to identify illegal apartments, sale of bootlegged cigarettes and buildings that pose a fire risk (Howard, 2012). The use of open data to support such 'pre-emptive government' can suggest that government agencies use data to control communities in top-down actions rather than empowering them. Far from supporting the ethos of community archives, the use of data by local government often runs counter to the spirit of fostering and nurturing communities.

As archivists become more concerned with curating huge data repositories documenting the use by government and big business of data to control the population, the idea of the community archive may come to seem marginal. There are other pressures militating against the ideals of open and free community engagement with the archive. The commercialisation of much of the UK archival heritage has gone largely unremarked (Prescott, 2014). Family history is big business; one of the most popular uses of the internet after pornography is genealogical research. Not surprisingly, wealthy corporations such as Ancestry and Findmypast have moved aggressively into this market. British archivists, short of money for new access initiatives but under pressure to maximise digital coverage of their collections, have been only too happy to make agreements with companies such as these, giving them exclusive rights to digital access to record series. As a result, many of the most important historic archive series, such as censuses, wills, rate books and church registers, are only available online if you can afford a £120+ annual subscription to one or other of these series (the committed researcher would need at least two subscriptions). How will community archives fit in with these commercial family history services? Increasingly, community archives contain important information about family and local history, but discovery of these resources can be problematic.

It might be tempting for community archives to increase their profile by entering into agreements with companies such as Findmypast. I personally hope they will not and that community archives will contribute to the development of a free, open and community-owned counterpart to the giant family history companies. By contrast with libraries and journal provision, the movement towards open access for archival material is quite small. FreeUKGenealogy (2019) provides free access to birth marriage and death registration, censuses and parish registers through the use of transcription by volunteers. There are potentially close links between this movement and community archives.

Big data, big tech, big history and big family history: all these tendencies within the archive world pose a threat to the vibrant community archive scene whose pursuit and celebration of history from below is frequently at odds with these larger corporate trends. It is striking how many of the issues presented by these threats to community archives are similar to those identified in the Mozilla Internet Health Report. Over-centralisation is just as much a threat to the preservation of archives as it is to the health of the internet. The community archive movement is inherently an open movement, because it seeks to ensure that everyone's voice is represented in the archival world. Issues around privacy, security and inclusion are just as vital in community archives as they are to the wider life of the internet.

Community archives need to make common cause with the approach taken by digital activists, such as those associated with Mozilla who gather to celebrate at the annual Mozfest in London. The values of Mozfest as described by its Executive Director Mark Surman are precisely those that need to animate community archives:

> A healthy Internet is one that's accessible to all; decentralized; bursting with vibrant, creative communities, trustworthy content, and groundbreaking ideas. It's an Internet where users control their data, and privacy and intellectual freedom thrive. An Internet not of passive consumers, but of active creators, building and shaping online tools and spaces. (MetaLAB (at) Harvard, 2018)

Community archives can and do contribute to the creation of these values on the internet. In order to do this, they need to avoid commercial solutions and promote decentralised solutions, such as Tim Berners-Lee's current Solid project (https://solid.mit.edu/). Community archives should seek out and promote open standards.

They need to adhere to best practice in terms of data security, ownership and privacy. By aligning themselves with internet activists such as Mozilla Foundation, community archives can promote a healthy internet in which all our voices can be held.

The community archives movement can potentially not only change the power relationships which surround the archive but can also help the internet realise its potential to create a more just, equal and happier world. The scale of the community archives movement is such that, if it becomes an activist movement to ensure that all our voices are preserved and heard in a digital world, it can realistically have a major impact on digital cultures.

The potential synergy between community archives and online activism is evident from the Occupy movement. While, as Paolo Gerbaudo (2014) has emphasised, the role of social media in fostering the initial call in 2011 to Occupy Wall Street can be exaggerated, social media was nevertheless important in creating publicity for events on the ground during the protest, enhancing the impact and 'reverberation' of the protests. Although a number of organisations, including the Smithsonian Museum and the New York Historical Society, collected printed ephemera relating to the Occupy demonstrations, it was evident from an early stage that it was also important to preserve the digital presence of the Occupy movement, and both the Internet Archive and the Roy Rosenzweig Centre for History and New Media at George Mason University archived digital material relating to the protests (Erde, 2014). The Tamiment Library and Robert F. Wagner Labor Archives at New York University also actively sought to document the events, although some members of Occupy were reluctant to work with New York University because of its developments in Greenwich village and its anti-union policies (Erde, 2014: 83). One issue in archiving the Occupy protests was a feeling that the archive itself should reflect the aspiration of the movement to be leaderless and anti-hierarchical. Jeremy Bold, a member of the Occupy Wall Street Archives Working Group, argued that they should create decentralised 'anarchives' and declared that the aim should 'NOT be merely in collecting the objects we determine have worth in the history of the movement, but trying to offer a framework in which everyone can define their history' (Erde, 2014: 81).

The most striking feature of the attempts to archive the Occupy protests is the emergence of a group of activist archivists who, recognising the potential of social media to record and protect social movements and document abuses of power, seek to support individuals and communities in using the internet to voice their concerns and opinions. As activist archivists, they seek to preserve the legacy of social movements for future generations and to help give voice and history to those who have been traditionally left out (Besser, 2012: 4–5). One of the founders of the group, Howard Besser, explained that:

> One of the earliest issues we encountered with Occupy was the prevalent notion that history is documented in book-length essays about famous people. Many people in Occupy could not see that someone in the future might be interested in the actions of an ordinary person like them. Now, a third of a century after Howard Zinn's *A People's History of The United States*, most progressive historians believe that history is made by ordinary individuals coming together to conduct acts in groups. And they believe that we can read history through archival collections of letters, post-cards and snapshots. Librarians, archivists and historians need to make the case to ordinary people that their emails, blogs and Flickr and Facebook postings are indeed important representations of early 21st century life that people in the future will want to access. And as librarians and archivists, we need to be aggressive about collecting these types of material and make concrete plans for access. (Owens, 2014)

In order to spread this gospel, the Activist Archivists produced a 'Why Archive' card to distribute to protestors, to explain the importance of groups taking responsibility for recording their activity (http://activist-archivists.org/wp/_p=994.html#).

The bullet points of the 'Why Archive' card chime in many ways with the key messages of the Internet Health Report:

WHY ARCHIVE?
- ACCOUNTABILITY: Archives collect evidence that can hold those in power accountable.
- ACCESSIBILITY: Archives make the rich record of our movements accessible. We can use them to ensure transparency, generate discussion, and enable direct action.
- SELF-DETERMINATION: We define our own movements. We need to create and maintain our own historical record.
- EDUCATION: Today's videos, flyers, webpages, and signs are material for tomorrow's skill-shares, classes, and mobilizations.

- CONTINUITY: Just as past movements inspire us, new activists will learn from the experiences we document. (Activist Archivists, 2012)

In order to promote the preservation of the rich digital materials produced by the Occupy movement, the Activist Archivists had to encourage precisely those messages about open standards, metadata and sharing that are prominent in the Internet Health Report. Six months after the first Occupy demonstration, more than half a million photographs had been posted to Flickr with the tag #Occupy and over 169,000 videos on YouTube. How far would these survive or be accessible? A study by one of the activist archivists found that YouTube and Vimeo mostly stripped out such key metadata as date, time and GPS location. In response, the Activist Archivists developed '7 Tips to Ensure our Video is Usable in the Long Term', which were expanded into more detailed 'Best Practices for Video Activists'.

The idea of a group of activist archivists actively intervening to make communities aware of the issues involved in using digital platforms to preserve their voice and actions for future generations is compelling. The commercial, technical and political pressures that favour big tech and large corporations over community action are powerful. If communities are to be able to continue successfully to use digital technologies, they will need the services of a larger cohort of activist archivists who can combine technical understanding with a commitment to creating a truly diverse and inclusive historical record. By promoting a healthy environment for community archives, activist archivists can also play a wider role in maintaining a healthy internet.

The health of our digital ecosystem is just as pressing an issue as the state of the earth's physical ecosystem (indeed, the two questions are closely interlinked). By promoting a diversity of voices on the internet and by encouraging a decentralised and inclusive view of information, community archives play an important part in ensuring a healthy internet. The relationship between the health of the internet and community archives will become even more important in the future, and community archives have a vital role to play in ensuring a flourishing digital ecosystem that works for us all.

References

Activist Archivists (2012) 'Why Archive?', [online], Available from: https://activistarchivists.wordpress.com/2012/10/19/why-archive-2/ [Accessed 13 October 2019].

Besser, Howard (2012) 'Archiving media from the Occupy Movement: Methods for archives trying to manage large amounts of user-generated audiovisual media' [online], Available from: http://besser.tsoa.nyu.edu/howard/Papers/besser-girona-occupy-paper.pdf [Accessed 23 January 2019].

Chenier, Elise (2016) 'Reclaiming the lesbian archives', *The Oral History Review*, 43(1): 170–82.

Cover, Rob, and Prosser, Rosslyn (2013) 'Memorial accounts: Queer young men, identity and contemporary coming out narratives online', *Australian Feminist Studies*, 28(75): 81–94.

Cover, Rob (2019) 'Memorialising queer community: Digital media, subjectivity and the Lost Gay # archives of social networking', *Media International Australia*, 170(1): 126–35.

Erde, John (2014) 'Constructing archives of the Occupy Movement', *Archives and Records*, 35(2): 77–92.

Flinn, Andrew (2010) 'Independent community archives and community-generated content', *Convergence*, 16(1): 39–51.

FreeUKGenealogy (2019) [online], Available from: https://www.freeukgenealogy.org.uk/ [Accessed 13 October 2019].

Furfaro, Daniele, Bain, Jennifer and Brown, Ruth (2018) 'Inside Cuomo's plan to have your face scanned at NYC toll plazas', *New York Post*, 20 July [online], Available from: https://nypost.com/2018/07/20/inside-cuomos-plan-to-have-your-face-scanned-at-nyc-toll-plazas/ [Accessed 23 January 2019].

Gerbaudo, Paolo (2014) *Tweets and the Streets: Social Media and Contemporary Activism*, London: Pluto Press.

Hale, Amy (2015) 'Marketing "Rad Trad": The Growing Co-Influence between Paganism and the New Right', in Ellwood, Taylor, Blanton, Crystal and Williams, Brandy (eds), *Bringing Race to the Table: Exploring Racism in the Pagan Community*, London: Immanion Press, pp 103–21.

Hitchcock, Tim (2014) 'Big data, small data and meaning' [online], Available from: http://historyonics.blogspot.com/2014/11/big–data–small–data–and–meaning_9.html [Accessed 23 January 2019].

Howard, Alex (2012) 'Predictive data analytics is saving lives and taxpayer dollars in New York City' [online], Available from: https://www.oreilly.com/ideas/predictive-data-analytics-big-data-nyc [Accessed 23 January 2019].

Karuk Tribe, Hillman, Lisa, Hillman, Leaf, Harling, Adrienne, Talley, Bari and McLaughlin, Angela (2017) 'Building Sípnuuk: A digital library, archives, and museum for indigenous peoples', *Collection Management*, 42(3–4): 294–316.

Keating, Rebecca (2018) 'The digital afterlife', Oxford Business Law Blog, 27 June [online], Available from: https://www.law.ox.ac.uk/business-law-blog/blog/2018/06/digital-afterlife [Accessed 22 January 2019].

Kim, Dorothy (2018) 'Medieval studies since Charlottesville', Inside Higher Education, 30 August [online], Available from: https://www.insidehighered.com/views/2018/08/30/scholar-describes-being-conditionally-accepted-medieval-studies-opinion [Accessed 22 January 2019].

MetaLAB (at) Harvard (2018) 'MozFest' [online], Available from: https://metalabharvard.github.io/projects/mozfest/ [Accessed 13 October 2019].

MTA Bridges and Tunnels (2016) 'RFI 16-63: All-Electronic Facial Detection and Recognition System at all TBTA Facilities' [online], Available from: https://www.documentcloud.org/documents/3428597-RFI.html [Accessed 13 October 2019].

Mozilla Foundation (2018) 'Internet health report 2018' [online], Available from: https://internethealthreport.org/2018/ [Accessed 13 October 2019].

Namaste, Justice (2018) 'The ever-evolving art of the coming-out video', *Wired* [online], Available from: https://www.wired.com/story/youtube-coming-out-videos/ [Accessed 22 January 2019].

NYC Open Data (2019) 'Open data project gallery' [online], Available from: https://opendata.cityofnewyork.us/projects/ [Accessed 13 October 2019].

Owens, Trevor (2014) 'Archiving from the bottom up: A conversation with Howard Besser' [online], Available from: https://blogs.loc.gov/thesignal/2014/10/archiving-from-the-bottom-up-a-conversation-with-howard-besser/ [Accessed 23 January 2019].

Poell, Thomas and van Dijck, José (2018) 'Social Media and New Protest Movements', in Burgess, Jean, Marwick, Alice and Poell, Thomas (eds) *The Sage Handbook of Social Media*, London: Sage, pp 546–61.

Prescott, Andrew (2014) 'Dennis the paywall menace stalks the archives' [online], Available from: http://digitalriffs.blogspot.com/2014/02/dennis-paywall-menace-stalks-archives.html [Accessed 23 January 2019].

Rieland, Randy (2018) 'Artificial intelligence is now used to predict crime. But is it biased?', *Smithsonian Magazine*, 5 March [online], Available from: https://www.smithsonianmag.com/innovation/artificial-intelligence-is-now-used-predict-crime-is-it-biased-180968337/ [Accessed 23 January 2019].

Ross, Alexander Reid (2017) 'A brief but very informative history of how fascists infiltrated punk and metal', *Noisey*, 18 August [online], Available from: https://noisey.vice.com/en_us/article/mbbg9p/a-brief-but-very-informative-history-of-how-fascists-infiltrated-punk-and-metal [Accessed 22 January 2019].

Sheridan, John (2018) 'Digital archiving: "Context is everything"' [online], Available from: https://blog.nationalarchives.gov.uk/blog/digital-archiving-context-everything/ [Accessed 22 January 2019].

Thomas, David and Johnson, Valerie (2015) 'From the Library of Alexandria to the Google Campus: Has the Digital Changed the Way We Do Research?', in Moss, Michael, Endicott-Popiovsky, Barbara and Dupuis, Marc (eds), *Is Digital Different? How Information Creation, Preservation and Discovery are Being Transformed*, London: Facet Publishing, pp 189–212.

Index

Printed in Great Britain
by Amazon

25663728R00165